Orange County North Carolina

Deed Book 6 & 7

- 1797-1799

(Volume #5)

By:
William D. Bennett, C.G.

This volume was reproduced from
A 1992 edition located in the
The Publisher's Private Library

All rights reserved. No part of this publication may be reproduced, stored in a retrieval system, transmitted in any form, posted on to the web in any form or by any means without the prior written permission of the publisher.

Please direct all correspondence and orders to:

www.southernhistoricalpress.com
or
SOUTHERN HISTORICAL PRESS, Inc.
PO BOX 1267
375 West Broad Street
Greenville, SC   29601
southernhistoricalpress@gmail.com

Originally published: Raleigh, NC, 1992
Copyright 1992 by: William D. Bennett
Copyright Transferred 2018 to:
Southern Historical Press, Inc.
Greenville, SC
ISBN #0-89308-961-3
All rights Reserved
Printed in the United States of America

ORANGE COUNTY RECORDS, VOLUME XI

CONTENTS

INTRODUCTION	vII
ORANGE COUNTY DEED BOOK 6	1
ORANGE COUNTY DEED BOOK 7	63
INDEX TO PERSONAL NAMES	117
INDEX TO PLACE NAMES	139

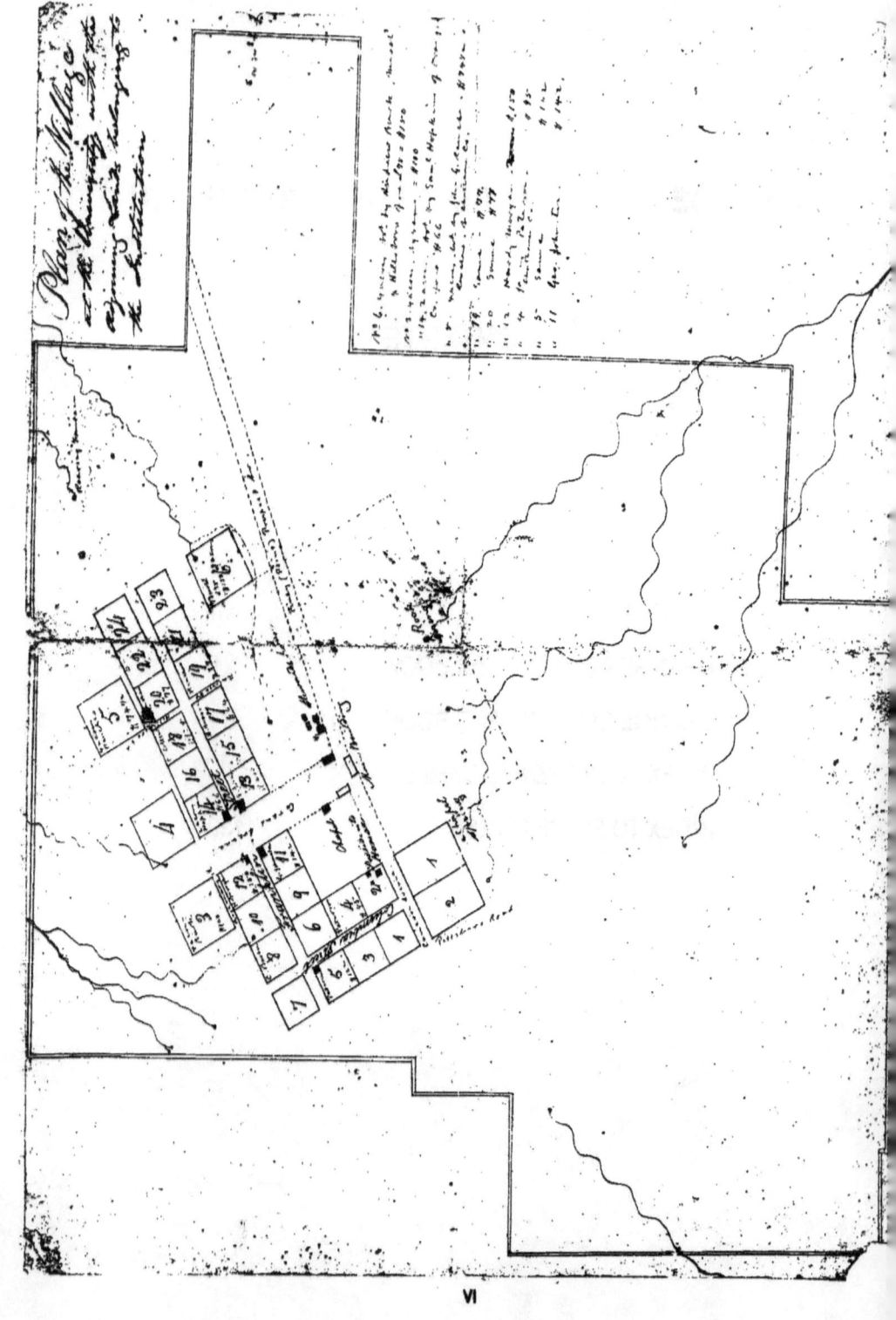

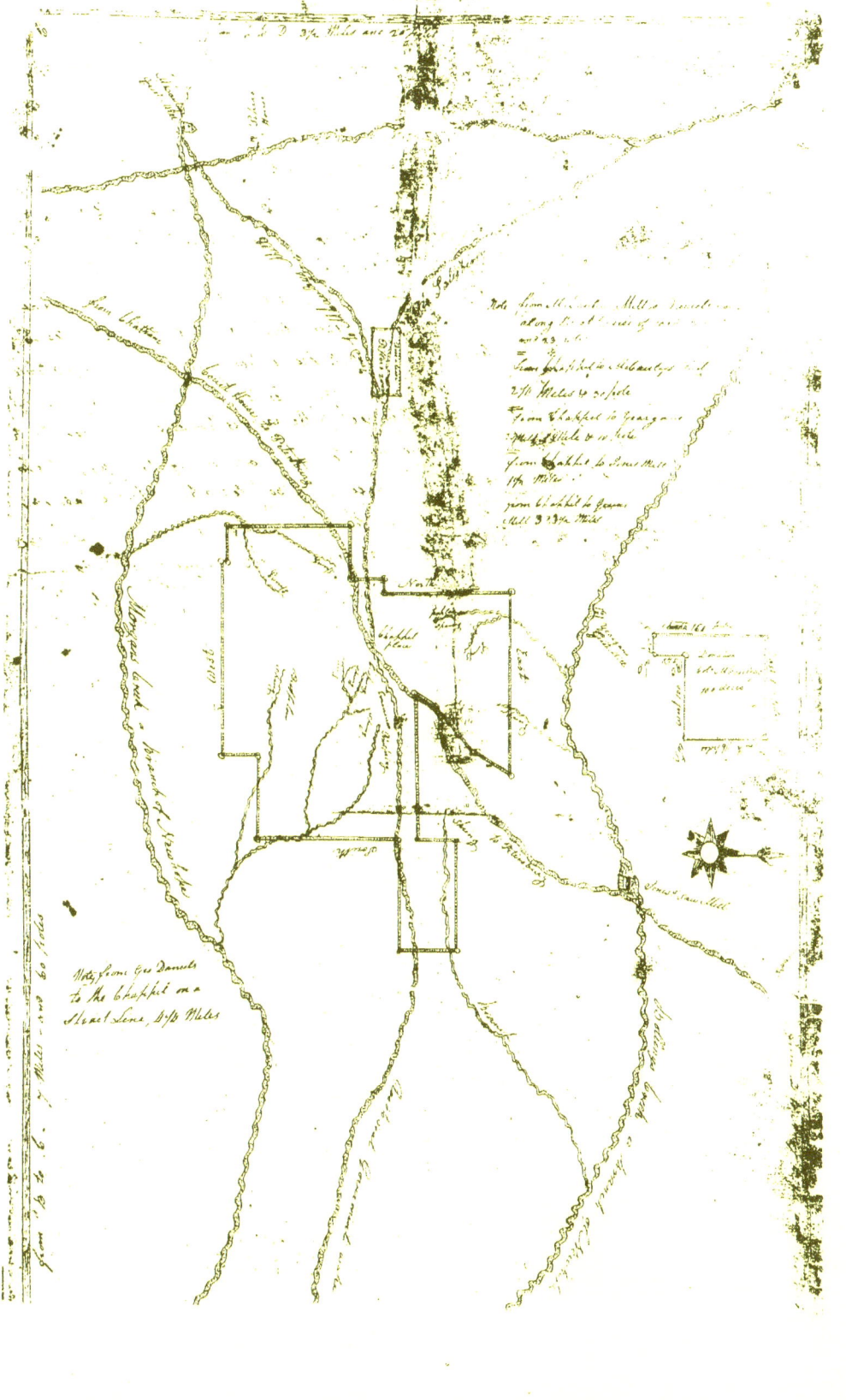

ORANGE COUNTY (NC) DEED BOOKS 6 & 7

INTRODUCTION

In Deed Books 6 and 7 there are a number of deeds concerning sale of lots in the "Village Adjacent to the Buildings of the University." These, of course, were lots in present Chapel Hill. The frontispiece is a survey made in 1792 by John Daniel of the general area showing the three tracts which had been donated for the use of the University of North Carolina. On the facing page is a survey made about 1797 of the immediate area which became the village. It will be noted that in the original plan there are twenty four two acre lots and six four acre lots. When this plat was originally made the Trustees of the University had sold the following lots: Lot #6 (4 acres) and Lot #3 (4 acres) to Andrew Burk a merchant in Hillsborough; Lot #14 (2 acres) to Samuel Hopkins of Orange County; Lot #5 (4 acres), Lot #19 (2 acres), and Lot #20 (2 acres) to John G. Rencher who is listed at this time as living in Chatham County; Lot #12 (2 acres) to Hardy Morgan; Lot #4 (2 acres) and Lot #5 (2 acres) to James Patterson of Chatham County; and Lot #11 (2 acres) to George Johnston. Later it appears that Christopher Barbee purchased Lot #8, Edmund Jones purchased Lot #13, a Moore purchased Lot #17, and a Collins purchased Lot #18. One unique proposal of the Trustees appears to have never been carried to conclusion. At one of their meetings, it was proposed that the buildings of the University be similar to the "Government Building." At that time, the only government building in the State was Tryon Palace. It should be noted that if covered colannaded walks were extended from "South Building" to "East Building" and "West Building," the three original buildings, you would have structures similiar to Tryon Palace.

In additon to deeds concerning the lots in the "Village Adjacent to the University," there are also included in these two deed books a number of references to lots adjoing the "Blue House" and the lot on which the "Blue House" stood in Hillsborough. The "Blue House" was an early mercantile building on the extreme southeast corner of Lot #25, at the junction of King and Churton Streets. It was diagonally across from the Market-House and Courthouse which were on Lot #1 and in an extremely advantageous position for trade. It was apparently a general store and bar. When deeds first mention it, it was owned by the Halifax firm of Young, Miller and Company (i.e., James Young, Andrew Miller, and George Alston of Halifax who had various connections in Glasgow, Scotland). The same company also owned and operated a well-known still-house on Lot #45 on East King Street, east of the Courthouse. The Still-house presumably supplied the bar of Young, Miller and Company's store. Early deeds mention the fact that the "Blue House" was "in the possession of Ralph McNair" (also of Halifax). McNair may merely have rented the "Blue House" or he may have owned it before its purchase by Young, Miller and Company.

The earliest known owner of the part of the lot where the "Blue House" stood was James Young of Glasgow. On 8 June 1771, Young sold that part of the lot at the corner to Thomas Blount of Edenton. Two days later, 10 June 1771, Blount sold the tract to "John Alston, James Young, James Morton, and Alexander Grindley, merchants in Glasgow, and Andrew Miller, William Littlejohn, and George Alston of North Carolina." At this time McNair was occupying the premises. However, the "Blue House" had already been built by this time. C. J. Sauthier's "Map of the Town of Hillsborough shows the "Blue House" lot in October 1768. (The Sauthier map was reproduced in "Orange County Records, Volume III, Deed Book 3.") The "Blue House" was evidently some forty feet long, according to Sauthier's measurements, and perhaps twenty four feet wide. There were outhouses to the north of it and a yard to the west and north. The "Blue House" lot was fifty five feet by fifty four feet, almost square.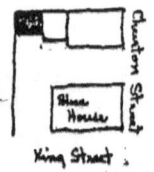

Various details of the operations of Young, Miller and Company are mentioned in *Colonial Records*." Andrew Miller was one of the firmest Tories in the Province. He employed Dr. Thomas Burke and John Kinchen to collect debts and do his legal work in Hillsborough, and there are various letters from Miller to Burke in the *Colonial Records*." Miller, it appears, refused to sign the Merchant's Association agreement not to export goods to Great Britain. Evidently Ralph McNair either managed his Hillsborough store (there was another Miller store in Granville County) or Young, Miller and Company absorbed McNair's debts. Miller's troubles mounted until he and his wife, Elizabeth, and their younger children were forced to flee to Bermuda where Miller died. His older sons, James and Charles Miller, were evidently on a ship, the Lady Margret, seized and taken to Philadelphia. Andrew Miller's property, including the "Blue House" lot and Lot #45, the Still-house lot, were confiscated by the State.

In October 1784, the General Assembly passed an act providing for the appointment of a one State Treasurer rather than a treasurer for each district. The State treasurer was to maintain his office in Hillsborough. In October 1785, John Nichols, High Sheriff of Orange County sold about two thirds of Lot #25 to Memucan Hunt, William Lytle, and Absalom Tatom. Two months later the General Assembly passed a resolution "that the House and Lott in the Town of Hillsborough commonly called the 'Blue House,' now confiscated and belonging to the State, be reserved for the use of the Public Treasurer." The "Blue House" was used as the State Treasury of North Carolina from 1 January 1786 to 1789. By November 1789, all books, papers, and money belonging to the State Treasury had been moved to Fayetteville. It is presumed that the "Blue House" stood vacant from 1789 until 1798. The Laws of 1797 provided that Henry Shepperd sell to the highest bidder the "Blue House," lot, and houses thereunto belonging.

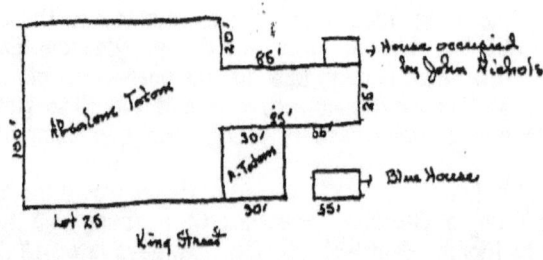

On 18 April 1798, Shepperd sold the "Blue House" to Catlett Campbell for six hundred and fifty pounds. Campbell's bond to John Haywood can be found in the Ernest Haywood Papers, Box 2, Folder 25, in the Southern Historical

later, 10 May 1804, Campbell sold the "Blue House" to William Whitted for one thousand seventy five pounds. Six years later, 27 August 1810, Whitted bought the remainder of Lot #25 from Dr. Barnabus O'Farrell. Following Whitted's death, Dr. James Webb, executor of the estate of William Whitted, deceased, sold Lot #25 to William Kirkland. No mention is made of the "Blue House" or of Young, Miller and Company. The present representatives of the Kirkland family do not know whether or not the Kirkland General Store on Kirkland's Corner, as it became known, occupied a new building or utilized the old "Blue House". Very likely Kirkland built a new structure. The present building on that corner was constructed in 1925.

The editor wishes to thank the University of North Carolina for permission to publish the two maps of Chapel Hill. The originals are to be found in the University Papers, University Archives, Library of the University of North Carolina at Chapel Hill. The editor wishes also to thank Virginia C. Forrest of Hillsborough for providing a copy of a monograph on the "Blue House" prepared by Dr. Mary Claire Engstrom. The discussion of the "Blue House" presented here is almost verbatim from Dr. Engstrom's monograph.

The following abbreviations have been used by the editor in these abstracts: N - North; S - South; E - East; W - West; ch. - chains; p. - poles; lk. - links; R. - River; Cr. - Creek; Br. - Branch. All other abbreviations found in these abstracts are those used by the Public Register when he was recording the deeds. It should be noted that there are a number of deeds in which words were omitted. The omitted words include directions, units of measure, and type of tree used as a corner.

ORANGE COUNTY (NC) DEED BOOK 6

P. 1, 13 August 1797, **Joseph Allison** of Orange to **Thomas Bradford** of "Macklenburg" County, Virginia, fifty pounds, 224 acres, in Sumner County, Tennessee, on N branch of Bradley Lick Cr. a fork of the East Fork of Stones R., begin at a white oak & hicory SE cor. to **James Saunders**, his line W 240 p. to a cedar & ash, S 182 p. to a stake, E 240 p. to a red oak & ash in **Saunder's** line, N his line to beginning; signed: **Joseph Allison**; witness: **David Ray, James Yarbrough**; proved August Term 1797 by **Yarbrough**, Delvd. **Thomas Bedford**.

P. 2, 3 April 1758, **William Craig** of Orange to **John Craig** of same, twenty pounds sterling, 237 1/2 acres, on Batts Cr. waters of Newhope, begin at a white oak, E to 3 persimmons, N 50 ch. to a white oak, W to a post, S to first station, part of a tract from **Granville** to **Craig** 6 September 1754; signed: **William (X) Craig**; witness: **William Reid, Alexr. Mebane**; acknowledged June Term 1758, registered in Book P, page 325 by **W. Churton**, P.R., Delvd. **John Gray**.

P. 3, 13 August 1797, **North Carolina** to **John Craig** [no residence given], fifty shillings per hundred acres, 25 acres, on waters of Newhope, adjoins **James Craig, William Barns** & his own land, begin at a hicory & red oak cor. of **James Craig**, his line E 34 ch. to his cor. a red oak, N 13 ch. 50 lk. to a black oak, E 11 ch. 50 lk. to 3 persimmons & a black jack on **William Barns'** line, sd. line S 71 ch. 50 lk. to a hicory **McCauley**'s cor., the same course in all 98 ch. to a stake, W 10 ch. to a stake in **Craig's** old line, sd. line N 14 ch. 50 lk. to his cor. a P. oak, W 35 ch. to a P. oak **James Craig's** cor., his line N to beginning, entered 26 January 1797, signed: **Saml. Ashe**; witness: **J. Glasgow**; [no probate record].

P. 4, 26 February 1787, **John Merrett** of Orange to **John Rhodes** of same, ten pounds, 42 acres, on E side of a branch of Newhope called Second Cr., begin at a pine **Merrett's** cor., S 82 p. to a stake on his line, W 26 p. to a pine, S 48 p. to a post oak, W 140 p. to a hicory, N 32 p. to a pine, W 100 p. to a pine, N 80 p. to a water oak, E 207 p. to a pine the first station, part of a tract from **North Carolina** to **Merrett** 13 March 1780; signed: **John (X) Merrett**; witness: **Littleberry Grisham, William Rhodes**; proved May Term 1787 by **William Rhodes**, Delvd. **John Rhodes**.

P. 5, 25 August 1795, **Boston Grave** of Montgomery County, Virginia, to **John Effland** of Orange, one hundred and fifty pounds, 129 acres, on waters of Stinking Quarter Cr. a water of Haw R., begin at 3 hicory saplins, S45E 21 1/2 ch. to a red oak cor. of **Jacob Graves**, his line S45W 60 ch. to his cor. stone, N45W 21 1/2 ch. to a stake in line of **John Graves**, his line N45E to first station, part of a larger tract purchased by **Boston Graves** of his father **John Graves, Henry McCulloh** to **John Graves**; signed: **Boston Graves**; witness: **James Garrett, Joshua Holt**; proved May Term 1797 by **Holt**, Delvd. **Joshua Holt**.

P. 7, 1 October 1796, **Thomas Hall & Nanny** his wife of Orange to **Thomas Gray** [no residence given], two hundred pounds, 340 acres, begin in a cor. pine in **David Hall's** line, E 64 1/2 ch. to a stake on **Zachariah Herndon's** line, N 34 1/2 ch. to a post oak, W 3 ch. to a pine, N 78 1/2 ch. to a black jack, W 3 ch. to a black jack, N 4 1/2 ch. to a pine, down branch 4 1/2 ch. to a poplar, W 59 1/2 ch. to a pine on **John Lee's** line, S 26 ch. to first station; signed: **Thomas Hall, Nanny (X) Hall**; witness: **John Bray, Mack Watson, John Green**; proved May Term 1797 by **Bray**.

P. 8, 17 October 1793, **Alfred Moore, John Haywood, William Richardson Davie, & Alexander Mebane** Esqs., on behalf of the **Trustees of the University of North Carolina**, to **John Carrington** of Orange, fifty five pounds, 2 acres, 1 lot in town adjacent to buildings of the University, on street #9, ; signed: **A. Moore, Jno. Haywood, W. R. Davie, Alexr. Mebane**; witness: **W. Watters**; proved May Term 1797 by **Bryson Dobbin** who proved handwriting of **William Watters** now deceased, Delvd. **James Carrington Junr**.

P. 9, 17 October 1793, **Alfred Moore, John Haywood, William Richardson Davie, & Alexander Mebane** Esqs. in behalf of the **Trustees of the University** to **John Carrington** of Orange, fifty two pounds, 2 acres, lot in town adjacen to University, Lot #8 in plan of town; signed: **Alfred Moore, John Haywood, W. R. Davie, Alexr. Mebane**; witness: **W. Watters**; proved May Term 1797 by **Bryson Dobbin** who proved handwriting of **Watters** now deceaseed, Delvd. **James Carrington Junr**.

P. 10, 10 January 1793, **John Elliott** of Orange, planter, to **William Carter** of same, planter, fifty pounds, 150 acres, on S side of Haw R., bounded on E by **Robert Morrison**, on S by his own land, begin at a bush his old cor. & on side of Big Cain Cr., E 6 1/2 ch. to a black oak, N 61 ch. to a spanish oak, W 61 1/2 ch. to a black oak, S 20 ch. to a stake, E 55 ch. to a hicory his other cor. of his deeded land, S 41 ch. to first station; signed: **John Elliott**; witness: **John Shy, Jesse Shy**; May Term 1797, **William Elliot** appeared in court and stated he was the only brother and heir at law of **John Elliot** Decd & also **Jane Elliot** widow and relict of **John Elliot** and severally acknowledged the deed, **Samuel Hill** swore that he was a close relative of **John Shy** now deceased and proved his handwriting, Delvd. **John Carter**.

P. 12, 14 November 1796, **Phillip Foust** of Sullivan County, Tennessee, to **Barnet Clap** of Orange, seventy pounds, 200 acres, on waters of Great Allamance, begin at a white oak a cor. of his deeded land, N45E 1 ch. 50 lk. to a post oak **John May's** cor., his line N45W 24 ch. to a post oak, N45E 31 ch. 50 lk. to a hicory on **John Albright's** line, S45E 38 ch. to a black oak, N45E 3 ch. to a hicory, S45E 22 ch. to a hicory, S45W 36 ch. to a hicory on his deeded land, N45W 36 ch. to beginning; signed: **Phillip Foust, Cathana (X) Foust**; witness: "Note the 2 signers names are wrote in dutch which I don't understand, JR"; proved May Term 1797 [witness not named], Delvd. **John Hufman**.

P. 13, 22 April 1797, **Thomas Steel** of Chatham to **Isaac Shugart** of Orange, one hundred pounds, [no acreage given], on S side of Haw R. & S side of Cain Cr., joins **William Helms, James Downing, & George Allen**, begin at a hicory, W 140 p. to a hicory, S 130 p. to a hicory, E 140 p. to a hicory, N 130 p. to first station; signed: **Thomas Steel**; witness: **James Newlin, John Newlin**; proved May Term 1797 by **James Newlin**, Delvd. **Jno. Carter**.

ORANGE COUNTY (NC) DEED BOOK 6

P. 14, 18 May 1797, **Joseph Holmes** to **Edmund Green**, both of Orange, one hundred and fifty pounds, 127 acres, on S side of Haw R., begin at a stone **George Albright's** cor. near a branch of Vunals Cr., along **Albright's** line N73W 34 ch. to a hicory, N45W 14 ch. to a hicory, S45W 23 ch. to a black oak **James Holms** cor., S45E 45 ch. to a persimmon his other cor., N45E 38 ch. to beginning; signed: **Joseph Homes**; witness: **Obed Green, William Ray**; proved May Term 1797 by **Ray**, Delvd. **Edmund Green**.

P. 15, 24 August 1796, **Moses Pearce** of Caswell to **John Hughes** of Orange, one hundred dollars, 100 acres, begin at a white oak, E 60 ch. to a red oak, S 20 ch. to a white oak, W 60 ch. to a red oak, N 20 ch. to first station; signed: **Moses Pearce**; witness: **Samuel Browning, Charles Taylor**; proved May Term 1797 by **Browning**, Delvd. **John Hughes**.

P. 16, 25 October 1782, **North Carolina** to **William Riley** [no residence given], fifty shillings per hundred acres, 200 acres, on North Fork of Little R., adjoins **Robert Jordan** & **John Riley**, begin at a stake, S 33 ch. to a stake in **John Riley's** line, E 60 1/2 ch. to a white oak, N 33 ch. to a post oak, W 60 1/2 ch. to first station; signed: **Alexr. Martin**; witness: **J. Glasgow**; [no probate record], Delvd. **Jas. Mebane**.

P. 17, 30 June 1797, **North Carolina** to **Mitch McDaniel** [no residence given], fifty shillings per hundred acres, 115 acres, on Marshalls Branch, begin at a gum on branch on **Strudwick's** line, with same S7W 24 1/2 ch. to a spanish oak on a rode, along same S20E 36 ch. to a red oak, N 4 ch. 90 lk. to a post oak - a conditional cor. between **McDaniels** & **Charles Kelley**, with conditional line N55E 10 1/2 ch. to a red oak, N46E 4 1/2 ch. to a R. O., N10W 2 1/2 ch. to a W. O., N11E 3 ch. to a post oak on Marshalls Branch, down same to beginning, entered 20 April 1778; signed: **Saml. Ashe**; witness: **J. Glasgow**; [no probate record], Delvd. **Mitch McDaniel**.

P. 18, 21 November 1796, **North Carolina** to **Jacob Allen** [no residence given], fifty shillings per hundred acres, 25 acres, on waters of Eno, begin at a black oak saplin in his line of another tract, E 8 ch. 40 lk. to a black oak saplin, S 30 ch. to a black oak saplin, W 8 ch. 40 lk. to a stake, N 30 ch. to first station; signed: **Saml. Ashe**; witness: **J. Glasgow**; [no probate record], Delvd. **Jacob Allen**.

P. 19, 30 June 1797, **North Carolina** to **James Prosser** [no residence given], thirty shillings per hundred acres, 72 acres, on waters of Little R., joins **William Ray, William Hopkins, Lazarus Tilley, James Williams**, & his own land, begin at a little white oak on **William Ray's** line & cor. to **Prosser's** Old Tract, on **Ray's** line N10E 20 ch. to a spanish oak cor. to **Ray, Hopkins**, & **Tilla**, E on **Tilla's** line 34 ch. 50 lk. to his cor. spanish oak on **James Williams'** line, along line S 20 ch. to a pine cor. to **Prosser's** Old Tract, his line to beginning, entered 10 February 1794; signed: **Saml. Ashe**; witness: **J. Glasgow**; [no probate record], Delvd. **Anthy. Rickets**.

P. 20, 17 October 1796, **North Carolina** to **Jacob Stout** [no residence given], fifty shillings per hundred acres, 45 acres, on waters of Cain Cr., joins his own &

John Allen's land & Chatham County Line, begin at a post oak on County Line, N 18 1/2 ch. to a black oak, W 24 1/2 ch. to a post oak John Allen's cor., S 18 1/2 ch. to a stake in County Line, County Line E 24 1/2 ch. to beginning; signed: Saml. Ashe; witness: J. Glasgow; [no probate record].

P. 21, 8 June 1797, North Carolina to John Sharp [no residence given], fifty shillings per hundred acres, 120 acres, begin at a post oak a cor. of Jacob Neese, W 88 ch. to a W. O. saplin a cor. of George Friddle, his line S6W 35 ch. to a W. O., S45E 28 ch. to a W. O., N 49 ch. to a stake, E 60 ch. to a stake, to first station, warrant dated 22 April 1796; signed: Saml. Ashe; witness: J. Glasgow; [no probate record], Delvd. Wm. Ray.

P. 21, 18 May 1789, North Carolina to John Coulter [no residence given], fifty shillings per hundred acres, 100 acres, on waters of Bolings Cr. of Newhope, bounded on E by Hardy Morgan, on W by Alexr. Piper, on N by John Bowles, begin at Morgan's cor. post oak, W 16 1/2 ch. to a post oak on Piper's line, N his line 15 1/2 ch. to his cor. post oak, W with line 14 1/2 ch. to a stake, N 24 1/2 ch. to a black jack on Bowles line, E with line 31 ch. to Morgan's cor. red oak, S with line 40 ch. to first station; signed: Sam Ashe; witness: J. Glasgow; [no probate record], Delvd. John McCauley (Irish).

P. 22, 10 August 1797, North Carolina to Frederick Loyd [no residence given], ten pounds per hundred acres, 50 acres, on waters of Morgans Cr., adjoins his own deeded land, begin at a R. O., N 16 ch. 50 lk. to a W. O., W 31 ch. to a spanish oak, S 16 ch. 50 lk. to a black jack, E 31 ch. to beginning, warrant dated 29 September 1797; signed: Saml. Ashe; witness: J. Glasgow; [no probate record], Delvd. F. Loyd.

P. 23, 10 August 1797, North Carolina to Richard Coop [no residence given], thirty shillings per hundred acres, 40 acres, on waters of Back Cr., adjoins James Whitsell, John McMiminy, George Boyd, & his own land, begin at a stake, N52W 14 ch. to a stake, W 22 ch. to a white oak, N 8 ch. to a stake, W 7 ch. 50 lk. to a poplar, S 17 ch. to a post oak, E 41 ch. to beginning; signed: Saml. Ashe; witness: J. Glasgow; [no probate record], Delvd. Richd. Coope.

P. 24, 5 April 1797, North Carolina to George Fossett [no residence given], fifty shillings per hundred acres, 56 acres, on waters of Stags Cr., adjoins his own land, begin at a black oak Andrew McCauley's cor., S 2 1/2 ch. to a black oak, E 13 1/2 ch. to a hicory Reuben Harper's cor., N 18 ch. to a black jack Harper's cor., E 23 ch. to a white oak Empson Bird's cor., S 18 1/4 ch. to a hicory Fossett's cor., his line W 79 ch. to a white oak Fossett's cor., N 4 ch. to a post oak in Andrew McCauley's line, his line to first station; signed: Saml. Ashe; witness: Wm. Hill; [no probate record], Delvd. Geo. Fossett.

P. 25, 5 April 1797, North Carolina to Daniel Warson [no residence given], fifty shillings per hundred acres, 18 acres, on waters of Scrub Cr., adjoins Isaac Dorris & his own land, begin at a black oak bush Warson's cor., N 16 1/2 ch. to a stake on side of a branch Isaac Dorris' cor., E 12 ch. to a stake in Dorris' line, S 14 ch. to a stake Warson's cor., S79W 12 1/2 ch. to first station; signed: Saml. Ashe; witness: Wm. Hill; [no probate record], Delvd. Daniel Wason.

P. 26, 10 August 1797, **North Carolina** to **Nathaniel Robinson** [no residence given], fifty shillings per hundred acres, 40 acres, on waters of Collins Cr., adjoins **John Durham, David Pasmore**, & his own land, begin at a P. O. on **Robison's** old line, S 18 ch. 50 lk. to a P. O. on **Lindsay's** line, E 22 ch. to a P. O. his cor., N 18 ch. 50 lk. to a P. O., W 22 ch. to beginning, warrant dated 20 January 1797; signed: **Saml. Ashe**; witness: **J. Glasgow;** [no probate record], Delvd. **John Millikin.**

P. 27, 30 June 1797, **North Carolina** to **Charles Millican** [no residence given], ten pounds per hundred acres, 150 acres, on waters of Cain Cr., begin at a post oak on James **Millican's** line, W 5 1/2 ch. to a white oak on **Strudwick's** line, with line N7E 30 ch. to a W. O., N70E 8 1/2 ch. to a R. O. & cor. of **Charles Kelley**, his line S 33 ch. to a R. O., E 25 ch. to a R. O., S 40 ch. to a P. O., W 31 ch. to a R. O. & hicory on **James Millican's** line, with line N 40 ch. to beginning, warrant dated 25 April 1785; signed: **Saml. Ashe**; witness: **Jas. Glasgow;** [no probate record], Delvd. **John Millikin.**

P. 28, 5 April 1797, **North Carolina** to **Jacob Huggons** [no residence given], fifty shillings per hundred acres, 60 acres, on waters of Staggs Cr., joins **Sutton Ward, John Smith,** & **John Millington**, begin at a stake in **Sutton Ward's** line, N 35 ch. to a red oak **Ward's** cor. on side of a branch, E 17 ch. 25 lk. to a post oak **John Smith's** cor., S 35 ch. to a hicory on **John Millington's** line, to first station; signed: **Saml. Ashe**; witness: **Wm. Hill;** [no probate record], Delvd. **Jacob Huggams.**

P. 28, 17 October 1796, **North Carolina** to **Alexander Robbs** [no residence given], fifty shillings per hundred acres, 277 acres, begin at a black oak **James Dickey's** cor., W 45 1/2 ch. to a white oak, N 45 1/2 ch. to a stake, W 3 1/2 ch. to a post oak, E 12 ch. to a black oak, S 21 ch. to a hicory, E 44 1/2 ch. to a maple, S 1 ch. to a gum, E 7 ch. to a black jack, S 34 ch. to a hicory, W 15 1/2 ch. to a white oak, S 9 ch. to beginning; signed: **Saml. Ashe**; witness: **J. Glasgow**; [no probate record], Delvd. **Wm. Dickey.**

P. 29, 16 July 1795, **North Carolina** to **George Sheridon** no residence given], ten pounds per hundred acres, 124 acres, on waters of Haw R., joins **David Pasmore** & **John Newland**, begin at a bush on Haw R., S45W 55 ch. to a white oak, S 26 1/2 ch. to a black oak, E 31 ch. to a stake, N 13 ch. to a black oak, W 4 ch. to a black oak on a branch, meanders of branch to a beach on Haw R., up river to first station; signed: **Richd. Dobbs Spaight;** witness: **J. Glasgow;** [no probate record], Delvd. **Thos. King.**

P. 30, 17 October 1796, **North Carolina** to **John Sloss** [no residence given], thirty shillings per hundred acres, 11 3/4 acres, on waters of Jourdan, begin at a post oak in his own former line, S with **William Stalcup's** line 4 ch. to a black jack, E with **Alexr. Robbs'** line 29 ch. 25 lk. to a W. O., N his line 4 ch. to a stake, W his own line 29 ch. 25 lk. to beginning; signed: **Saml. Ashe**; witness: **J. Glasgow**; [no probate record], Delvd. **Hardy Hurdle.**

P. 31, 10 August 1797, **North Carolina** to **Thomas Lasley** [no residence given], fifty shillings per hundred acres, 150 acres, on waters of Little Cain Cr., joins

James McBride, John Pickard, & Hawfields Old Road, begin at a post oak a cor. of **John Pickard** Junr., S33E 17 ch. to a post oak a cor. of **John Pickard Senr.**, his line E 33 ch. to a W. oak near the road, N40E 5 ch. to a red oak on a branch, N12W 43 ch. 50 lk. to a post oak on road, W 12 ch. to a post oak, to beginning, entered 14 September 1778; signed: **Saml. Ashe**; witness: **J. Glasgow**; [no probate record], Delvd. **Thos. Lasley.**

P. 32, 30 June 1797, **North Carolina** to **Reubin Smith** [no residence given], fifty shillings per hundred acres, 19 acres, on waters of Little Cain Cr., joins **Hugh Rae** & his own land, begin at a red oak a cor. of another tract of **Smith's**, N 12 ch. to a red oak, W 16 ch. to a red oak on **Ray's** line, S 12 ch. to a post oak **Ray's** cor., his line E 16 ch. to beginning, warrant dated 3 May 1797; signed: **Saml. Ashe**; witness: **J. Glasgow**; [no probate record], Delvd. **Reuben Smith.**

P. 33, 10 August 1797, **North Carolina** to **Reubin Smith** [no residence given], ten pounds per hundred acres, 200 acres, on waters of Haw R., begin at a post oak, E 22 ch. to a P. O., S34W 48 ch. to a hicory, W 16 ch. to a red oak, N 4 1/2 ch. to a stake, W 22 1/2 ch. to a P. O., N 35 ch. to beginning, warrant dated 25 April 1785; signed: **Saml. Ashe**; witness: **J. Glasgow**; [no probate record], Delvd. **R. Smith.**

P. 34, 8 June 1797, **North Carolina** to **John Reeves** [no residence given], thirty shillings per hundred acres, 50 acres, on waters of Suggs Cr. of Haw R., adjoins his own land & **Empson Bird**, begin at a post oak **Reeves'** cor., N 19 ch. to a black oak **Empson Bird's** cor., E 30 1/2 ch. to a post oak, S 9 ch. to a post oak on **Reeves'** line, his line W 8 ch. to a hicory, S 10 ch. to a post oak, W 22 1/2 ch. to first station, warrant dated 1 October 1793; signed: **Saml. Ashe**; witness: **J. Glasgow**; [no probate record], Delvd. **John Reeves.**

P. 35, 15 July 1797, **Andrew Murdock** Sheriff of Orange to **Absalom Tatom** of Hillsborough, 61 pounds, 185 acres, land of **William Watters** Esq. deceased to satisfy judgement of two hundred fifty four pounds four shillings three pence and cost recovered by **William Kirkland & Company** and judgement of four hundred one pounds eighteen shillings ten pence & cost recovered by **William Cain & Company**, on the Occaneechee Mountain near Hillsborough, sold 20 May last, begin at a pine a cor. of **Carrigan's** Old Place now **William Whitehead's**, W 61 ch. to a hicory, S 28 ch. to a black oak, E 7 ch. to a black oak, S 43 ch. to a stake, E 15 ch. to a black jack, N60E 48 ch. to center of 3 post oaks about 100 yards SE of the Cool Spring, 6 ch. to beginning, **Walter Alves & Emilia** his wife to **Watters** 8 June 1793; signed: **Andrew Murdock**; witness: **J. Estes, John Whitehead**; acknowledged August Term 179, Delvd. **A. Tatum.**

P. 37, 28 July 1797, **Andrew Murdock** Sheriff of Orange to **Jacob Neese** of same, fifty pounds one shilling, foreclosure obtained by **Governor of North Carolina** against **James Williams** on mortgage dated 5 June 1784 which was security for payment of fifty one pounds with 152 acres as collateral, adjoins **Jacob Ross & McCullock**, on waters of Great Allamance, begin at a post oak on another line of **McCullock's** land, S 31 ch. to a stake, W 49 ch. to a stake, N

31 ch. to a stake, E 49 ch. to first station, sold 3 July last, ninety four pounds seventeen shillings one farthing principal & seventeen pounds nine shillings four pence costs due to State; signed: **Andrew Murdock**; witness: **R. Bell, James Green**; acknowledged August Term 1797, Delvd. **Andrew Murdock.**

P. 39, 10 July 1797, **Andrew Murdock** Sheriff of Orange County to **John Rhea** of same, one hundred seven pounds ten shillings, decree of foreclosure obtained by **Governor of North Carolina** against **James Williams** on mortgage dated 5 June 1784 for forty four pounds six shillings eight pence for purchase of 214 acres, on waters of Little R., adjoins **Duke, Nehemiah Edge, Thomas King**, & land of **McCullock**, begin at a black oak **John Duke's** cor., S 46 ch. to a post oak, continued 17 ch. to a stake, W 34 ch. to a black oak, N 63 ch. to a white oak, E 34 ch. to first station, eighty two pounds nine shillings one farthing principal & seven pounds six shillings eleven pence three farthings costs due on mortgage, sold 3 July last; signed: **Andrew Murdoch**; witness: **Robert Harris, William Montgomery**; acknowledged August Term 1797, Delvd. **Wm. Montgomery.**

P. 41, 4 July 1797, **Andrew Murdock** Sheriff of Orange to **Richard Bennehan** of same, two hundred seventy two pounds, land of **James Williams** mortgage of two hundred thirty three pounds, 461 acres, on waters of Little R., adjoins **Charles Horton, Patrick Clark**, and **William Ray** & a tract of **Henry Eustace McCulloh**, begin at a black oak a cor. of **William Ray & Patrick Clark**, E 74 ch. to a stake, N55W 5 ch. to a post oak, N 63 ch. to a stake, W 70 ch. to a black oak, S 65 ch. to first station, one hundred and forty four pounds eight shillings eleven pence one farthing principal & seventeen pounds nineteen shillings four pence half penny interest due on mortgage, sold 3 July last, ; signed: **Andrew Murdock**; witness: **David Ray, James Yarbrough**; acknowledged August Term 1797, Delvd. **Richd. Bennehan.**

P. 43, 1 April 1797, **Andrew Murdock** Sheriff of Orange to **Robert Marley** of Guilford, sixty nine pounds, 208 acres, levy on lands of **Adam Marley** & **Thomas Vincent** for one hundred fifteen pounds nine pence recovered by **John Warren** Assignee &c., sold 5 February 1797, on waters of Deep Cr., begin at a hicory on W bank of creek, N 9 ch. to a stake, E 16 ch. 50 lk. to a post oak, N 12 ch. 25 lk. to a post oak, E 29 ch. 25 lk. to a black oak, S 5 ch. 50 lk. crossing creek continued in all 54 ch. 25 lk. to Deep Cr., up creek to first station; signed: **Andrew Murdock**; witness: **William Hall, John McKerall**; acknowledged August Term 1797, Delvd. **H. Hurdle.**

P. 45, 20 July 1797, **Andrew Murdock** Sheriff of Orange to **William Montgomery** of same, eighty eight pounds one shilling, 226 acres, **Governor** vs **James Williams**, mortgage for two hundred thirty three pounds, on waters of Flat R., adjoins **John Duke & McCulloh**, begin at a black oak **Duke's** cor., S 46 ch. to a post oak continued 17 ch. to a stake, E 36 ch. to a stake, N 63 ch. to a stake, E 36 ch. to a stake, N 63 ch. to a stake, W 36 ch. to first station, ninety nine pounds fifteen shillings four pence principal seventeen pounds ten shillings four pence costs due, sold 3 July last, signed: **Andrew Murdock**; witness: **Thomas Rhew, John Rhew**; acknowledged August Term 1797, Delvd. **Wm.Montgomery.**

P. 48, 28 July 1797, **Andrew Murdoch** Sheriff of Orange to **Daniel Albright** of same, forty pounds, 159 acres, **Governor** vs **James Williams**, mortgage for fifty eight pounds six shillings eight pence, on N side of Great Allamance, adjoins **Joseph Houseman** & land of **McCulloh**, begin at a poplar on side of Great Allamance, N 33 ch. to a stake, E 49 ch. to a stake, S 31 ch. to a stake, W 15 ch. to a stake, S 7 ch. to Great Allamance, up creek to first station, suit for fifty eight pounds six shillings eight pence & seventeen pounds ten shillings eight pence costs, sold 3 July 1797; signed: **Andrew Murdoch**; witness: **Robert Bell, James Green**; acknowledged August Term 1797, Delvd. **Andrew Murdock**.

P. 50, 10 July 1797, **Andrew Murdoch** Sheriff of Orange to **Robert Harris** of same, seventy one pounds one shilling, 117 acres, **Governor** vs **James Williams**, mortgage for fifty nine pounds, on S side of Flat R., adjoins **Willm. Horton, Reason Ricketts, John Dicks**, & land of **McCulloh**, begin at an elm on side of Flat R., S 17 ch. to a gum, E 107 ch. to a black oak, N 5 ch. to a pine on side of Flat R., up river to first station, levy for one hundred and nine pounds fourteen shillings eight pence principal & interest & seventeen pounds elevern shillings six pence costs, sold 3 July 1797; signed: **Andrew Murdock**; witness: **William Montgomery, Thomas Pinnier**; acknowledged August Term 1797, Delvd. **Robt. Harris**.

P. 52, 8 July 1797, **Andrew Murdock** Sheriff of Orange to **Henry Snotterly** of same, fifty pounds one shilling, 184 acres, **Governor** vs **James Williams**, mortgage for thirty four pounds, on S side of Great Allamance, adjoins **George Friddle, Conrad Pile**, & **McCulloh's** land, begin at a stake on the side of the Allamance, S 49 ch. to a black oak, E 38 ch. to a post oak, N 48 ch. to a stake on the side of Allamance, up creek to first station, payment due from **Williams** five years after 5 December 1782, levy for sixty one pounds principal and interest & seventeen pounds twelve shillings two pence costs, sold 3 July 1797; signed: **Andrew Murdock**; witness: **R. Bell, James Green**; acknowledged August Term 1797, Delvd. **Andrew Murdock**.

P. 54, 10 July 1797, **Andrew Murdock** Sheriff of Orange to **Andrew Gibson** of same, merchant, eighty pounds, 270 acres, **Governor** vs **James Williams**, mortgage dated 5 June 1784 for fifty six pounds thirteen shillings four pence, on waters of Great Allamance, joins **Michael Charles, Shadrack Holt, Jacob Wilhite**, & Guilford County Line, begin at a black oak, N30E 52 ch. to a hicory, N45W 49 ch. to a black oak, S 93 ch. to a stake on Guilford County Line, E 23 ch. to first station, levy for one hundred five pounds eight shillings & seventeen pounds ten shillings six pence costs, sold 3 July 1797; signed: **Andrew Murdock**; witness: [none named]; acknowledged August Term 1797, Delvd. **James Patterson**.

P. 56, 30 June 1797, **North Carolina** to **Jacob Harder,** [no residence given] fifty shillings per hundred acres, 200 acres, on waters of Boyds Cr., joins **John King** & others, begin at a post oak, E 20 ch. to a stake, S 6 ch. to a stake, E 20 ch. 50 lk. to a stake, S 45 ch. to a stake, W 40 ch. 50 lk. to a stake, N 51 ch. to beginning, warrant dated 8 March 1797; signed: **Saml. Ashe**; witness: **J. Glasgow**; [no probate record], Delvd. **H. Hurdle**.

P. 57, 6 August 1785, **James Freeland** Sheriff of Orange to **John McCandless** of same, twenty pounds, 230 acres, levy against **William & John Rielley** for sixteen pounds four shillings five pence recovered by **James Mebane**, land sold was property of **John Reilly**, sold 10 May 1785, on waters of Little R., begin at a R. O. a cor. of **James Baldridge** on **McCulloh's** Line, his line S 27 ch. 50 lk. to a B. O., another of his lines W 60 ch. to his cor. B. J., S 2 ch. to **Armstrong's** cor., his line E 50 ch. to a B. J., S 39 ch. 25 lk. to a R. O., E at 16 ch. crossing the Road leading from Hillsborough to Paynes Tavern the course continued 1 ch. to a W. O. **Armstrong** & **Robert Jordan's** cor., the same course on **Jordan's** line in all 37 ch. to his cor. a pine, N 47 ch. 75 lk. to a B. O. in the road a cor. to **Jordan** & **James Mebane**, the course continued on **Mebane's** line in all 68 ch. 75 lk. to a P. O. **Baldridge's** cor., his line W 25 ch. 50 lk. to first station; signed: **James Freeland**; witness: **David McCandless, Robert Wasson**; proved August Term 1797 by **David McCandless**, Delvd. **John McCandless**.

P. 59, 8 July 1797, **Michael Robinson Senior** of Orange to **John Latta Senior** of same, two hundred pounds, 392 acres, on both sides South Fork of Little R., adjoins **Robert McCulloh**, begin at a black oak **Robert McCulloh's** cor., E 79 ch. to a hicory, S 25 ch. to a stake, SW 35 ch. to a post oak, S 29 ch. to a hicory, W 25 ch. to a white oak, S 40 ch. to a stake, W 19 ch. to a black oak, N 94 ch. to first station, tract of land where **Michael Robinson Junior** now lives, **North Carolina** to **Michael Robinson** 13 March 1780; signed: **Michael Robinson**; witness: **Robert Walker, John Riggs**; proved by **Walker** [no date given], Delvd. **Jno. Latta Senr.**

P. 60, 10 December 1796, **Benjamin Smith** of Brunswick County to **James Hogg** of Orange, nineteen hundred & one third dollars, 1/64 share in lands in Kentucky, on 17 March 1775 the Cherokee Nation sold **Richard Henderson, John Williams, Thomas Hart, Nathaniel Hart, John Luttrell, William Johnston, James Hogg, David Hart,** & **Leonard Henley Bullock** all of North Carolina a tract on waters the River Kentucky, Green River, Cumberland, Powell, & Clinch R. & other branches of the Ohio (1/8 part to each man except **David Hart** & **Leonard Henly Bullock** who each received 1/16), on 27 August 1777 Hogg sold part of his share to **William Dry** of Brunswick County 1/4 of his 1/8 part or 1/32 part of the two deeds from the Indians, **William Dry** sold **Richard Quince** 1/2 of his share or 1/64 part, **Quince** sold his share to **General Benjamin Smith** of Brunswick County; signed: **Benjamin Smith**; witness: **A. Tatom, John Hogg**; proved May Term 1797 by **Absalom Tatom**; affidavit of **James Carson**, presiding Justice of Court of P&QS of Orange, that attestation was made in due form, affidavit of **Abner B. Bruce**, Clerk of Court, that **Carson** was Presiding Justice, Delvd. **James Hogg**.

P. 63, 5 September 1785, **Margaret Wall**, widow, of Orange to **John Kelley**, farmer, of same, forty pounds, her life estate in lands devised to her, **Isaac Holder's** will dated 13 January 1767 bequeathed to his son, **Isaac Holder, Jr.**, the tract where **Isaac Holder Sr.** lived, 2/3 of which he was to receive when he reached 21 and the remainder at the death of **Isaac Holder's** wife, if **Isaac Holder Jr.** died without issue the land was to be divided between **Margaret Douglass** daughter of **John Douglas**, **Anne Holdeness** daughter of **John Holdeness**, **Fanny Wood** daughter of **John Wood**, **John Holdeness** son of **Thomas Holdeness Junr.**, & **Thomas Kelley** son of **John Kelley**, **Margaret Douglass** is now **Margaret Wall**, widow of **John Wall**; signed: **Margaret Wall**;

witness: **Samuel Clenny, Barnaby (+) Grimes**; proved August Term 1797 by **Grimes**, Delvd. **John Kelley**.

P. 65, 27 August 1785, **Fanny Wood** [no residence given] to **John Kelley** of North Carolina, forty pounds, her life estate in lands devised to her by **Isaac Holder Senr.** repeat of above; signed: **Fanny (X) Wood**; witness: **Samuel Clenny, John Wood**; proved August Term 1797 by **John Wood**, Delvd. **John Kelley**.

P. 67, 10 July 1778, **Robert Marley & Martha** his wife of Orange to **Benjamin Chapman** of same, two hundred pounds, 90 acres 8 perches, on Buck Quarter Cr., begin at a post oak, S7 1/2 20 perches, S57E 32 perches, S53E, S63E 36 East, S87E, S37E, S30E, E 56 perches to a black oak, S 162 to a dogwood & sweet gum. W 142 76 to a black oak, W 7 68 to beginning, from **Granville** 27 February 1759; signed: **Robery Marley, Martha Marley**; witness: **Jno. Kelley**; proved August Term 1797 by **Kelley**, Delvd. **John Kelley**.

P. 68, 15 May 1796, **Joseph Noey** of Orange to **John Noey** of same, one hundred pounds, 230 acres, formerly claim of **H. E. McCulloh**, confiscated to the use of the State, on S side of Haw R., on waters of Ulias Cr., adjoins tract #47, begin at a white oak, N70W 15 ch. to a white oak, N30E 20 ch. to a post oak, N 5 ch. to a stake, N30E 20 ch. to a post oak, N 5 ch. to a stake, E 40 ch. to a black oak, S10W 51 ch. to a stake, S 20 ch. to a black oak, to first station; signed: **Joseph Noey**; witness: **George Noey, Joseph Rich, J. V. Patterson**; proved August Term 1797 by **Patterson**, Delvd. **Garrald Burrow**.

P. 69, 7 July 1797, **Everard Garret** of Orange to **Ludwick Albright Junior** of same, three hundred silver dollars, 173 acres, on waters of Little Allamance, begin at a red oak **Jeremiah Holt's** cor., E 10 1/2 ch. to a stake, S45E 10 ch. to a stake, N45E 7 ch. to a stake, E 44 1/2 ch. to a stake, N 5 1/2 ch. to **Michael Holt's** cor., N45W 19 ch. to a red oak, S52W 25 ch. to a red & white oak, N65W 37 ch. to a persimmon, S45W 15 ch. to a red oak on **Jeremiah Holt's** line, his line to beginning part of a tract from **Henry E. McCulloh** to **John Powell Senr.**; signed: **Everard Garret**; witness: **John Holt, William Dickson**; proved August Term 1797 by **John Holt**, Delvd. **John Powell**.

P. 71, 8 June 1797, **North Carolina** to **Adam Smith**, [no residence given] fifty shillings per hundred acres, 23 acres, adjoins his own land, begin at a sweet gum, S 40 ch. to a post oak, S70E 13 ch. to a stake **Smith's** cor., his line N20W 38 ch. to beginning, warrant dated 6 June 1796; signed: **Saml. Ashe**; witness: **J. Glasgow**; [no probate record].

P. 71, 12 October 1784, **Benjamin Rainey** of Orange & **Nancy** his wife to **Michael Holt** of same, four pounds, 12 acres, on S side of Haw R., begin at a stone in **George Holt's** field, E 15 ch. to a white oak grub on Old Holts Spring Branch, S10E the meanders of creek 18 ch. to a stake, N45W to beginning, part of a larger tract from **North Carolina** to **Rainey**; signed: **Benjamin Rainey, Nancy (X) Rainey**; witness: **John Williams, Christopher Holt**; proved August Term 1786 by **Christopher Holt**, Delvd. **Jno. Powell**.

P. 73, 19 January 1779, **John Powell & Mary** his wife of Orange to **Elias Powell Junior** of same, fifty pounds, 139 acres, on S side of Haw R., begin at a white oak **Elias Powell Senr.'s** cor., S43W 89 p. to a red oak, N45W 250 p. to a hicory saplin, N45E 89 p. to a black jack, S45E 250 p. to first station, part of 970 acres from **Henry McCulloh** to **John Powell Senior**; signed: **John Powell, Mary (X) Powell**; witness: **William Rainey**; proved May Term 1784 by **Rainey**, Delvd. **John Powell**.

P. 74, 1 May 1796, **William Shepperd** Attorney for the **Trustees of the University of North Carolina** to **Joseph Homes** of Orange, two hundred and seventy pounds, 360 acres, on S side of Haw R., begin at a red oak, S45W 84 ch. to a white oak, N45W 33 ch. to a red oak, N45E 20 ch. to a black oak, N45W 12 ch. to a post oak, N45E 64 1/2 ch. to a white oak, S45E 45 ch. to beginning; signed: **William Shepperd** Attorney; witness: **H. Shepperd, Aaron Sharpe**; proved August Term 1797 by **Sharpe**, Delvd. **Joseph Homes**.

P. 76, 16 August 1797, **Charles Dunnagan** of Orange to **James Dunnagan** of same, one hundred pounds, 100 acres, begin at a white oak on bank of Little R. on N side near mouth of **Charles Dunnagan's** Spring Br. that is opposite against, up river 43 ch. to a stake, E 52 ch. to river, up river to beginning, land lies on N side of Little R., tract of land taken up by **Charles Dunnagan** & surveyed by **James Smith** DS in 1779; signed: **Charles (X) Dunnagan**; witness: **William Dunnagan, Sharwood Dunnagan**; acknowledged August Term 1797, Delvd. **James Dunnagan**.

P. 77, 30 June 1797, **North Carolina** to **William Roberts**, [no residence given] fifty shillings per hundred acres, 195 acres, on waters of Flat R., begin at a W. O., N29E 46 ch. to a pine, N 12 ch. to a stake, W 47 ch. to a stake, S 52 ch. to a stake, E 24 ch. to beginning, warrant dated 16 July 1796; **Saml. Ashe**; witness: **J. Glasgow**; [no probate record], Delvd. **Willm. Roberts**.

P. 78, 12 January 1797, **Thomas Hart & Ellenor** his wife Orange to **William Whitted Junior** of Hillsborough, one hundred dollars, [no acreage given], on waters of Eno, bounded by **Whitted** on W, **Peter Hart** on S, by house of **Benjamin Thornton** on E, & **Ralph Fossett** on N, begin at a stake the NW cor. of tract, S 13 ch. to a stake, E 25 ch. to a spanish oak, N 13 ch. to a stake, W 25 ch. to beginning, part of tract from his father **James Hart** to **Thomas**; signed: **Thomas Hart, Elliner (X) Hart**; witness: **Absalom Tatom, John Whitted**; proved August Term 1797 by **Tatom**, Delvd. **Jas. Whitted**.

P. 79, 28 August 1797, **John McKerrall** of Orange to **Adam Whitsell** of same, eighty one pounds ten shillings, 163 acres, on waters of Gunn Cr., begin at **Ludwick Albright's** cor. red oak, S45W 23 ch. to a black oak, N45W 56 ch. to a red oak, N45E 37 ch. to a stake, S45E 41 ch. to a stake, S45W 15 ch. to a hicory, S45E 5 ch. to first station, **North Carolina** to **Andrew Ross** 4 June 1784 & **Sheriff of Orange** to **McKerrall** 18 October 1796; signed: **John McKerrall**; witness: **David Ray, Andrew Murdock**; proved August Term 1797 by **Murdock**, Delvd. **Adam Whitsell**.

P. 81, 5 April 1797, **North Carolina** to **Samuel Wilson**, [no residence given] fifty shillings per hundred acres, 84 acres, on waters of Little R., adjoins **Robert Beverly, Andrew Griffin,** & his own land, begin at a black oak, W 8 1/2 ch. to a black jack, **Robt. Burney's** cor., E 42 1/2 ch. to a stake in **Andrew Griffin's** line, N 14 ch. to a post oak on **Samuel Willson's** line, W 34 ch. to a stake **Willson's** cor., S 29 ch. to first station; signed: **Saml. Ashe**; witness: **Wm. Hill**; [no probate record], Delvd. **Saml. Willson.**

P. 81, 28 August 1797, **John Dunnavan** of Orange to **George McCraw** of same, fifty pounds, 51 acres, begin at a red oak on the Great Road leading to **Faucetts** a cor. of **William Dickey**, 29 ch. to a hicory, E 14 ch. to a hicory, N 2 1/2 ch. to a post oak, W 21 ch. to a black oak, S36E 15 ch. to a white oak, S52W 4 ch. to a black oak on side of the Road, up road to first station; signed: **John ( ) Dunnavan**; witness: **John Sloss, Alex (X) Ross**; proved August Term 1797 by **Sloss**, Delvd. **Hardy Hurdle.**

P. 83, [blank] July 1788, **North Carolina** to **James Adams**, [no residence given] fifty shillings per hundred acres, 150 acres, on both sides of Shirleys Br. waters of Stones Cr., bounded on N on Caswell County Line, begin at a post oak on Caswell County Line, S 30 ch. to a post oak W 50 ch. to a post oak, N 30 ch. to a stake, E 50 ch. to first station; signed: **Samuel Johnston**; witness: **W. Williams**; [no probate record].

P. 83, 9 April 1796, **Trustees of the University of North Carolina** to **Nathaniel Harris** of Orange, thirty three pounds, 220 acres, on both sides of Flat R., begin at a white oak on bank of river, N55E 54 ch. to a red oak, S 68 1/2 ch. to a black oak, W 43 ch. crossing Flat R. to a hicory, N crossing river 37 ch. to beginning; signed: **William Shepperd** Commissioner & Attorney; witness: **Jesse Rice, William Ray**; proved August Term 1797 by **Ray**, Delvd. **Nathl. Harris.**

P. 85, 19 August 1797, **James Hogg** Esq. of Orange to **Joseph Taylor** of same, eighty pounds, 100 acres, on waters of Eno, formerly occupied by **Mrs. Jane Anderson & James Anderson, Jane Anderson & James Anderson** to **Hogg** at request of **William Hill** Esq., **Hogg** to **George Alsworth**, now occupied by **Alsworth**, [no metes or bounds description]; signed: **James Hogg**; witness: **John Taylor, George Alsworth**; proved August Term 1797 by **Alsworth**, Delvd. **Joseph Taylor.**

P. 86, 28 August 1797, **Benjamin Yeargan** of Orange to **Garrett (Jarratt) Yeargin** of same, five hundred pounds, 457 acres, on waters of Lick Cr., begin at a white oak **Samuel Hays'** cor., his line N 150 p. to a white & red oak, E 86 p. to **Couch's** cor., E his line 186 p. to a white oak his cor., S 248 p. to a white oak, W 40 p. to a hicory **Barbee's** cor., S his line 37 p. to a white oak, W **Hardy Morgan's** line 208 p. to a white oak his cor., N his line 162 p. to a pine, W 18 p. to beginning; signed: **Benjamin Yeargain**; witness: **James Green**; acknowledged August Term 1797, Delvd. **John McCauley (Irish).**

P. 87, 26 May 1785, **Charles Abercromby** of Orange to **William Deshays** of same, forty pounds, 180 acres, on waters of Newhope, begin at a white oak on **John Mitchem's** line, W 80 p. to a red oak, S 120 p. to a red oak, W 60 p. to a white oak saplin, S 180 p. to a black jack, E 120 p. to a black jack on on

William Rhodes line, along line 40 p. to a white oak, E on line 5 1/2 p. to a pine, N to first station; signed: **Charles Abercrombie**; witness: **John Meacham**; proved November Term 1785 by **Meacham**, Delvd. **Joseph Nix**.

P. 89, 9 April 1797, **Henry Nolner** of Petersburg, Virginia, to **Williams Dickins** of Granville, five hundred and fifty five dollars, 555 acres, 2 tracts, begin at a hicory cor. formerly **Gibson's**, E to Deep Cr., down creek to Flat R., up river to a W O, N to first station, 125 acres, 2nd. tract, begin at a P O near the Old Mill Path, W 50 ch. to a W O, N 65 ch. to a B O, E cross the river 84 ch. to a stake, S 34 ch. to a W O, up river to mouth of a branch below Mill Seat, up branch to a W O, along **Carrington's** line to the Old Mill Path, S on Old Mill Path to first station, 430 acres; signed: **Henry Nolner**; witnesas: **Ephriam Frazier, John (+) Russell**; proved August Term 1797 by **Frazier**.

P. 90, 16 March 1797, **Robert Barnwell** to **Richard Cope** both of Orange, one hundred and fifty dollars, 100 acres, on waters of Quaker Cr., begin at a black oak on W side of creek, W 10 ch. to a black oak, S7W 7 1/2 ch. to a black oak, W 20 ch. to a stake, N 33 ch. to a black oak bush, E to a persimmon on bank of creek, down creek to first station, part of 200 acres from **North Carolina** to **Barnwell** 9 November 1784, recorded in Book M No. 2 Folio 66; signed: **Robert (X) Barnwell**; witness: **Thomas Lynch, Moses Lynch**; proved August Term 1797 by **Thomas Lynch**, Delvd. **Richd. Coope**.

P. 91, 4 February 1796, **Andrew Gibson** of Guilford to **Thomas Carmichael** of Orange, one hundred and fifty pounds, 140 1/2 acres, begin at a hicory, E 15 1/2 ch. to a black jack, N 14 ch. to a black oak, E 31 to a black oak, S 8 1/2 to a black oak, 10 ch. to a W. O., S 23 1/2 to a post oak, W 40 ch. to a black jack, N46W to beginning; signed: **Andrew Gibson**; witness: **Joseph Sloss, James Ross**; acknowledged August Term 1797, Delvd. **Joseph Barber**.

P. 93, 3 December 1796, **David Witherspoon** of New Bern to **John Umpstead** of Orange, fifty pounds, 360 acres, 2 tracts, first tract on waters of Foresters Cr., known as **Theophilus Thompson** Tract, Sheriff of Orange to **Witherspoon**, begin at a black jack **Nichols'** cor., W 48 1/2 ch. to a red oak, N 34 ch. to a post oak, E 48 1/2 ch. to a stake on **Nichols'** line, S 34 ch. to beginning, 210 acres, another tract on Foresters Cr. waters of Little R., adjoins **Robert Smith, William Anderson, Henry Stile, & Theophilus Thompson**, begin at a black jack on **Nichols'** line, N 18 1/2 ch. to a black oak, W 60 ch. to a white oak **Isaac Gaddes'** cor., S 16 ch. to a hicory, W 18 ch. to a red oak, S 16 ch. to a white oak on **Stiles'** line, W 22 ch. to a white oak **Thompson's** line, N 13 1/2 ch. to a post oak, E 48 ch. to first station, 150 acres, Sheriff of Orange to **Witherspoon**; signed: **D. Witherspoon**; witness: **S. Benton, Rd. W. Freeor(?)**; proved August Term 1797 by **Samuel Benton**, Delvd. **John Umpstead**.

P. 94, 30 August 1797, **Walter Aives** of Orange to **Richmond Harris** of same, two hundred pounds, 166 acres, in fork of Flat & Eno R., adjoins **Richard Benehan & Richmond Harris, James Harris** to **Walter Aivis** 5 November 1794, devised to **James Harris** by will of his father **James Harris** as an undivided half, to **James Harris** from **Thomas Webb & William Wallace, James Harris** had bequeathed other half to **Richmond Harris**, [no metes or bounds description];

signed: **Walter Alvis**; witness: **Gavin Alves;** proved August Term 1797 by **Gavin Alves,** Delvd. **W. Alves.**

P. 96, 10 June 1797, **Owen Lindley** of Orange to **William Whitted, Jr.**, of Hillsborough, two hundred and fifty one dollars, 60 1/2 acres, on waters of Eno R., begin at a stake on **Hugh Finley's** line E along **Finley's** line 25 ch. to a white oak, N 20 ch. 20 lk. to a red oak cor. of land **Whitted** purchased from **Peter Hart,** W along **Whitted's** line 25 ch. to a hicory, S along the line of land **Whitted** purchased from **Stephen Hart** 34 ch. 20 lk. to beginning, **Stephen Hart** to **Owen Lindley** for shares of **Stephen Hart** and heirs of **Samuel Hart** from estate of **James Hart**; signed: **Owin Lindley**; witness: **A. Tatom, John Strother**; proved August Term 1797 by **Tatom,** Delvd. **Jas. Whitted.**

P. 97, 1 June 1791, **Andrew Gibson** of Guilford to **James Ross** of Orange, one hundred pounds, 150 acres, begin at a black jack oak on **Widow Denning's** line, E 10 ch. to **William Boyle's** cor. on a post oak, S 19 ch. to a black oak, the course continued 14 ch. to a black jack, W 57 ch. to a post oak, N 16 ch. to a post oak, W 17 ch. to a post oak, N 7 ch. to a post oak, E 17 ch., continued 44 ch. to a stake, N 10 ch. to first station; signed: **Andrew Gibson**; witness: **Thomas Carmichael, James Lett Junr.**; acknowledged August Term 1797, Delvd. **Joseph Barber.**

P. 99, 25 May 1797, **Stephen Tatom** of Orange to **Fowler Jones** of same, thirty shillings, 1 acre, on waters of Camp Cr., begin at a maple on N side of Lick Br., N 8 p. to a stake, W 20 p. to a stake, S 8 p. to branch, down **Mary Anderons** Branch to beginning; signed: **Stephen (X) Tatom**; witness: **William Tatom, Elijah Parrish**; acknowledged August Term 1797.

P. 100, 8 September 1796, **John King** of Orange, planter, to **James Mitchell** of same, planter, one hundred pounds, 398 1/2 acres, on waters of Morgan Cr., begin at **Charles King's** cor. on a hicory, N 90 p. to a red oak saplin, W 112 p. crossing creek & continued 169 p. to a black oak, S 227 p. to a white oak, E 281 p. to a red oak on creek, up creek to first station; signed: **John King, Sarah (+) King**; witness: **John Mitchell, John McCauley**; proved August Term 1797 by **John Mitchell,** Delvd. **James Mitchell.**

P. 101, 29 September 1794, **John Griffeth** & wife **Jennett** of Orange to **Peter Walker** of same, one hudred and thirty pounds, 128 acres, begin at a white oak, S 32 ch. to a stake, W 40 ch. to a hicory **Thomas Lapsley's** cor., N 32 ch. to a stake, W 40 ch. to first station, on both sides of West Fork of Back Cr. a branch of Haw R., **Zachariah Kaydle** to **Benj. Kaydle,** Granville to **Zachariah Kaydle** 25 October 1753, **Benjamin Kaydle** to **John Douglass** 22 February 1760, **John Douglass** to **Thomas Hart,** by sd. **Hart** sold by Act of Assembly to **John & Robert Tinnin** 3 October 1792 signed **Alexander Mebane** Sheriff, **John & Robert Tinnin** to **John Griffeth** 2 September 1780; signed: **John Griffith, Jenet Griffith**; witness: **John Walker, Andrew Walker**; acknowledged before **Sterling Harris & Empson Bird** August Term 1797.

P. 103, 16 August 1790, **David Lapsley** of Orange to **William Walker** of same, one hundred and forty pounds, 250 acres, on waters of Back Cr., begin at a red oak on **Joseph Thompson's** line, E 37 1/2 ch. to a red oak, N cross the branch of Back Cr. 6 1/2 ch. to a hicory, W 37 1/2 ch. to a stake on **Edward Linch's** line, S along **Lapsley's & Thompson's** line to first station, surveyed 22 August 1760 for **Thomas Lapsley Senior, Granville** to **Lapsley** 1761, willed by **Thomas Lapsley Senior** to **David Lapsley**; signed: **David Lapsley**; witness: **James Mumford, Joseph Moore**; proved August Term 1797 by **Moore**, Delvd. **Thos. Johnston.**

P. 105, 8 September 1796, **John King** of Orange, planter, to **James Mitchell** of same, planter, one hundred pounds, 100 acres, on Morgans Cr. waters of New Hope, begin at a stake, S 25 ch. to a red oak, W 40 ch. to a stake & marked saplins, N 25 ch. to a stake, 40 ch. to first station; signed: **John King, Sarah (X) King**; witness: **John Mitchell, John McCauley**; proved August Term 1797 by **John Mitchell**, Delvd. **James Mitchell.**

P. 106, 30 January 1797, **Peter Hart** of Orange to **William Whitted, Junr.** of Hillsborough, ninety dollars, 36 acres, on waters of Eno, bounded by sd. **William** on W & N, by **Benjamin Thompson** on E, & by **Owen Linley** on S, begin at a stake the SW cor., 14 ch 40 lk. to a hicory, E 25 ch. to a red oak, N 14 ch. 40 lk. to a spanish oak the SE cor. of Division No. 1, W 25 ch. to beginning, **James Hart** to son **Peter Hart**; signed: **Peter Hart**; witness: **Ralph Faucett, William Rider**; proved August Term 1797, Delvd. **Jas. Whitted.**

P. 107, 26 Augusat 1797, **Thomas Bradshaw** of Orange to **Joseph Steel** of same, fifty pounds, 27 1/2 acres, formerly claimed & sold as **John Thompson's**, begin at a stake in a field on a line of **Steel's** Old Tract, along line S 12 lkk. & 87 lk. to a white oak, S20W 14 ch. 50 lk. to a post oak near Thompsons Br., up branch 20 ch. 35 lk. to a post oak bush on branch, E 21 ch. 50 lk. to beginning; signed: **Thomas Bradshaw**; witness: **Charles Christmas, William Shaw**; proved August Term 1797 by **Christmas**, Delvd. **James Crutchfield.**

P. 109, 7 August 1797, **John Thompson** of Orange to **William Fitch** of same, three hundred and seventy five pounds, 300 acres, on Little R., begin at a R. O., N 35 ch. to a B. O., E 54 ch. to a B. O., S 64 ch. to a R. O., W 12 ch. to a poplar, S 5 ch. to a W. O., W 10 ch. to a B. O., N 34 ch. to a B. O., W 32 ch. to first station, **North Carolina** to **John Thompson** 3 September 1779; signed: **John Thompson**; witness: **James Baldrige, Malcomb Baldrige**; acknowledged August Term 1797, Delvd. **William Fitch.**

P. 110, 29 June 1797, **Jonathon Clenney** of Hillsborough to **Samuel Clenny** of Hillsborough, two hundred and thirty five pounds, [no acreage given], on waters of Buck Water Cr., bounded by **William Cain's** land formerly **Timothy Cain's** land, **Stephen Carrol's** land formerly **John Cain's** land, **William Clenny's** land on the S by lands of **John Woods Sheriff**, on W by lands willed to sd. **Samuel** by his father & **John Kelley's** land on N, part of a tract formerly property of **Samuel Clenny** Decd. & willed to **Jonathon** by will dated 2 July 1795, [no metes or bounds description]; signed: **Jonathon Clenny**; witness: **A. Tatom, John McKerall**; proved August Term 1797 by **Absalom Tatom**, Delvdd. **Saml. Clenny.**

P. 112, 28 July 1797, **Everard Garret** of Orange to **John Holt Junior** of same, one hundred pounds, 100 acres, on both sides of Little Allamance, place formerly purchased by **William Garrett**, begin on a red oak on **William O'Neal's** line near a big road, N80E 36 1/2 ch. to a cor. of pointers, N40E 10 ch. to a stake on **Ephriam Cook's** line, his line S45E 12 ch. to a stone **John Albright's** cor., his line S50W 53 ch. to a red bud, N32W 13 ch. to a red oak a cor. of **William Dixon**, his line to beginning, part of a larger tract from **John Powell Senior, Henry McCulloh** to **John Powell Senior**; signed: **Everard Garrett**; witness: **John Powell, William Dickson**; proved August Term 1797 by **William Dixon**, Delvd. **John Powell**.

P. 113, 21 August 1797, **Robert Watson** of Rowan to **Alexander Russell** of Orange, seventy five pounds, 125 acres, on Rocky Branch of Haw Cr., begin at fork of branch **Mahon's** cor., his line N2W 4 1/2 ch. to an ash on branch, N10E 9 ch. to a black oak, N18W 20 ch. to a black jack, leaving **Mahon's** line running S85W 11 ch. to a black jack, S52W 21 ch. to a white, S65W 13 1/2 ch. to a black jack **Russel's** cor., S31E 9 ch. to a stake, continuing **Russel's** line S70E 25 ch. to a hicory, N70E 21 ch. to beginning, **Richard Foster** to **Samuel Watson, Samuel Watson** to **Robert Watson**; signed: **Robert Watson**; witness: **John Malcomb, John Foust**; proved August Term 1797 by **Malcomb**, Delvd. **Alexr. Russell**.

P. 115, 28 July 1797, **Everard Garrett** to **William Dixon**, both of Orange, three hundred dollars, 127 acres, on waters of Little Allamance, begin at a persimmon, S45W 15 ch. to a red oak, N 65 ch. to a stake, N80E 20 ch. to a red oak **John Holt's** cor., his line S25E 1 1/2 ch. to a red oak; S32E 13 ch. to a red bud a cor. of **John Holt's** & **John Albright's**, to beginning, **Henry E. McCulloh** to **John Powell**; signed: **Everard Garrett**; witness: **John Powell, John Holt**; proved August Term 1797 by **Holt**, Delvd. **John Powell**.

P. 116, 4 October 1796, **Joseph Sears** of Orange to **David Holliberton** of Wake, one hundred and nineteen pounds, 238 acres, on Woolf Branch of Elibees Cr., begin at a hicory called **Tucker's** Corner on Wake County Line, with line S15W 160 p. to a red oak & pine formerly a hicory a cor. of **Shadrack Forrest**, his line N75W 180 p. to a post oak **Forrest's** other cor., N 272 p. to a pine **Elias Turner's** cor., S38E 60 p. to a pine on a branch **Turner's** other cor., E 40 p. to a white oak in **Turner's** line, his line S 8 p. to his cor. hicxory, his other line E 150 p. to a stake in the County Line, with line S15W 32 p. to a pine **Tucker's** cor. on a branch, his line N15W 180 p. to a post oak cor. formerly a hicory, S15W 66 p. to 2 black jacks, S75E 10 p. to first station, **North Carolina** to sundry persons; signed: **Joseph Sears**; witness: **John Alston, Ethed. Tucker**; proved August Term 1797 by **Alston**.

P. 118, 8 August 1797, **Richard Henderson, Thomas Hart, Nathaniel Hart, William Johnson, James Hogg, John Luttrell, John Williams, David Hart,** & **Leonard Henly Bullock** by Articles of Agreement dated 6 January 1775 became tenants in common according to the Laws of Englands to a tract of land purchased from the Cherokee Tribe of Indians, lying on Ohio R. & waters thereof, including Cumberland R., by Act of General Assembly 1780 entitled "An Act to Invest Certain Lands in Fee Simple in **Richard Henderson & Others**"

200,000 acres was granted to **Richard Henderson, Thomas Hart, John Williams, William Johnston, James Hogg, David Hart, & Leonard Henly Bullock**, the Heirs & Assigns or Devisees of **Nathaniel Hart** Deceased, & the Heirs & Assigns or Devisees of **John Luttrell** Deceased, to **Landon Carter** Heir of **John Carter** Decd. & Heirs of **Robert Lewis**, land to be laid out in one survey, Begin at the Old Indian Town in Powells Valley, down Powells R. not less than 4 miles in width on one or both sides to junction of Powells & Clinch R., down Clinch R. on one or both sides not less than 12 miles in width for compliment of 200,000 acres, 10,000 acres of tract to be laid off for Heirs of **Carter** & **Lewis** at the lower end, land granted in consdideration of expense, trouble, & risque in making the purchase of the Cherokee Indians, at a meeting of the members & copartners & representaives of others deceased held at Hillsborough 16 January 1797 it was agreed that the part of the Company (190,000 acres surveyed & returned by **Stokley Donaldson** to Secretary of State) be divided between original parties, their heirs & assigns, Company known as **Richard Henderson & Company**, lands lying on Powells R. in Powells Valley be divided as follows: Lots on plat designated Lot 1A & 2N (6,500 acres) assigned to **John Umpstead** assignee of **John Luttrell**, Lot 1B & 2M to **Thomas Hart**, Lot 1I & 2C to heirs & assigns of **Richard Henderson** as follows: NE half of Lot 1 to **Robert Burton** & SW half to heirs of **Richard Henderson** NE moiety of Lot 2 to **Robert Burton**, SW moiety to heirs of **Richard Henderson** Deceased, Lot 1L & 2D to **Walter Alves** in right of his wife heir of **William Johnston**, Lot 1E & 2F to heirs of **Nathaniel Hart**, Lot 1G & 2Y to heirs of **David Hart** & heirs of **Leonard Henly Bullock** as follows: NE moiety of Lot 1 to heirs of **David Hart** & SW moiety of sd. lot to heirs of **Leonard Henly Bullock**, NE moiety of Lot 2F to heirs of **David Hart** & SW moiety of sd. lot to heirs of **Leonard Henly Bullock** dividing line to run paralell to NE end of grant N45W, Lot 1H & 2P to **James Hogg**, Lot 1O & 2K to **John Williams**, each lot containing 6,500 acres; land on Clinch R. divided as follows: Lot 1A & 2C to **James Hogg**, Lot 1C & 2B to **John Williams**, Lot 1H & 2D to Heirs of **Nathaniel Hart**, Lot 1E & 2H to Heirs & Devisees of **Richard Henderson** as follows: NE moiety of 1E to **Robert Benton** & SW moiety to Heirs of **Richard Henderson** Deceased & NE moiety of 2H to **Robert Benton** & SE moiety to Heirs of **Richard Henderson** Deceased the last two lots divided by a line running N45W, Lot 1F & 2G to Heirs & Devisees of **David Hart** & Heirs & Devisees of **Leonard Henly Bullock** as follows: NE moiety of 1F to Heirs of **David Hart** & SW moiety to Heirs of **Leonard Henly Bullock** & NE moiety of 2G to Heirs of **David Hart** & SW moiety to Heirs of **Leonard Henly Bullock** the lots to be divided by a line running paralell to line of NE end of grant, Lots 1D & 2A to **John Umpstead** assignee of **John Luttrell**, Lot 1B & 2E to **Walter Alves** in right of his wife heir of **William Johnston**, Lots 1C & 2F to **Thomas Hart**, each lot containing 5,300 acres, agreement is between **John Williams** & **James Hogg** surviving copartners of **Richard Hendertson & Co.**, **Nathaniel Hart** heir of **Nathaniel Hart**, **Walter Alvis** in right of his wife heir of **William Johnston**, **Henry Reeves** attorney for **Thomas Hart**, **Richard Benton** devisee & executor of **Leonard Henly Bullock**, **John Umpstead** assignee of **John Luttrell**, **Joseph Hart** one of the heirs of **David Hart**, **Leonard Henderson** devisee of **Richard Henderson** & attorney in fact for **Archibald Henderson** devisee of **Richard Henderson** & guardian of **John Henderson** (infant); signed: **Jo. Hart, John Umpstead, Henry Purviance** attorney for **Thomas Hart, Nathl. Hart, L. Henderson**; witness: **John Williams, James Hogg, Richard Bullock**,

Walter Alves; acknowledged Granville Co. 9 August 1797 before **M. Hunt & M. Bullock**, certification by **A. Henderson** that **Memacan Hunt & Micajah Bullock** were Justice of Peace dated 10 August 1797.

P. 130, 5 April 1797, **John McMurey** of Parson [Person] to **John Whelley** of Orange, seventy five pounds, 150 acres, on branches of South Hico, begin at a pine on the Ridge Path, S12SW 13 1/2 ch., S30W 6 1/2 ch., S15W 10 ch., S25W 6 1/2 ch., S28W 31 ch. to a black oak cor., E 29 1/2 ch. to a white oak, N6E 34 ch. to a red oak on side of a path, along same N79E 12 ch. to a red oak, N 29 1/2 ch. to a stake, W to beginning; signed: **John McMurrey**; witness: **William Keling, George Eubank**; acknowledged August Term 1797, Delvd. **Willm. Helling.**

P. 132, 18 February 1793, **Matthew Forrest** of Orange to **Alexander Kirkpatrick** of same, sixty one pounds, 50 acres, on N side of Haw R. on Haw Cr., begin at a black oak saplin in **McDaniel's** line, E 45 1/2 rods to a hicory, N15 1/2E 16 1/2 ch. to an ash on Haw Field Branch, down branch to a beach at mouth, down creek to a post among some rocks at the foot of the Pine Hill, a direct course to beginning, part of a tract from **North Carolina** to **Eli McDaniel** 3 September 1779; signed: **Matthew Forrest**; witness: **William Trousdale**; proved August Term 1797 by **Trousdale**, Delvd. **Moses Cox.**

P. 133, 8 August 1795, **Richard Clemments** to **Samuel Chizenhall** both of Orange, one hundred pounds, 150 acres, part of a tract deeded to **Richard Clemments**, begin on a white oak tree on **Thomas Wood's** line, W to a pine on **William Chizenhall's** line, S along **Chizenhall** to a red oak saplin, E to a red oak on **Thomas Wood's** line, down line to beginning; signed: **Richard Clemments**; witness: **Clement Chizenhall, John Clements**; proved August Term 1797 by **Clement Chizenhall.**

P. 134, 20 October 1795, **Zebedee Hicks** of Caswell to **Richard Cope** of Orange, one hundred sixty six pounds, 200 acres, on waters of Back Cr., begin at a black oak on side of a Great Road leading to Hillsborough, S50E 49 ch. to a black jack, S 15 ch. to a stake in an Old Field, 57 ch. to a post oak, N 48 ch. to a post oak, E 19 ch. to first station; signed: **Zebedee Hicks**; witness: **Adam Sharpe, John Whitsell**; proved August Term 1797 by **Sharpe**, Delvd. **Richd. Coope.**

P. 136, 28 August 1797, **Alexander Kirkpatrick** to **Moses Cox** both of Orange, forty pounds, 50 acres, on N side of Haw R. on Haw Cr., 50 acres, begin at a black oak saplin in **McDaniel's** line, E 45 1/2 rods to a hicory, N47E 16 1/2 ch. to a red oak on Hawfields Branch, down branch to a beach at mouth, down creek to a post oak among some rocks at foot of Pine Hill, a direct course to beginning, part of a tract from **North Carolina** to **Eli McDaniel** 3 September 1779; signed: **Alexander Kirkpatrick**; witness: **William Trousdale, Robt. Trousdale**; acknowledged August Term 1797, Delvd. **Moses Cox.**

P. 137, 10 April 1797, **William Dickens** of Granville & **Robert Dickens** of Person to **Henry Nolner** of Petersburg, Virginia, five hundred and fifty five dollars, 555 acres, several tracts, first tract begin at a hicory cor. formerly **Gibin's**, E to Deep

Cr., down creek to Flat R., up river to a white oak, N to first station on Orange County Line, 125 acres, second tract begin at a post oak near the Old Mill Path, W 50 ch. to a white oak, N 65 ch. to a black oak, E crossing river 85 ch. to a stake, S 34 ch. to a white oak, up river to mouth of a branch below the Mill Seat, up branch to a white oak, along **Carrington's** line to the Old Mill Path, S along Old Mill Path to first station, 430 acres; signed: **William Dickens, Robert Dickens**; witness: **Ephriam Frazier, John (+) Russell**; proved August Term 1797 by **Frazier**, Delvd. **Henry Nolner**.

P. 140, 2 day of 4th month commonly called April 1790, **Peter Stout** of Orange, planter, to **Jacob Stout** of same, one hundred pounds, 59 acres, on Cain Cr., part of a tract from **Granville** to **John Wright** 2 March 1755, **Wright** to **Peter Stout** 13th of ninth month 1762, begin at a bush on S side of Cain Cr., S 79 p. to a black oak, W 100 p. to a post oak in **John Allen's** line, with **Allen's** line N 81 p. to Cain Cr., down creek to first station; signed: **Peter (X) Stout, Margaret (X) Stout**; witness: **John Allen, Benjamin Piggott**; proved August Term 1797 by **Allen**, Delvd. **John McPherson**.

P. 141, 16 February 1797, **John Kennedy Senior** of Orange to **Thomas Kennedy** of same, fifty pounds, 94 acres, begin at a black oak a cor. of his other tract, N63E 7 ch. to a black oak, N15W 9 ch. to a persimmon, N57E 15 ch. 25 lk. to a white oak at side of branch, down branch to mouth to an ash on side of Haw or Buffalow Cr., down creek to a post oak at mouth of a branch, up branch to first station; signed: **John Kennedy**; witness: **William Clendenin, Sterling (X) Moore**; proved August Term 1779 by **Moore**, Delvd. **Thos. Atkinson**.

P. 143, 13 May 1797, **Philemon Hodges** of Cumberland to **Benjamin Yeargan** of Orange, thirty pounds, 30 acres, bounded by **Yeargan** on S, **John Caldwell** on W & **Hodges** on N, includes all land on S side of Schoolhouse Branch & branch is a dividing line between **Hodges** & **Benjamin Yeargan** as far as the head of a branch & then a direct W course to **Calwell's** line; signed: **P. Hodges**; witness: **Samuel Hays, Jarratt Yeargan**; proved August Term 1797 by **Jarratt Yeargan**, Delvd. **John McCauley (Irish)**.

P. 144, 28 November 1796, **Charles King** of Orange to **Baxter King** of same, sixty five pounds, 50 acres, on waters of Morgans Cr., begin at a black jack & post oak in **William King's** line, along linbe E to a cor. stake, S along line of marked trees to a hicory in **Charles King's** line, W his line to a post oak cor., N to beginning; signed: **Charles King**; witness: **John Moseley, Saml. Moseley**; acknowledged August Term 1797, Delvd. **John McCauley (Irish)**.

P. 145, 7 September 1796, **James Gibbons** to **Jacob Waggoner** [no residence given], forty nine pounds paid by **Henry Waggoner**, 300 acres, on waters of Little R., adjoins **John Brown, Samuel Torringtine, Alexander Torringtine**, & **James Hagan**, begin at a black oak on **John Brown's** line, E 12 ch. to a hicory, N 16 1/2 ch. to a white oak, E 33 1/2 ch. to a black oak, N 28 ch. to a white oak, W 7 1/2 ch. to a hicory, N 46 ch. to a post oak, W 38 ch. to a white oak, S 4 ch. to first station, "unto the said son"; signed: **James Gibbins**; witness: **William Hall, James Lawson, James Wilson**; proved August Term 1797 by **Hall**, Delvd.

Wm. Hall.

P. 146, 5 April 1797, **John McMurrey** of Person to **Benjamin Whelley** of Orange, twenty seven pounds, 45 acres, on one of the branches of South Hico, begin at a post oak a cor. of **William Kaling**, N 32 ch. to a red oak on a path, along same S29W 12 ch. to a red oak, S6SW 34 ch. to a white oak, E 16 ch. to beginning; signed: **John McMurrey**; witness: **George Eubank, William Kiding**; acknowledged August Term 1797, Delvd. **Wm. Keeling**.

P. 148, 26 August 1797, **James Millikin** of Orange to **John Millikin** of same, fifty pounds, 50 acres, on waters of Little Cain Cr., begin at a post oak, S 13 1/2 ch. along **Charles Millikin's** line to a B. O., W 41 1/2 ch. to a W. O. on **Robert Millikin's** line, N 13 1/2 ch. to a white oak, E 41 1/2 ch. to first station; signed: **James Millikin**; witness: **Archabald Campbell, William Moore**; proved August Term 1797 by **Campbell**, Delvd. **John Millikin**.

P. 149, 12 March 1797, **John McMurrey** of Person to **George Eubank Senior** of "said county", twenty five pounds, 50 acres, on Middle Fork of Hico, begin at a poplar a cor. of **William Kealing**, W 26 ch. 50 lk. to a white oak on creek, S 13 ch. 15 lk. to a white oak, E 26 ch. 50 lk. to a stake **William Kealing's** line, with same N to beginning, also for ten pounds five shillings, 20 1/21 acres, on waters of Hico, begin at a cor. of **William Kieling** on Person County Line, 3 1/2 ch. to a poplar a cor. of **John McMurrey**, along line 33 ch. to a W., N 3 1/2 ch. to a pine on "Parson" County Line of **George Eubank**, along line to first station; signed: **John McMurrey**; witness: **Edward Gaines, George Eubank**; acknowledged August Term 1797, Delvd. **Thos. Eubank**.

P. 150, 14 September 1796, **John Haney & Stephen Conger** of Orange & **Joseph Dorris** of Robinson County, Tennessee, to **William Ozburn** of Orange, one hundred pounds, 48 acres, begin at a black oak **Martin Hurdle's** cor., N 8 ch. to a spanish oak on side of a branch, down branch N50W 25 1/2 ch. to a hicory stump on N side of Deep Cr., N89W down creek 13 ch. to a hicory on bank of Stoney Cr., down creek S36E 18 ch. to a stake, S25W 10 1/2 ch. to a black oak, E 24 ch. to beginning; signed: **John Haney, Stephen Conger, Joseph Dorris**; witness: **Hardy Hurdle, Joseph Ming, Martin Hurdle Junior, Joseph Dorris Junior**; proved August Term 1797 by **Hardy Hurdle**, Delvd. **Hardy Hurdle**.

P. 152, 19 August 1797, **George Alsworth** of Orange to **Joseph Taylor** of same, twenty pounds, 38 1/4 acres, on waters of Eno, adjoins **Joseph Moore, Robert Smith, & Ralph Williams, Samuel Thomspon** to Alsworth, begin at a post oak cor. of **Joseph Moore's** New Survey & line of the Old Survey, W 17 1/2 ch. to a hicory **Moor's** & **Smith's** cor., N 16 ch. to a stake, E 15 ch. to a white oak **William's** cor., N 3 ch. to a stake, E 2 1/2 ch. to a black oak **Moor's** cor., S 19 ch. to first station; signed: **George Ailsworth**; witness: **John Taylor, Robert Taylor**; "Whereas the above mentioned land was bid of by me at a Sheriff's Sale to satisfy a judgment obtained against **George Ailsworth** by **William Hill** of New Hanover and whereas **George** has fully indemnified me for the money I paid the Sheriff, be it known that I fully release & quit cvlaim to **Joseph Taylor** my right to the land, 19 August 1797"; signed: **James Hogg**; witness: **John**

ORANGE COUNTY (NC) DEED BOOK 6

Taylor, Robert Taylor; proved August Term 1797 by **Robert Taylor**, Delvd. **Joseph Taylor**.

P. 154, 23 May 1797, **Ephriam Frazier** of Orange to **John Green** of same, one hundred pounds, on N side of Flat R., 228 acres, part of 2 tracts surveyed by **John Carrington & Thomas Gipson**, begin at a dogwood on side of a branch, S 146 p. to a hicory, S50E 80 p. to a post oak, E 34 p. to a post oak, S 20 p. to a red oak, W 2 1/2 p. to a white oak on side of a branch, down branch to a persimmon, S23W 64 p. to an ash on the Road that formerly led from Granville to Hillsborough, W 20 p. to a mulberry near Flat R., up river to mouth of Deep Cr., up Deep Cr. to mouth of Little Cr., up Little Cr. to first station; signed: **Ephriam Frazier**; witness: **Willm. Frazier, Abraham (X) Parker**; proved August Term 1797 by **Parker**, Delvd. **Abraham Parker**.

P. 156, 21 November 1796, **William Courtney** of Hillsborough to **George Johnston** of Orange, three hundred pounds, 627 acres, three tracts, first on both sides of New Hope, 627 acres, begin at a red oak **Allen's** line, E 148 red oak, N 100 to a stake, W 12 black jack, N 160 white oak, W 132 stake **Hall's** line, S 84 his cor. gum, E 6 stake, S 188 to first station, second tract **North Carolina** to **Courtney** 3 Sept. '79, 185 acres, on both sides of New Hope, begin at a white oak on **Alexander Mebane's** line on N side of creek, E 23 p. to his cor. stake, continues 97 p. to a hicory, S 40 p. to a beach, E 22 p. to a white oak in **William Rhodes'** line, S his line 22 p. to a red oak, E 24 p. to a red oak, S 200 p. to a white oak saplin, W 83 p. to a black jack, N 106 p. to a black oak, W 83 p. to a black oak, N 184 p. to first station, tract where **Courtney** has had a mill, third tract, 152 acres, half of a tract from **North Carolina** to **Mark Patterson & Joseph Cobb** 18 May '89, on waters of New Hope, N half of tract, sold by **Sheriff** to **Courtney**, begin at a white oak, E 40 ch. to a black jack, S 30 1/2 ch. to a stake, E 53 ch. to a white oak, S 5 ch. to a walnut, W 83 ch. to a stake, N 23 1/2 ch. to a post oak, W 10 ch. to a black jack, N 12 ch. to first station; signed: **William Courtney**; witness: **Jo. Courtney**; proved August Term 1797 by **Jo. Courtney**, Delvd. **John McCauley (Irish)**.

P. 158, 26 August 1797, **Charles Millikin** of Orange to **John Millikin** of same, two hundred pounds, 150 acres, on waters of Little Cain Cr., begin at a P. O. om **James Mileken** line, W 5 1/2 ch. to a W. O. on **Strudwick's** line, with line N7E 30 ch. to a W. O., N70E 8 1/2 ch. to a R. O. cor. to **Chs. Cilley**, his line S 33 ch. to a R. O., E 25 ch. to a R. O., S 40 ch. to a P. O., W 31 ch. to a r. o. & hicory on **James Millikin's** line, with line N 40 ch. to first station; signed: **Charles Millikin**; witness: **Archibald Campbell, William Moore**; proved August Term 1797 by **Campbell**, Delvd. **Thos. Millikin**.

P. 160, 24 September 1796, **John Swann** of New Hanover, Esquire, to **George Clenney** of Hillsborough, taylor, two hundred pounds, 2 acres, 2 lots, in Hillsborough, Lot # 112 bounded on N by Tryon Street, on W by by Lot #111, on S by Lot #121, on E by Wake Street, Lot #93, bounded on E by Wake Street, on N by Lot #94, on W by Lot #92, on S by Tryon Street; signed: **John Swann**; witness: **John Hogg, S. Benton**; proved August Term 1797 by **Saml. Benton**, Delvd. **James Clenny**.

P. 161, [blank] April 1797, **William F. Strudwick** of Orange to **John Pugh** of same, ninety nine pounds, 68 acres, on Haw Cr., bounded by **William Gorden, Jeremiah McCracken,** & land occupied by **John Wilson,** begin at an ash on side of creek, up creek to a maple, N69E 22 ch. to a white oak, S46E 7 1/2 ch. to a hicory, N70E 2 1/2 ch. to a branch, N80E 7 ch. to a black oak, N35W 25 ch. to a black oak on Haw Cr., down creek to first station; signed: **William F. Strudwick**; witness: **Reuben Smith, Jesse Cate**; proved August Term 1797 by **Smith**, Delvd. **Thomas Adkinson.**

P. 163, 9 May 1797, **John Woods Senior** of Orange to **David Woods** of same, one hundred pounds, 165 acres, on waters of Little R., part of 2 tracts known as Tracts #22 and #28, begin at a heap of stones in **Thomas Woods** line, S55E 42 ch. to a black oak, S15W 52 ch. to a black jack, W 112 ch. to a black jack **John Nichols'** cor., N10W 55 1/2 ch. to a black oak **Nichols'** other cor., W 11 1/2 ch. to a black oak saplin **Thomas Woods'** cor., N25E 32 1/2 ch. to first station; signed: **John Woods**; witness: **James Latta Junr., Thomas Woods**; acknowledged August Term 1797, Delvd. **Thomas Woods.**

P. 164, 15 December 1795, **William F. Strudwick** of Orange to **Jonathon Jones** of same, one hundred pounds, 100 acres, on Little Back Cr., begin at a hicory at mouth of a branch on creek, down creek S60W 41 ch. to 2 sweet gum saplins, S8E 23 1/2 ch. to a stake, N65E 44 ch. to a hicory, N18W 25 ch. to beginning; signed: **W. F. Strudwick**; witness: **Thomas (X) Jones, Eliza Shepperd**; proved August Term 1797 by **Thomas Jones**, Delvd. **Jonathon Jones.**

P. 165, 1 March 1796, **John Waggoner** of Orange to **Stephen Smith** of same, sixty five pounds, 65 acres, begin at an ash on bank of North Fork of Little R., S with **William Campble's** line 23 1/2 ch. to a red oak **Robert McCullock's** cor., W his line 29 ch. to a post oak, N with **Robert Hall's** line 21 1/2 ch. crossing creek to a black oak, down creek 12 1/2 ch. to a black oak, E 3 1/2 ch. to a black oak, S8W 7 1/2 ch. to 2 white oaks on creek, down creek to first station; signed: **John (X) Waggoner**; witness: **Wm. Hall, Robert Hall, Michael Robinson**; proved August Term 1797 by **William Hall**, Delvvd. **Willm. Hall.**

P. 167, 5 June 1797, **Martha Ray**, widdow, to **John Holmes** both of Orange, ninety pounds, 188 acres, begin at a black oak **J. Lindley's** line, W 53 ch. to a post oak **Tinnin's** line, S ____ to a post oak, E 22 1/2 ch. to a white oak, N45E 13 ch. to a white oak, S45E 13 ch. to a post oak, E 10 ch. to a black gum, N to beginning, part of a larger tract from **Henry Eustace McCulloh** to **William Ray** Deceased; signed: **Martha Ray**; witness: **James H. Ray, George Foust**; proved August Term 1779 by **Foust.**

P. 168, 10 June 1795, **Robert Morrison** of Orange to **John Shy** of same, forty pounds, 14 3/4 acres, begin at an elm & sugar tree on W side of Haw R. at mouth of a branch, W 21 ch. to a mulberry on side of a branch, S 20 1/2 ch. to a black oak on head of a branch, down branch 80 p., N to a black oak on bank, down N bank so as to reserve 1/2 rod of bank for **Robert Morrison** to first station, part of a tract from **Granville** to **Zachariah Marten** 24 June 1751 **Marten** to **James Swaffer, Swaffer** to **James Dickey** Esq., **Dickey** to **Laurance**

Thompson Esq., **Thompson** to **Laurance Thompson Junior**, Thompson to **Moses Emery**; signed: **Robert Morrison**; witness: **Nathaniel Carter, Nathaniel Edwards**; proved August Term 1797 by **Carter**, delivered to **Jesse Varnel**.

P. 169, 27 April 1796, **William Lytle** of North Carolina to **George Claney** of Hillsborough, ten pounds, 2 acres, 2 lots in Hillsborough, Lots #73 & #74, bounded on E by Wake Street, on N by Queen Street, on W by Hazell Street, on S by Tryon Street & Lots #92 & #93; signed: **William Lytle**; witness: **Henry Terrell, John Barton**; acknowledged August Term 1797, Delvd. **Jas. Clinney**.

P. 170, 1 May 1797, **John Woods Senior** of Orange to **Thomas Woods**, eighty pounds, on waters of Little R., 80 acres, part of Tract No. 29, begin at a stake in line of Tract No. 30, S31W 58 ch. to a black oak saplin on **John Nichols'** line, W 4 1/4 ch. to a white oak a cor. of Tract No. 28 & No. 29, N 30 ch. to a black oak **William Woods** cor., N45E 27 1/4 ch. to a gum in line of Tract No. 30, E with line to first station; signed: **John Woods**; witness: **James Latta Junr., David Woods**; acknowledged August Term 1797, Delvd. **Thos. Wood**.

P. 172, 26 August 1797, **Henry Moore** of Orange, planter, to **James Watson** Senior of same, planter, four hundred pounds, 203 3/4 acres, on E side of Horse Cr., begin at creek, E 39 1/4 ch. to **Thomas Horton's** white oak cor., S 13 1/4 ch. to a stake, E 12 3/4 ch. to a stake, S 7 ch. 20 lk. to a black jack, E 15 ch. 60 lk. to a post oak, S 17 ch. 30 lk. to a white oak, W 20 ch. same line of marked trees 2 degrees S 43 ch. to a post oak on creek, up creek to first station; signed: **Henry Moore**; witness: **James Moore, John Watson**; proved August Term 1797 by **James Moore**, Delvd. **James Watson Senr.**

P. 173, 20 August 1792, **Samuel Allen** of Orange to **Joseph Sears** of same, one hundred pounds, 83 acres, on waters of Ellebees Cr., begin at a hicory in the County Line on S side of Woolf Branch, N75W 180 p. to a white oak, N15E 76 p. to a sweet gum on a branch, S75E 180 p. to a pine in County Line, S15W 76 to beginning; signed: **Samuel (X) Allen**; witness: **Saml. Alley, John Chandler**; proved August Term 1797 by **Samuel Alley.**

P. 175, 17 September 1787, **Thomas Lloyd** of Orange to **William Walker** of same, one hundred eighty four pounds, 158 acres, begin at a black oak on **Joseph Thompson's** line, N 29 ch. to a stake about 2 ch. E of a marked white oak, W 10 ch. to a rock, N 32 ch. to a hicory, S 16 ch. to a post oak, E 7 ch. to a post oak, S 43 ch. to a post oak, W 7 ch. to first station, 128 acres is part of a tract from **Zachariah Cadle** to Thomas Lapsley, **Thos. Lapsley Sr.** to Thomas **Lapsley Jr.** 13 August 1759, other 30 acres by will of **Thomas Lapsley Sr.** to **Thomas Lapsley Jr.**, Thomas Lapsley Jr. to **Thomas Lloyd Junior** 13 September 1787; signed: **Thomas Lloyd Jr.**; witness: **Edward Pickett, Peter Walker**; proved August Term 1797 by **Pickett**.

P. 176, 18 July 1797, **William Ozburn** of Orange to **Robert Marley** of Guilford, sixty pounds, 48 acres, begin at a black oak **Martin Hurdle** cor., N 8 ch. to a spanish oak on side of a branch, down branch N50W 25 1/2 chains to a hicory stump the N side of Deep Cr., N89W down creek 13 ch. to a hicory on bank of Stoney Cr., down Stoney Cr. S36E 18 ch. to a stake, S25W 10 1/2 ch. to a black oak, E 24 ch. to beginning; signed: **William Ozbern, Margaret (X) Ozbern**; witness: **Joseph Ming, Hardy Hurdle**; proved August Term 1797 by **Hurdle**, Delvd. **Hardy Hurdle**.

P. 178, 9 June 1797, **Joseph Taylor** of Granville to **William Laws** of Orange, two hundred pounds, 149 1/2 acres, begin at a black oak in **Benehan's** line on E side of Mill Cr., by **Benehan's & Guisse'** line S56W 80 p. to a post oak **Guisse'** cor. his line S34E 320 p. to a dogwood **Joseph Taylor's** cor., his line N7E 36 p. to a red oak his cor., his line N30E 30 p. to a maple his cor., his line N13E 26 p. to a post oak his cor., his line N23W 18 p. to a post oak his cor., his line N18E 13 p. to a pine his cor., his line N31W 24 p. to a maple standing on W side of Mill Cr., up branch to beginning; signed: **Joseph Taylor**; witness: **Micajah Bullock, George Laws Junr., Peyton Medison**; proved August Term 1797 by **Medison**, Delvd. to **Willm. Roberts**.

P. 179, 22 April 1794, **William Walker** to **Robert Walker**, both of Orange, one hundred pounds, 100 acres, on waters of Little R., begin at a hicory, W along **Michael Robinson's** line to a spliced hicory or stake, S along **Walker** to a black oak saplin, E to a post oak run by **John Riggs & Walker**, N to first station; signed: **William Walker**; witness: **Jonathan Nichols, John Walker**; proved August Term 1797 by **Nichols**, Delvd. to **John Latta junr.**

P. 181, 20 May 1797, **John Sloss** of Orange to **Alexander Robbs** of same, fifteen dollars, 11 3/4 acres, on waters of Jourdans Cr., begin at a post oak in his own former line, E with **Alexander Robbs'** line 29 ch. & 25 lk. to a white oak, N with his line 4 ch. to a stake, W with his own line 29 ch. 25 lk. to beginning, **North Carolina** to **Sloss** 17 October 1796; signed: **John Sloss**; witness: **William Dickey, James Faucett**; acknowledged August Term 1797, Delvd. to **Hardy Hurdle**.

P. 182, 3 May 1797, **Memucan Hunt** of Granville to **William Palmer** of Orange, one hundred & twenty five pounds, 1 acre, in Hillsborough, 400 lk. in length, 250 lk. in breadth, Lot #22, **Commissioners** of Confiscated Property to **Hunt**, estate of **Edmund Fanning**, grant dated 25 August 1786; signed: **M. Hunt**; witness: **Thomas Owen, Jett Burton, Wm. Norwoo**d; proved August Term 1797 by **William Norwood**, delivd. **Willm. Palmer**.

P. 183, 30 August 1797, **David Holliburton** of Orange, planter, to **Shadrick Forrest** of same, planter, three hundred silver dollars, 238 acres, different tracts, on Woolf Br. on Ellibees Cr., begin at a large hicory in Wake County Line, with line S15W 160 p. to a red oak & pine formerly a hicory a cor. of **Forrest**, his line N75W 180 p. to a post oak **Forrest's** other cor., a line N 272 p. to a pine Elias **Turner's** cor., S38E 60 p. to a pine on a branch **Turner's** other cor. E 40 p. to a white oak **Turner's** line, his line S 18 p. to his cor. hicory, his other line E 150 p. to a stake on the County Line, with line S15W 32 p. to a pine now **Phipps'** cor. on a branch, his line first N75W 180 p. to a post oak cor. formerly a hicory, S15W 66 p. to 2 black jacks, S75E 180 p. to first station, it being land grants to sundry persons from **North Carolina** & conveyed to **Holliburton**; signed: **David H. Burton**; witness: **John Humphries**; acknowledged August Term 1797, Delvd. **Shadrack Forrest**.

P. 184, 19 August 1790, **Jane Anderson** of Orange, widow, & **James Anderson** of same, yeoman, son and heir of **William Anderson** deceased to **Andrew Burke** of same, Esq., one hundred pounds, 110 acres, on waters of Eno, begin at a post oak, W 25 ch. to a B. O., N 46 ch. to a B. O., E 25 ch. to a white oak, S 46 ch. to first station, bounded on E side by **Gaddis**, on S & W by **Smith**, **North Carolina** to **William Anderson** 3 September 1779; signed: **Jane (X) Anderson, James Anderson**; witness: **Alexr. Mebane, Willm. Kirkland**; proved August Term 1797 by **Kirkland**.

P. 186, 10 August 1797, **North Carolina** to **Caleb Harvey**, [no residence given] fifty shillings per hundred acres, 95 acres, on Big Cr., adjoins **Whitted, Thompson, Cantrel, Cloud**, and his land, begin at a post oak **Cloud's** cor., N 78 ch. to a spanish oak & black jack **Whitted's** NE cor., E 4 ch. to a black jack, S partly on **Thompson's** line 35 ch. to his cor. red oak, E 6 ch. 50 lk. to a black oak near **Harvey's** old cor., his line S 16 ch. 50 lk. to a white oak, W 10 ch. to a black oak bush, S 6 ch. crossing Big Cr. to a black oak, E crossing creek 30 ch. 50 lk. to a red oak on **Combs'** line, S sd. line 20 ch. to a spanish oak & black oak, to beginning, entered 11 November 1796; signed: **Saml. Ashe**; witness: **J. Glasgow**; [no probate record].

P. 187, 25 January 1797, **John Barnett** [name appears as **John Bennett** in body of deed] of Wake County to **Edmond Herndon** of Orange, one hundred pounds, 112 acres, on North East Cr. of New Hope, begin at a post oak, N 160 p. to a stake, W 110 p. to a pine, S with his line 20 ch. to his cor. post oak, E 5 ch. to a stake, S 110 p. to a black oak saplin, E 100 p. to first station; signed: **John Bennett**; witness: **John Scoggin, Zachariah Herndon**; proved August Term 1797 by **Zachariah Herndon**, Delvd. **Edmd. Herndon**.

P. 189, 20 April 1797, **Sack Mize** of Orange to **Only Owens** of same, one hundred pounds, 100 acres, on Camp Cr., waters of Nap of Reeds, begin on bank of Camp Cr. on **Samuel Carey's** line, E his line 116 p. 50 lk. to a pine, S to **Wilborn's** line, his line to Camp Cr., up creek to first station; signed: **Sack (X) Mize, Mornig (X) Taton**; witness: **Kedrick Mize, Henry (X) Walker, John (X) Jenking**; proved August Term 1797 by **Jenking**.

P. 190, 17 eighth month commonly called August 1797, **Jacob Stout** of Orange, planter, to **John MacPerson** of Chatham, one hundred & sixty pounds, 104 acres, on Cain Cr., begin at a bush on S side of Cain Cr., S 153 p. to a post oak in the County Line dividing Orange & Chatham Counties, W along line 98 p. to a stake in **John Allen's** line, along **Allen's** line N 155 p. to Cain Cr., down creek to first station; signed: **Jacob Stout, Judith (X) Stout**; witness: **John Alan, Enoch Macpherson**; proved August Term 1797 by **John Allen**, Delvd. **Jno. McPherson**.

P. 192, 5 January 1797, **James Faucett** of Orange to **William Whitted Junior** of Hillsborough, nine hundred dollars, 300 acres, joins the Commons of the Town of Hillsborough on the W, formerly property of **Edmund Fanning**, sold by **Commissioners** of Confiscated Property to **John Estes** 25 August 1786, begin at a pine on side of Occoneechy Mountain, N 67 ch. to a black jack on the line of the Town of Hillsborough, W 45 ch. to a black jack on **Courtney's** line, S 67 ch. to a stake on the side of the mountain, E 45 ch. to beginning; signed: **James Faucett**; witness: **A. Tatom, William Carrington**; proved August Term 1797 by **Tatom**, Delvd. **Jas. Whitted.**

P. 193, 30 March 1797, **Stephen Tatom** of Orange to **John Jenkins** of same, thirty pounds, 50 acres, on Camp Cr., part of tract willed to **Stephen Tatom** by his father **Stephen Tatom**, begin at a pine **Wilborn's** line, W 9 p. to a stake **William Mangrum's** cor., S his line 142 p. to a maple in the Lick Br., down branch to a maple on the side of branch, N 70 p. to a white oak on bank of Camp Cr., up creek to **Wilborn's** line, W 118 p. to a black jack **Wilborn's** cor., N his line 90 p. to first station; signed: **Stephen (X) Tatom**; witness: **Thomas Flint, Joseph (I) Waller**; acknowledged August Term 1797.

P. 194, 10 July 1797, **Robert Ray** to **George Foust**, both of Orange, one hundred & thrity three pounds, 140 acres, on Great Allamance Cr., begin at a hicory on bank of creek on cor. of an Old Field, N35W 16 ch. 50 lk. to a hicory on creek **James H. Ray's** cor., his line S50W 6 ch. 25 lk. to a heap of stones, sd. line N70W 23 ch. 50 lk. to a poplar, N22W 3 ch. 50 lk. to a stake on bank of creek on N side, N meaders of same 13 ch. to a stake opposite mouth of a branch & a B. O. cor. of **Foust**, his line S18E 25 ch. to a post oak, S46E 11 ch. to a white oak, S79E 12 ch. to a persimmon, S12W 24 1/2 ch. to a stake in Fayetteville Road **Pain's** line, along line E 15 ch. to a B. J., N30E 15 ch. to a stump on a branch, N 22 ch. to a hicory, E 20 ch. to beginning; signed: **Robt. Ray**; witness: **James Tinnin, John Homes**; proved August Term 1797 by **Homes**, Delvd. **Geo. Lay Senr.**

P. 196, 15 August 1797, **John Linch** of Orange to **James Hart** of same, three hundred pounds, 200 acres, on Deep Cr., a branch of Stoney Cr., bounded by land of **James Dickey** & **Edward King**, begin at a black oak cor. of **James Dickey**, N32W 30 1/2 ch. to a black oak, N7W 16 ch. to a white oak, N20E 15 ch. to a hicory, N 25 ch. to a black oak, E 25 ch. to a post oak, S 80 ch. to a post oak, 11 1/2 ch. to first station, **North Carolina** to **Robert Mains** 9 November 1784, conveyed to **James Dickey**; signed: **John Linch**; witness: **Richard Hargraves, John Paul**; proved August Term 1797 by **Paul**, Delvd. **James Hart.**

P. 197, 22 April 1794, **William Walker** to **Robert Walker**, both of Orange, one hundred pounds, 100 acres, bought of **James Riggs Junior**, on waters of Little R., begin at mouth of Black Jack Cr. the conditional line between **John Riggs** & **James Riggs**, up creek to a hicory, N to a post oak saplin, E to a black oak cor., N along **Walker's** line to a hicory on the Old Line the line made consentable between **Thomas, John, & James Riggs**, W to a post oak, S to a hicory, W to a white oak, S to river, down river to first station; signed: **William Walker**; witness: **Jonathan Nickols, John Walker**; proved August Term 1797 by **Nickols**, Delvd. **Jno. Latta.**

P. 199, 30 August 1797, **John Davis** of Orange to **Elisha Bevill** of same, fifty pounds, 50 acres, on Presswoods Cr., waters of New Hope, begin at a white oak **Hays'** beginning cor., W to a red oak **Davis'** cor., S crossing creek to a hicory, an E course to a stake on **Hays'** line, along Main Road with **Hays'** line to first station; signed: **John (X) Davis**; witness: **Benjamin Yeargan, Charlotte Hinton Yeargan**; proved August Term 1797 by **Benjamin Yeargan**, Delvd. **Elisha Bevell**.

P. 200, 18 December 1794, **Abraham Davis** of Orange to **Ephriam Frazier** of Granville, two hundred & sixty pounds, 238 acres, on N side of Flat R., part of 2 tracts surveyed by **John Carrington & Thomas Dixon,** begin at a dogwood on side of a branch, S 146 p. to a hicory, S50E 80 p. to a post oak, E 34 p. to a post oak, S 20 p. to a red oak, W 242 p. to a white oak on side of a branch, down branch to a persimmon, S23W 64 p. to an ash on the Road that formerly led from Granville to Hillsborough, W 20 p. to a mulberry near Flat R., up river to mouth of Deep Cr., up creek to mouth of Little Cr., up Little Cr. to first station; signed: **Abraham Davis**; witness: **Arthur Frazier, Abraham Parker**; proved August Term 1797 by **Parker**, Delvd. **Abraham Parker**. P. 202, 15 May 1794, **Benjamin Roney** of Orange to **James Roney** of same, one hundred & fifty pounds, 150 acres, on Scrub Cr. a branch of Quaker Cr., bounded on N by **John Waldraven**, begin at a black jack, W 50 ch. to a hicory, N 40 ch. to a black jack, E 50 ch. to a white oak, S 30 ch. to first station, where Roney formerly lived, ; signed: **Benjamin Roney**; witness: **John Walker, Hugh McAdam**; proved August Term 1797 by **Walker**, Delvd. **James Roney**.

P. 203, 11 May 1797, **Philemon Hodges** of Cumberland to **John Davis** of Orange, fifty pounds, 50 acres, on Presswoods Cr., waters of New Hope, begin at a white oak **Hays** beginning cor., W to a red oak **Davis'** cor., S crossing creek to a hicory, an E course to a stake in **Hays'** line, along the Main Road with **Hays'** line to first station; signed: **P. Hodges**; witness: **Benjamin Yeargan, Samuel Hays**; proved August Term 1797 by **Yeargan**, Delvd. **John Davis**.

P. 204, 24 February 1797, **William Rhodes** of Orange to **George Johnston** of same, ten pounds, 22 acres, begin at a white oak, E 7 ch. 25 lk. to a post oak, S cxrossing New Hope 30 1/2 ch. to a red oak, W 7 ch. 25 lk. to a black oak saplin, N crossing New Hope 30 1/2 ch. to first station; signed: **Willm. Rhodes**; witness: **Mann Paterson, Daniel Watson**; proved August Term 1797 by **Patterson**, Delvd. **John McCauley (Irish)**.

P. 205, 16 April 1796, **Trustees of University of North Carolina** to **Colba Jackson** of Orange, twelve pounds, 60 acres, on waters of Stinking Quarter Cr., begin at a stake a cor. of **George Friddle's**, S45E 16 ch. to a black oak, E 3 ch. to a stake, S25E 22 ch. to a P. O., N45E 22 ch. to a P. O., N45W 33 ch. to a white oak, W 9 ch. to a stake, to first station; signed: **Willm. Shepperd**, Atty.; witness: **William Ray, Thomas Whitted**; proved August Term 1797 by **Whitted**, Delvd. **John Powell**.

P. 207, 7 April 1787, **James Bozwell** of Orange to **Thomas Laycock** of same, seventy pounds, 165 acres, begin at a red oak, S across the river 30 ch. to a red oak, E 55 ch. to a white oak, N 30 ch. to a red oak saplin, W crossing the river to first station; signed: **James Bozwell**; witness: **Jno. Kelly, Jacob Richards**; proved August Term 1797 by **Kelly**, Delvd. **Thos. Laycock**.

P. 209, 15 October 1796, **Lewis Garner** of Orange to **John Hughes** of same, twenty pounds, 36 acres, on E side of a branch, part of an Old Tract of **Garner's,** begin on side of branch at an ash, E 17 1/2 ch. to the Old Cor. black jack, S 20 ch. to a post oak, E 7 ch. to a post oak, S 13 ch. to a post oak, N 6 1/2 ch. to branch to a white oak, up branch to first station, part of a larger tract from **North Carolina** to Garner; signed: **Lewis (X) Garner;** witness: **John Haney, Thomas (X) Lafferty;** proved August Term 1797 by **Lafferty,** Delvd. **Wm. Hutchell.**

P. 210, 5 August 1797, **Mary Heriot, George Heriot, William Hairiot, Daniel Tucker, John Heriot,** & **Robert Heriot** of George Town South Carolina, Executrrix & Executors to the estate of **Col. Robert Heriot** deceased to **Shadrack Simmons** & **Leonard Dozer** Esquires of District of George Town, power of attorney to sell one three hundred and eighty fourth part or share of an undivided tract known as Transylvania & one other tract lying on branches of the Ohio and adjoing the same, sd. tracts sold by **William Dry** of Brunswick County, North Carolina, to **Robert Heriot** deceased 22 June 1778; signed: **Mary Heriot, George Heriot, Will. Heriot. Danl. Tucker, John Od. Heriot, Robert Heriot;** witness: **John Davis, B. W. Tucker;** proved before **Francis G. Dellesseline,** J. P., 5 August 1797 by **John Davis.**

P. 214, 9 November 1784, **North Carolina** to **William Love,** [no residence given] fifty shillings per hundred acres, 280 acres, on both sides of Jourdans Cr., adjoins **Jacob Cantrell** & entry of **James Scott,** begin at abeach on side of Jourdans Cr. on a line of **James Scott,** W 28 ch. to a post oak, N 33 ch. to a black oak, W 4 ch. to a black oak, N 40 ch. to a white oak, E 40 ch. to a sassafrass, S 40 ch. to a black oak, E 9 ch. to an elm, down creek to first station; signed: **Alex. Martin;** witness: **J. Glasgow;** [no probate record], Delvd. **Wm. Love.**

P. 215, 8 June 1797, **North Carolina** to **John McCrory,** [no residence given] fifty shillings per hundred acres, 100 acres, begin at a stake on his first line 35 ch. from his beginning cor., W 17 ch. to a stake, S35W 6 ch. to a stake, W 22 ch. to a stake, N20W 49 ch. to a stake, N50W 20 ch. to a stake, N15W 6 ch. to a stake, N40W 19 ch. to a stake, N50E 3 ch. to a stake, N40W 15 ch. to a stake, N 17 ch. to a stake **McCrory's** line, along same S50W 17 ch. to a W. O., S 17 ch. to a W. O., S40E 22 ch. to a hicory, S50W 4 ch. to a hicory, S40E 19 ch. to a white oak, S15E 6 ch. to a W. O. on Back Cr., up same SE 22 ch. to a gum, S20E 45 ch. to a P. O., E 22 ch. to a B. O., N45E 8 ch. to a hicory, E 18 ch. to a B. O., N 22 ch. to first station, warrant dated 20 December 1796; signed: **Saml. Ashe;** witness: **J. Glasgow;** [no probate record], Delvd. **John McCrory.**

P. 216, 19 July 1797, **North Carolina** to **John McCrory,** [no residence given] fifty shillings per hundred acres, 120 acres, on waters of Boyds Cr. within his own line, begin at a black oak, E 57 1/2 ch. to a black jack his own cor., S 74 1/2 ch. to a stake on **Freelands** line, W 4 ch. to a stake, N 57 1/2 ch. to a stake, W 53 1/2 ch. to a stake on his own line, N 17 ch. to first station, entered 12 December 1796; signed: **Saml. Ashe;** witness: **J. Glasgow;** [no probate record], Delvd. **John McCrory.**

P. 217, 29 November 1797, **Samuel Benton** of Orange to **Mrs. Mary Watters,** one hundred pounds, a negro man named **Cesar**; signed: **S. Benton**; witness: **John Taylor**; proved November Term 1797 by **Taylor**.

P. 217, 16 July 1795, **North Carolina** to **John Long, David Coble, & Adam Smith**, [no residences given] ten pounds per hundred acres, 60 acres, adjoins **John Rudolph** & **John Coble**, begin at **Smith's** cor., S20W 50 ch. to a post oak, N20E 31 1/2 ch. to a hicory, S50E 8 ch. to a stake, S75E 30 ch. to first station; signed: **Richard Dobbs Spaight**; witness: **J. Glasgow**; [no probate record], Delvd. **David Patterson**.

P. 218, 10 August 1797, **North Carolina** to **David Dranbery**, [no residence given] fifty shillings per hundred acres, 77 acres, lying on S & W cor. of this county, adjoins Chatham County Line on S, Randolph County Line on W & **Springer** on N, begin on Chatham & Orange cor., N 68 p. to a black jack **Springer's** cor., E 182 p. along **Springer's** line to a persimmon, S 68 p. to Chatham Line, W to beginning, warrant dated 31 May 1796; signed: **Saml. Ashe**; witness: **J. Glasgow**; [no probate record], Delvd. **David Patterson**.

P. 219, 16 July 1795, **North Carolina** to **John Caldwell**, [no residence given] ten pounds per hundred acres, 70 acres, on waters of New Hope Cr., bounded on N by **Daniel Booth**, on E by **John Weems**, on S by **Benjamin Yeargan**, begin at a white oak a cor. of **William McCauley** & **Daniel Booth**, S 97 p. to a white oak a cor. of **McCauley**, E 116 p. to a pine a cor. of **John Weems**, N 97 p. to a pine & white oak pointers in **Daniel Booth's** line, W with his line 160 p. to first station; signed: **Richard Dobbs Spaight**; witness: **J. Glasgow**; [no probate record], Delvd. **Jno. McCauley (Irish)**.

P. 220, 18 May 1789, **North Carolina** to **Isaac Rawls**, [no residence given] ten pounds per hundred acres, 100 acres, on waters of Back Cr., bounded on E by **Andrew Smith**, begin at **Smith's** cor. red oak, S 25 ch. to a white oak, W 40 ch. to a post oak, N 25 ch. to a black jack, E 40 ch. to first station; signed: **Sam. Johnston**; witness: **J. Glasgow**; [no probate record], Delvd. **Jacob Huggams**.

P. 221, 4 September 1797, **Alexander Piper** of Orange to **William Brewer** of Chatham, five hundred pounds, 380 acres, on Morgans Cr., begin at a cor. sugartree at mouth of a branch on **Samuel Piper's** line, up branch to a sweet gum, along a line of marked trees to a cor. black oak on **William Partin's** line, along **Partin's** line to a sweet gum in a branch, down branch to a hicory, along a line of marked trees to a maple on Morgans Cr., up creek to a white oak on **Mathew McCauley's** line, his line to **Edmund Jones'** line, along **Jones'** line to the cor. sugartree on **Samuel Piper's** line, land bought of **Thomas Connally** & **Benjamin Hagwood**, part of each tract, **Hagwood's** deed dated 9 November 1784; signed: **Alexander Piper, Sarah Piper**; witness: **Mathew McCauley, Abraham Piper, James Powell**; proved November Term 1797, Delvd. **John McCauley (Irish)**.

P. 222, **Robert Bell** of Orange to **Col. William Shepperd** of same, five hundred pounds, negroes **Davie, Fann, Doll, Suxy, Hester, Fann, & Sophia**; signed: **R. Bell**; witness: **Charles Christmas, J. Williams**; proved November Term 1797 by **Christmas**.

P. 223, 23 August 1780, **Benjamin Cornell** of Orange & **Sarah** his wife to **John Galbreath** of same, five thousand pounds, 160 acres, on waters of Mill Cr. bounded all round by **Dickson, Bunch, Standford, & Beason**, begin at a B. O., W 10 ch. to a W. O., S 2 ch. to a W. O., SE 4 ch. 50 lk. to a B. O., E 4 ch. to a W. O., S 7 ch. to a B. O. E 5 ch. to a W. O., S 13 ch. to a B. O., E 3 ch. to a B. O., S 14 ch. to a P. O., E 11 ch. to a persimmon, N W. O. & 1/2(?) to a B. O., E 12 ch. to a W. O., N 1 1/2 ch. to a W. O., E 23 ch. to a hicory, N 16 ch. to an ash, down branch to first station, **North Carolina** to **Cornell** 3 July 3rd year of Independence; signed: **Benjamin Cornell, Sarah Cornell**; witness: **Moses Crawford, John Campbell**; proved November Term 1797 by **Crawford**, Delvd. **Hardy Hurdle**.

P. 225, 30 June 1797, **North Carolina** to **John Galbreath**, [no residence given] fifty shillings per hundred acres, 94 acres, on waters of Back Cr., begin at a post oak cor. to **Strudwick, Galbreath's** line W 24 ch. 50 lk. to a stake **Charles Standford's** cor., his line S 33 ch. 25 lk. to his other cor. on **Standford's** line, his line E 31 ch. to a stake on **Strudwick's** line, his line to beginning, entered 25 January 1797; signed: **Saml. Ashe**; witness: **J. Glasgow**; [no probate record], Delvd. **H. Hurdle**.

P. 226, 27 February 1796, **James Patterson** of Chatham to **George Johnston & Samuel Hopkins** both of Orange, for love & goodwill for my 2 friends, all right & title granted by **Hardy Morgan** respecting the timber on land of **Morgan, Johnston & Hopkins** entitled to all pine trees fit for sawing from the mouth of Little Cr. of Morgans Cr. to **Samuel Allen's** line and W of Morgans Wagon Path that leads into the Chapel Road, also all the sweet gums on the Lowgrounds of Morgan, also all pine fit for sawing on a 140 acre tract the S part of the **Patterson** Tract adjoining **Christopher Barbee**, right & title to pines on land of **Abraham Allen**; signed: **J. Patterson**; witness: **John McCauley, Jane Puckett**; proved November Term 1797 by **McCauley**.

P. 227, 29 November 1797, **James Moore**, Administrator of **William Watters** Decd. to **Samuel Benton** [no county of residence given for either], eighty pounds, bill of sale for a negroe boy named **Peter**; signed: **James Moore**; witness: **Jno. Taylor**; proved November Term 1797 by **John Taylor**, Delvd. **Colo. S. Benton**.

P. 227, 25 February 1794, **William Christmas** of Franklin County to "my nephew" **Noial Graves Christmas** son of brother **Nathaniel Christmas**, [no consideration given], one negroe wench named **Neise** willed by my father **John Christmas** to me; signed: **William Christmas**; witness: **Nathaniel Christmas, Thomas Christmas**, proved November Term 1797 by **Nathaniel Christmas**.

P. 228, 2 August 1777, **Ralph McNair** lately of Orange, attorney, to **Thomas Estis** of same, planter, one hundred & twenty five pounds, 280 acres, on waters of New Hope, all the remainder of 480 acres from **Granville** to **John Caragan**, purchased by **McNair** in 2 parcels from **William Gibson & James Scarlett**, **McNair** has already sold 200 acres to **George Reeves**, begin at **George Reeves'** cor. tree on the Old Last Line 125 p. N from the SE cor. of the Original Tract, N 125 p. to the NE cor. of the Original Tract, W along the Old Line 256 p.

to the NW cor., S along the Old Line 175 p. to **George Reeves'** other cor., 125 p. N from the SW cor. of the Original Tract, E crossing the Cleared Ground & formerly the dividing line between **George Reeves** & **Thomas Estis** 256 acres to first station; signed: **Ralph McNair**; witness: **Jas. Anderson, John Telfair, Will: Burges**; proved November Term 1797 by **Anderson**, Delvd. **Betty Carrall**.

P. 230, 11 September 1797, **John Daniel** of Orange to **Joseph Booth**, seventy pounds, bill of sale for one negroe boy namerd **Harry** aged about nine years; signed: **John Daniel**; witness: **William Merritt, William O'Kelly**; acknowledged November Term 1797.

P. 230, 16 October 1797, **John Daniel** of Orange to **Robert Campbell** of same, thirty pounds, 1 acre, in the village adjacent to the **University of North Carolina**, 1/2 of Lot #16 in plan of village, westward half of lot, to be divided by a line to begin on the Main Street, N28W across the lot; signed: **John Daniel**; witness: **Robert T. Daniel, Charles Campbell**; acknowledged November Term 1797, Delvd. **Jno. McCauley (Irish)**.

P. 231, 29 November 1797, **Lewis Hornaday** of Cane Creek Settlement of Orange County to **Jacob Nugant** of same, two hundred & thirty pounds, 220 acres, begin at a white oak, S180 p. to bank of Cane Cr., W 180 p. along bank of Cane Cr. to a black oak, N 180 p. to a stone near a black oak saplin, W 40 ch. to a post oak, N 5 ch. to a white oak, E 64 ch. to a hicory, N 2 1/2 ch. to a hicory, 12 1/2 ch. to a hicory, S 4 ch. to a stake, E 22 ch. to a post oak, S 2 1/2 ch. to a post oak, 25 ch. to a hicory, N 8 1/2 ch. to a white oak which is the first station; signed: **Lewis (H) Hornerday**; witness: **Andrew Morrow**; proved November Term 1797 by **Morrow**, Delvd. **Jacob Nugant**.

P. 233, 29 July 1795, **James Smith** of Spartanburgh, South Carolina, to **Samuel Smith** of Orange, fifty pounds, 100 acres, on Back Cr. of Haw Cr. a branch of Haw R., begin at a hicory on S side of the northernmost creek, S5W 45 ch. to a black oak, S85E 23 ch. to a black oak, N5W 45 ch. to a stake, N85W 23 ch. to beginning, Entry No. 361, surveyed 18 September 1778, Grant No. 181, recorded in Orange County registers Book L folio 107, 29 July 1795; signed: **Jas. Smith**; witness: **John Bunch, George Bunch**; proved November Term 1797 by **John Bunch**, Delvd. **James Mebane**.

P. 234, 2 October 1797, **Hugh Tedford** of Orange to **John Gardner** of Rockingham County, two hundred & twenty pounds, 220 acres, in Orange & Guilford Counties, where he now lives, part of one of tract **Thomas Tedford Senr.** Decd. died possessed of, willed to **Robert Tedford** & sold to **Hugh Tedford** a legatee, begin at a post oak cor. of Original Survey, W with line 385 p. crossing the County Line & Haw R. to a stake, N crossing river & Fishing Cr. 45 p. to a willow oak on bank of creek on **James Warnion's** line, E his line 120 p. to a black oak, N his line 67 1/2 p. to a hicory near a path, E crossingf the County Line 265 p. to a frowning oak, S 112 p. to first station; signed: **Hugh Tedford**; witness: **William Walker, A. Boyd, Emanuel James**; proved November Term 1797 by **Walker**, Delvd. **J. Gardner**.

P. 235, 30 November 1797, **Andrew Murdock** Sheriff of Orange to **James**

Carrington Junior of same, thirty one pounds, 1 lot, 1 acre, Lot # 9, in town adjacent to the buildings of the University, levy on land **John Carrington, Senior, Andrew Burke,** and **James Carson** for two hundred pounds, the **Trustees of the University of North Carolina** recovered against **John Carrington** father to **James Carrington Junior** (parties thereto); signed: **Andrew Murdock**; wit: **James Green, George Horner**; acknowledged November Term 1797, Delvd. **Jno. McCauley (Irish).**

P. 237, 10 July 1797, **Andrew Murdock** Sheriff of Orange to **George Horner** of same, planter, one hundred and seventy one pounds, 325 acres, on waters of Flat R., adjoins **Arthur Mangum, William Smallwood,** and **McCulloh**, levy against **James Williams,** deceased, for one hundred and forty pounds, begin on a pine **Arthur Mangum's**, S55W 116 ch. to a hicory, E 97 ch. to a black oak, N 68 ch. to first station; signed: **Andrew Murdock**; witness: **James Green, Thomas Watts**, proved November Term 1797 by **Green**, Delvd **George Horner.**

P. 239, 24 May 1797, **Henry Lewis Lutterloh** of Chatham to **Elizabeth Sharpe Senior** [no residence given], one hundred pounds, negro girl slave named **Fillis**; signed: **H. Lewis Lutterloh**; witness: **William Norwood**; proved November Term by **Norwood.**

P. 240, 10 July 1797, **Andrew Murdock** Sheriff of Orange to **Eli McDaniel** of same, fifty one pounds one shilling, 132 acres, on Cunalls (?) Cr. a branch of Haw R., adjoins **Peter Woolfe**, begin at a post oak, S45W 44 ch. to a post oak, S45E 30 ch. to a post oak, 45E 44 ch. to a stake, N45W 30 ch. to first station, levy against **James Williams** for twenty five pounds; signed: **Andrew Murdock**; witness: **James Green, Thomas Lasley**; proved November Term 1797 by **Green**, Delvvd. **Saml. ODaniel.**

P. 242, 30 November 1796, **Jacob Rich** of Orange to **Cason Caps** of same, twenty seven silver dollars, 13 1/2 acres, on N side of Great Allamance, begin on bank of creekm on a spanish oak, N35E 15 ch. & 50 lk. to a stake, S 5 ch. to a black oak, S60E 5 ch. to a hicory, S25W 4 ch. & 50 lk. to an elm on bank of creek, up creek to beginning; signed: **Jacob Rich, Philepina (X) Rich**; witness: **James H. Ray, Luke Pryor**; proved November Term 1797 by **Ray**, Delvd. **James H. Ray.**

P. 243, 30 November 1796, **Andrew Murdock** Sheriff of Orange to **James Carrington Junior**, twenty one pounds, 1 lot, 2 acres, on blank street, Lot # 8, levy against **John Carrington, Andrew Burke,** and **James Carson** for two hundred pounds recovered by the **Trustees of the University of North Carolina**, levied on lands of **John Carrington** father of **James Carrington**; signed: **Andrew Murdock**; witness: **James Green, George Horner**; acknowledged November Term 179, Delvd. **Jno. McCauley (Irish).**

P. 245, 20 August 1777, **Leonard Henly Bullock** of Granville to **William Dry** Esquire of Brunswick, two thousand pounds, one eight share of **Richard Henderson & Company**, by deed dated 17 March 1775 the Cherokee Nation of Indians sold **Richard Henderson, Thomas Hart, Nathaniel Hart, John Williams, John Luttrell, William Johnson, James Hogg, David Hart,** and

Leonard Henly Bullock the tract now known as Transylvania on the River Ohio, begining at the Ohio R. at the mouth of Caintucky R. known by the English as Louisa R., up river & most northerly fork of same to the head spreing, SE to Top Ridge of Powells Mountain, westwardly along ridge to point from which a NW course will strike the head spring of the most southwardly br. of the Cumberland R., down river to Ohiuo R., up Ohio to beginning, also a tract beginning on Holsten R. where the course of Powells Mountain strikes same, up river to where the Virginia Line crosses it, W along line by **Col. Donaldson** to a point six english miles E of the Long Island in Holsten R., a direct course tro the mouth of the Great Canaway until it reaches the top ridge of Powell Mountain, W along ridge to beginning, deeded to aforesaid as tenants in common and not as joint tenants, one eighth to **Richard Henderson**, one eighth to **Thomas Hart**, one eighth to **Nathaniel Hart**, one eighth to **John Williams**, one eighth to **John Luttrell**, one eighth to **William Johnston**, one eighth to **James Hogg**, one sixteenth to **David Hart**, one sixteenth to **Leonard Henly Bullock**; signed: **Leonard H. Bullock**; witness: **Richard Henderson, Gaiht. Bullock**; proved in Raleigh 9 December 1797 before **John Williams,** Judge of Superior Court, Delvd. **James Hogg.**

P. 249, 22 May 1778, **John Luttrell** of Chatham to **William Dry** of Brunswick, one thousand pounds, one eighth of the purchase made by **Richard Henderson & Company** from the Cherokee Indians, **Dry** to pay his proportinate share of expenses; signed: **J Luttrell**; witness: **Henry Gifford, Mathew Jones**; proved in Raleigh 9 December 1797 before **John Williams** Judge of Superior Court, Delvd. **James Hogg.**

P. 250, 30 April 1778, **John Williams** of Granville to **William Dry** Esquire of Brunswick, two thousand pounds, one fourth part of his **(John Williams)** share of the land purchased by **Richard Henderson & Company** (see P. 245); signed: **Jno. Williams**; witness: **Jacob Blount, Robert Summer**; proved 7 December 1797 before **John Williams** Judge of Superior Court.

P. 253, 22 August 1777, **John Williams** of Granville to **William Dry** Esquire of Brunswick, two thousand pounds, one fourth of his **(John Williams)** share of **Richard Henderson & Company**; signed: **Jno. Williams**; witness: **Robert Burton, Adam Rice**; proved 7 December 1797 before **John Haywood** Judge of Superior Court.

P. 256, 27 August 1777, **Thomas Hart** Esquire of Orange to **William Dry** Esquire of Brunswick, two thousand pounds, one quarter part of his **(Thomas Hart's)** share of the land purchased by **Richard Henderson & Company**; signed: **Thomas Hart**; witness: **Thomas H. Hill, James Hogg**; proved in Raleigh before **Jno. Williams** JSL&E 6 December 1797 by **Hogg.**

P. 260, 29 September 1794, **William Smother** to **Joseph Sillivan**, both of Orange, fifty two pounds, 130 acres, on both sides of Big Cr. of Haw R., bounded on S by **William Hatchett**, on W by **John Smothers**, begin at a post oak, E 26 ch. to a black, N 50 ch. to a red oak, W 26 ch. to a black jack, S 50 ch. to first station, part of a tract granted to **William Smothers**; signed: **William Smothers, Ann (X) Smothers**; witness: **William Hatchett, Edward Hatchett**;

proved November Term 1797 by **William Hatchett**, Delvd. **Wm. Hatchett.**

P. 261, 9 October 1797, **Benjamin Smith** to **James Hogg** [no residence given], [no consideration given], 27 August 1777 **James Hogg** sold **Col. William Dry** of Brunswick one fourth of one eighth share or one thirty ssecond part of whole purchase from Indians, 22 June 1778 **William Dry** sold **Daniel Tucker** of George Town District, South Carolina, one twelfth undivided share of the one thrity second part recorded in Book D folio 98 to 100 in George Town District, 24 March 1796 **Tucker** sold to **Benjamin Smith** a moiety of the one twelfth part, moiety sold is one seven hundred and sixty eighth part of the whole purchase; signed: **Benjamin Smith**; witness: [none listed]; acknowledged in Raleigh before **Jno. Williams** JSCL&E 9 December 1797.

P. 263, 9 December 1797, **Benjamin Smith** of Brunswick to **James Hogg** of Orange, {consideration not given], one sixty fourth share of land of **Richard Henderson & Company**, 27 August 1777 **Thomas Hart** to **William Dry** of Brunswick one fourth of his share or one undivided thirty second, 22 February 1778 **Dry** to **Benjamin Smith** then of Charleston, South Carolina, now of Brunswick County one sixty fourth part of the tract from the Cherokee Indians; signed: **Benjamin Smith**; witness: [none listed]; acknowledged before **Jno. Williams** JSCL&E in Raleigh 9 December 1779.

P. 266, 5 August 1797, **Charles Brown** of District of Georgetown, South Carolina, to **Shadrach Simmons** and **Leonard Dozer** Esquires of same, power of attorney, to sell one third part of one hundred and twenty eighth part of land of **Richard Henderson & Co.**, 22 June 1778 **William Dry** of Brunswick to **Joseph Brown** of Georgetown, South Carolina, father of **Charles Brown**, vested in **Charles Brown** since death of father; signed: **C. Brown**; witness: **Jos. Blyth**, **John Davis**; proved Georgetown District, South Carolina before **George Hariott** 5 August 1797 by **Joseph Blyth**; affidavit of **J. Cornelius**, Notary Public of South Carolina, that **Hariott** was a justice.

P. 269, 28 July 1797, **George Heriot** of Georgetown District, South Carolina, to **Shadrack Simons & Leonard Dozer** of same, power of attorney, to sell three fourths share (the other fourth having been sold to **Capt. James Mitchell**) of tract named Transylvania and another tract lying on branches of Ohio & adjoining same, share of **Heriot** is three hundred and eighty fourth part, **William Dry**, Esq., of Brunswick County, North Carolina to **Heriot** 22 June 1778; signed: **Geo. Heriot**; witness: **Ezra Pugh**; proved Georgetown District, South Carolina, before **John Keith**, Esq., 28 July 1797; affidavit of **Cornelius Dupee**, Notary Public of South Carolina, that **Keith** is a justice.

P. 271, 2 August 1797, **Joseph Brown** of Charleston, South Carolina, to **Shadrach Simons & Leonard Dozer** of Georgetown District, power of attorney, to sell a one third share of an undivided one hundred and twenty eighth part of a tract called Transylvania and a tract lying on the branches of the Ohio & adjoining same, **William Dry** of Brunswick County, North Carolina to deceased father **Joseph Brown** of Charleston 22 June 1778, now vested in grantor; signed: **Joseph Brown**; witness: **Henry Bennett, Francis Ley**; proved Charleston District, South Carolina, before **James Bentham**, Esq., 2 August 1797 by **Francis Ley**; affidavit of **John Mitchell,** Notary Public of South Carolina that **Mitchell** is a justice.

P. 275, 22 June 1778, **William Dry,** Esq., of Brunswick County, North Carolina, to **George Heriot** of Georgeton, South Carolina, merchant, eioght hundredand thirty three pounds six shillings eight pence, one undivided twelfth part of **William Dry's** one two and thirtieth part [one three hundred and eighty fourth part] in the **Henderson Company** lands; signed: **Wllm Dry;** witness: **Jos. Brown, Wilson Dalgett;** appended is a deed from **Shadrack Simons & Leonard Dozer,** Esq., of Georgetown District, South Carolina, to **James Hogg** [no residence given], two hundred and ninety three dollars, share of **George Heriot** in land conveyed to him by **William Dry** excepting share sold to Mr. **Mitchell** of South Carolina, dated 17 November 1797; signed: **Shadrack Simons, Leonard Dozer;** witness: [none listed]; acknowledged 17 November 1797 in Cumberland County, North Carolina, before **C. D. Howard & Robt. Donaldson;** affidavit of **Jos. Winston,** Clk., that **Howard & Donaldson** are justices; affidavit of **Soloman Cohen** of George Town before **William Heriot** that signature of witness, **Joseph Brown,** is that of **Joseph Brown,** deceased, 18 September 1793; receipt of **William Dry** for money from **Heriot** witnessed by **Joseph Brown & Wilson Dalzell.**

P. 280, 20 June 1778, **William Dry,** Esq., of Brunswick County, North Carolina, to **Joseph Brown,** Esq., of George Town, South Carolina, two thousand five hundred pounds, one sixth of **William Dry's** undivided share in the **Henderson Company** purchased from **James Hogg** (one hundred and twenty eighth part); signed: **William Dry;** witness: **George Heriot, Wilson Dalzett;** deed from **Shadrack Simons & Leonard Dozer** of Georgetown District, South Carolina, to **James Hogg,** seven hundred and eighty two dollars, two thirds of the aforementioned deed, by virtue of power of attorney from **Charles Brown** and **Joseph Brown** lawful representatives of their father **Joseph Brown** each claiming for himself one third of the deed from **Dry** to **Brown,** dated 17 November 1797; signed: **Shadrack Simons, Leonard Dozer;** witnesses: [none listed]; acknowledged by both **Simons & Dozer** 17 November 1797 in Cumberland County before **C. D. Howard & Robt. Donaldson;** affidavit of **Jos. Winslow** that **Howard & Donaldson** are justices.

P. 284, 22 June 1778, **William Dry,** Esq., of Brunswick County, North Carolina, to **Robert Heriot** of George Town, South Carolina, eight hundred thirty three pounds six shillings eight pence, twelfth part of **William Dry's** undivided share in the **Henderson Company** purchased from **James Hogg** (a three hundred and eighty fourth part of the whole); signed: **Wllm. Dry;** witness: **Jos. Brown, Wilson Dalzell;** deed from **Shadrack Simons & Leonard Dozer** of Geo. Town District, So. Carolina, to **James Hogg,** three hundred ninety & a half dollars, by power of attorney from **Mary Heriot, George Heriot, William Heriot, Daniel Tucker, John Heriot, & Robert Heriot** legal representatives of **Robert Heriot,** right to aforementioned tract; signed: **Shadrack Simons, Leonard Dozer;** witness: [none listed]; acknowledged 17 November 1797 before **C. D. Howard & Robt. Donaldson** of Cumberland County, North Carolina; affidavit of **Jos. Winslow** that **Howard & Donaldson** are justices dated 17 November 1797; affidavit of **George Heriot** of George Town District, South Carolina that **Daniel**

Tucker swore that signature of **Jos. Brown** was his handwriting, 3 October 1793.

P. 289, 1 December 1797, **North Carolina** to **John Kelley**, [no residence given] fifty shillings per hundred acres, 67 1/2 acres, on waters of Buck Water, bounded on N by **Copeland** & his own land, on E by his & **John Wood's** land, on S by **William Whitehead**, on W by **Copeland**, begin at a red oak saplin, S 7 ch. to a black jack, W 8 1/2 ch. to a stake **Wood's** cor., S 16 3/4 ch. to a white oak **Whitted's** cor., W 18 1/2 ch. to a post oak, S 8 ch. to a white oak, W 5 to a black oak saplin, N 33 1/4 ch. to a hicory, E 32 ch. to first station, entered 9 May 1795; signed: **Sam Ashe**; witness: **Jas. Glasgow;** [no probate record], Delvd. **John Kelley.**

P. 290, 1 December 1797, **North Carolina** to **John Kelley,** [no residence given] fifty shillings per hundred acres, 100 acres, on Buck Water Cr., begin at a maple in Finchers Br., W 60 ch. crossing Buck Water twice to a stake formerly a black oak tree **Houlden's** cor., S 5 ch. crossing creek to a stone **Houlden's** cor., E 1/2 ch. to a red oak, S 2 ch. to a black oak **Kelley's** cor., E 22 1/2 ch. to a white oak **Kelley's** cor., S 57 ch. to a small red oak on **Lewis'** line, E 9 1/2 ch. to a post oak, N3E **John Wood's** line 7 ch. to a black oak, E **Wood's** line 19 1/2 ch. to mouth of Frenchers Br., up branch to beginning, entered 30 January 1797; signed: **Sam Ashe;** witness: **J. Glasgow;** [no probate record], Delvd. **John Kelley.**

P. 291, 20 January 1796, **Samuel Gattis** of Orange to **Nathaniel King** of same, one hundred pounds, 200 acres, in Saint Thomas District, begin at a post oak, W 20 ch. to a red oak, N 100 ch. to a white oak, E 20 ch. to a white oak, S to beginning; signed: **Samuel Gattis, Margret Gattis;** witness: **Alexander Gattis, William Gattis;** proved November Term 1797 by **William Gattis**, Delvd. **Jno. McCauley (Irish).**

P. 293, 10 May 1796, **Samuel Gattis** of Orange to **Nathaniel King** of same, twenty five pounds, 75 acres, near Presswood Cr., part of a tract from **Granville** to **Gilbert Strayhorn** 27 February 1759 registered in Book E Page 225, begin at a stone in the SW cor. of tract in a branch, N 57 ch. to a white oak saplin, E 52 p. & 10 ft. to a white oak saplin, S 57 ch. to a stake in the old field, W 52 p. 10 ft. to beginning; signed: **Samuel Gattis, Margret Gattis;** witness: **Alexander Gattis, William Gattis;** proved November Term 1797 by **William Gattis**, Delvd. **Baxter King.**

P. 294, 18 November 1797, **Umphrey Williams** of Orange to **Jeremiah Piggott** of same, seventeen dollars, 50 acres, on waters of Rocky Cr., part of 570 acres from **North Carolina** to **Williams** 17 November 1790, begin at a black oak, N80W to a black jack 100 p., N10W 44 p. to a spanish oak saplin **Buckingham's** cor., N63E 100 p. to a black oak, S10E 110 p. to a spanish oak, N80W 3 p. to beginning; signed: **Umphrey (+) Williams;** witness: **Edmund Green, Susannah (X) Boggs;** proved November Term 1797 by **Green**, Delvd. **Benj. Bickell.**

P. 295, 9 October 1797, **Obed Green** of Orange to **Nicholas Holt** of same, one hundred pounds, 123 acres, on waters of Vernals Cr., begin at a white oak, S25W 35 ch. to a stake on Harmon's Rd., N25E 40 ch. on road to a stake, E 9 ch. to a stake, N 15 ch. to a stake, E 28 ch. to first station; signed: **Obed Green;** witness: **Edmund Green,** *Jonnoye albright* **Albright;** proved November Term 1797 by **Edmund Green,** Delvd. **Obed Green.**

P. 296, 9 November 1796, **Ishom Hawkins** of Halifax to **John Jenkins** of Orange, forty five pounds, 108 1/2 acres, begin at a red oak near Pee Cr., N 35 ch. to a post oak, E 5 ch. to a red oak, N 25 ch. to a red oak, E 11 ch. to a red oak, S 44 ch. to a red oak, E 21 ch. to a post oak, S 16 ch. to a small post oak the dividing line between **John Coal** & sd. land, W the dividing line 22 ch. to a white oak **Cole's** cor., N6W 8 1/4 ch. to a post oak **Cole's** cor., S81W 11 ch. to a red oak **Cole's** cor., S2W 7 ch. to a white oak **Cole's** cor. of another tract, W his line to first station; signed: **Isham (X) Hawkins;** witness: **John Justiss, James Roan, Lewis (X) Roan;** proved November Term 1797 by **James Rowan,** Delvd. **Jno. Jenkins.**

P. 297, 28 September 1797, **Stephen Wilson** of Orange to **William Gess** of same, two hundred dollars, 121 acres, on waters of Mountain Cr., begin at a black oak saplin **Dollar's** cor., S8W 30 ch. to a red oak bush, W8N 32 3/4 ch. to a stake, N 12 3/4 ch. to a stake, N35E 15 ch. to a black jack, E 10 ch. to a hicory, N16E 35 ch. to a black oak, to first station; signed: **Stephen Wilson;** witness: **Thomas Latta Senr., John Latta Junr.;** proved November Term 1797 by **John Latta Junior,** Delvd. **Willm. Gess.**

P. 299, 28 November 1797, **Samuel Smith** of Orange to **James Mebane** of same, twenty five pounds, 100 acres, on Back Cr. of Haw Cr. a branch of Haw R., begin at a hicory on the S side of the northern most creek, S5W 45 ch. to a black oak, S85E 23 ch. to a black oak, N5W 45 ch. to a stake, S85E 23 ch. to beginning; signed: **Saml. Smith;** witness: **Andrew Murdock, William McCauley;** acknowledged November Term 1797, Delvd. **Jas. Mebane.**

P. 300, 15 September 1797, **John Carrington** of Orange to **Chuza Hopkins** of same, fifty pounds, fortieth part of an acre, a certain small piece of land containing a spring, part of a tract **Hopkins** bought of **Carrington,** begin at a white oak, E 2 rods to a red oak, S 2 rods to a red oak, W 2 rods to a red oak, N to first station; signed: **John Carrington;** witness: **Jno. Latta Junr., John Mangum;** proved November Term 1797 by **John Latta Junr.,** Delivdd. **Jno. Latta Junr.**

P. 301, 10 December 1795, **James Murray** of Orange to **William Faucett** of same, one hundred and thirty five pounds, 152 acres, on W side of Owens Cr., begin at a red oak, S 50 ch. 31 lk. to a post oak, E with **McAdams'** line 8 ch. 80 lk. to pointers, S with his line 8 ch. 50 lk. to a sweet gum by the creek, up creek 38 ch. to a black oak by the creek, N4E 6 ch. 70 lk. to a black oak, W 78 ch. to pointers by a small branch, N11W 35 ch. 234 lk. to a hicory in the old line, W along line to first station; signed: **James Murray;** witness: **William Love, Robert Mitchell;** acknowledged November Term 1797, Delivd. **Wm. Fossett.**

P. 302, 7 March 1797, **William Stroud** of Orange to **David Simmons** of

Chatham, fifty pounds, 100 acres, on waters of Raibons Cr. waters of New Hope, begin at the mouth of **John Ivey's** Spring Branhc where it empties into creek, up branch to a fork near the path that leads from **John Ivey's** to **James Loyd**, up W prong to head spring, S to **John Ivey's** line, W on line to the Haw Br., down branch to creek, down creek to beginning; signed: **William Stroud**; witness: **John Jolley, Boling Jolley**; proved November Term 1797 by **Boling Jolley**, Delivd. **David Simmons**.

P. 303, 15 April 1797, **Jesse Cate** of Orange to **Thomas Griffin** of same, one hundred pounds, 58 acres, on Marshals Br., begin at a gum on branch, S7W 24 1/2 ch. to a R. O. on the Fayetteville Road, along same N54W 27 1/2 ch. to an elm on road in a Dralight, down meanders of Dralight 12 1/2 ch. to Marshals Br., up branch to beginning; signed: **Jesse Cate**; witness: **William Moore, Saml. Doning**; proved November Term 1797 by **Moore**, Delivd. **Thos. Griffin**.

P. 305, 22 November 1794, **Christopher Holt** of Orange to **Absalom Holt** of same, fifty pounds, 180 acres, on S side of Haw R. on waters of Little Allamance, begin at a post oak saplin, S 150 p. to a spanish oak, E 192 p. to a post oak, N 150 p. to a black jack, W 192 p. to beginning, part of a larger tract from **Granville** to **Michael Holt Senior**, reference to **Absalom Holt** as son of **Christopher Holt**; signed: **Christopher (+) Holt**; witness: **Reuben Holt, Thos. Cole, Geo. Holt**; proved November Term 1797 by **George Holt**, Delivd. **Absalom Holt**.

P. 306, 19 October 1797, **Nicholas Holt** of Orange to **Obed Green** of same, two hundred and fifty pounds, 231 acres, on waters of Rock Cr., begin at a black oak **Benjamin Picket's** cor. on **Joshua Picket's** line, with **Benjamin Picket's** line S45E 30 ch. to a red oak & cor., along his other line S30W 18 ch. to a white oak, S80E 18 ch. to a hicory saplin, N70E 15 ch. to Harmons Road, along road N25E 40 ch. to a stake, W 41 ch. to a black oak & **Joshua Picket's** cor., his line S45W 20 ch. to beginning; signed: **Nicholas ( ) Holt**; witness: **Edmund Green, Joshua Piggott**; proved November Term 1797 by **Edmund Green**, Delivd. **Obed Green**.

P. 307, 1 May 1796, **Trustees of the University of North Carolina** to **Obediah Green & Nicholas Holt** of Orange, seventy pounds sixteen shillings, 354 acres, begin at a white oak, W 38 1/2 ch. to a stake, S 10 ch. to a stake, W 50 ch. to a red oak, N15W 9 ch. to a red oak & cor. of **Joshua Picket**, his line S45W 20 ch. to a black oak **Benjamin Picket's** cor., his line S45E 30 ch. to a red oak cor. of **Picket**, S30W 18 ch. to a white oak on **Picket's** line, S82E 20 ch. to a stake on a branch, N70E 50 ch. to a hicory, N29E 48 ch. to beginning; signed: **William Sheppard**, attorney; witness: **H. Sheppard**, "something in Dutch"; proved November Term 1797 by [blank], Delivd. **Obed Green**.

P. 309, 28 January 1797, **Mathew Lindsey** of Orange to **William Lindsey** of same, three hundred pounds, 274 acres, on head of West Fork of Eno R., part of two tracts, **John Logue** to **Mathew Lindsey & North Carolina** to **Lindsey** granted in 1779, begin at the creek, W 55 ch. to a P. O., N 15 ch. to a P. O., E 15 ch. to a P. O., N 41 1/2 ch. to a B. J., E 55 ch. to a P. O., S 25, E 8 ch., S 3 1/2 ch. to a B. O. on S side of a branch, down branch to creek, down creek to first station; signed: **Mathew Lindsey**; witness: **Jos. Allison, Samuel Maden**; proved November Term 1797 by **Joseph Allison**, Delivd. **Wm. Lindsey.**

P. 310, 8 June 1797, **James Warnock** of Guilford to **William Walker, Rachel Hunter, & Mary Hunter** of Rockingham, fifty pounds, 73 acres, on waters of Haw R., begin at a post oak, S 79 p. to a black oak their dividing cor. standing near a branch, W through the survey crossing two branches of the river 148 p. to a post oak standing in the Rockingham County line & being a cor. of their other dividing cor., with that line N 79 p. to a walnut, E to first station; signed: **James (O) Warnock**; witness: **A. Phillips, James Warnock, Thomas Larimer**; proved November Term 1797 by **James Warnock**, Delivd. **Isaac Brackin.**

P. 311, 2 February 1796, **Jesse Nevill** of Orange to **Daniel Stevens** of same, eighty pounds, 80 acres, begin at **Pomfret Herndon's** Old Wagon Road where **George Hagwood** built a cabbin, along road a small space nearly N to a white oak marked on left hand of road, nearly W along a marked line to a sweet gum saplin on the head of Bird Br., down branch to m̦outh of Wikes Spring Br., up Wike Spring Br. to the spring, nearly S up the drain to a bunch of maples in the branch that runs from the Woolfe Pit into the Meadows Fork of Prices Cr., down branch to creek, down creek to Steven's line, N along his line to a hicory in the Old Field, E to beginning; signed: **Jesse Nevill**; witness: **John Willson, Benjamin Nevill**; proved November Term 1797 by **Willson**, Delivd. **Daniel Stephens.**

P. 313, 18 June 1796, **William Mebane** of Orange to **Thomas Cole** of same, three hundred and fifty pounds, 300 acree, on Haw R., begin at a hicory a cor. of **Henry Suver**(?) land, his line S 29 ch. to a post oak cor. of **James Murrow**, W 28 ch. to a post oak, S 10 ch. to a post oak, W 10 ch. to a stake, N 20 ch. to a red oak, W 30 ch. to a post oak, N7E 70 ch. to a white oak & red oak on S bank of Haw R., down river to beginning including river 20 ch., also including mill & mill race; signed: **Wm Mebane**; witness: **James Murray Junr., Absalom Holt**; proved November Term 1797 by **Holt.**

P. 314, 13 April 1792, **James Hunter** of Orange to **Sion Bobbitt** of same, one hundred pounds, 100 acres, part of a survey of **Charles Ashley's** lying on N side of Dyals Cr. including the plantation where **Robert Thompson** formerly lived, begin at **Arthur Mangum's** line on Dyal Cr., W on line to **Willm. McFarlan's** cor. a dead hicory, S on **McFarlan's** line to the first branch, down branch to Dyals Cr., up creek to first station; signed: **James Hunter, Christian Hunter**; witness: **James (X) Horner, Taylor Duk**; proved November Term 1797 by **Horner**, Delivd. **Sihon Bobbitt.**

P. 315, 5 First Month 1797, **Stephen Hart** of Orange rto **Owen Lindley** of same, ninety pounds, 60 1/2 acres, begin at a hicory on **William Whitehead's** line, S 10 ch. 10 lk. to a stake, continued same course 24 ch. 20 lk. to a stake, E 25 ch. to a white oak, N 14 ch. 10 lk. to a hicory, same course continued in all 24 ch. 20 lk. to a red oak, W 25 ch. to first station; signed: **Stephen Hart, Catherine (O) Hart**; witness: **Henry Fossett, James Thompson**; proved November Term 1797 by **Thompson.**

P. 316, 1 November 1797, **Henry McCollum** of Hillsborough to **Elizabeth Williams** of Orange, fifteen pounds, 1/2 acre, lot in Hillsborough, part of Lot # 129, bounded on N by Kings Street, on E by Lot # 130, on S by Margaret Lane, on W by **Jonathon Copeland's** claim being part of the same lot; signed: **Henry McCollum**; witness: **James Roberts, S. Harris**; proved November Term 1797 by **Harris**, Delivd. **Elizabeth Williams**.

P. 317, 13 Ninth Month 1796, **Allen Edwards** of Orange to **Isaac Harvey** of same, three hundred and thirteen pounds, 117 acres, on N side of Cain Cr., begin at a white oak **Thomas Lindley's** cor., E 80 p. to a post oak the dividing cor., S to red oak on bank of creek, down creek to mill dam, down race to **Thomas Lindley's** line, N to first station, part of tract granted by will by **Hugh Laughlin** to his daughters 24 Second Month 1765; signed: **Allen (X) Edwards**; witness: **Thomas Lindley, Eli Harvey**; proved November Term 1797 by **Lindley**, Delivd. **Thos. Lindly**.

P. 319, 30 Eighth Month 1796, **James Woody, James Allen, James Mathews, Nathaniel Morrison, & John Hackney** all of Orange to **Allen Edwards** of same, three hundred and thirteen pounds, 117 acres, on N side of Cain Cr., begin at a white oak **Thomas Lindley's** cor., W 80 p. to a post oak the dividing cor., S to a red oak on bank of creek, down creek to the mill dam, down the race to **Thomas Lindley's** line, N tto first station, being part of the land devised to them from **Hugh McLaughlan** by will dated 25 Second Month 1765; signed: **Nathl. Morrison, James Matthews, James Woody, James Allen, John Hackney**; witness: **Jonathon Lindley, Thomas Lindley**; proved November Term 1797 by **Thomas Lindley**.

P. 320, 25 January 1797, **James Patterson** of Chatham to **George Johnston & Samuel Hopkins** both of Orange, eighty pounds, 10 acres, begin at a hicory saplin on Bolands Cr., W to **Benjamin Yeargan's** line, S crossing creek to a stake on bank, E to the road, N with Old Road to beginning, with a saw mill formerly the property of **Hardy Morgan**; signed: **James Patterson**; witness: **John McCauley, John Puckett**; proved November Term 1797 by **McCauley**, Delivd. **Geo. Johnston**.

P. 321, 19 October 1793, **Alfred Moore, John Haywood, William Richardson Davie, & Alexr. Mebane**, Esq., Commissioners, on behalf of the **University of North Carolina** to **John Caldwell** of Orange, twenty nine pounds, 2 acres, one lot in town adjacent to the buildings of the University, on Franklin Street, Lot # 24; signed: **A. Moore, John Haywood, W. R. Davie, Alexr. Mebane**; witness: **W. Watters**; proved November Term 1797 by **Samuel Benton** who swore to the handwriting of **William Watters**, Delivd. **Jno. McCauley (Irish)**.

P. 322, 28 December 1795, **William F. Strudwick** of Orange to **Nathaniel Christmas** of same, twenty pounds, 47 acres, on waters of Little Cain Cr., begin at a post oak on **Charles Christmas'** line, S27E [should read S47E] 197 ch. to a P. O. **Durham's** cor., his line W 26 1/2 ch. to a spanish oak, S 5 ch. to an R. O. on a branch, up branch N35W 32 1/2 ch. to a stake a cor. of **Charles Christmas**, his line E to beginning; signed: **W. F. Strudwick**; witness: **Thomas Watts**; proved November Term 1797 by **Watts**.

P. 323, 13 January 1797, **George Johnston** of Orange to **Mathew McCauley** of same, one hundred and seventy pounds, 200 acres, begin at a red oak, E along a line of marked trees to the Mill Cr., down creek to fork, up the south creek to where **Jesse Nevill's** line crosses, along **Nevill's** line to a cor. red oak saplin on top of a hill by **Nevill's** Mill, N along marked trees to first station; signed: **Geo. Johnston**; witness: **W. H. Haywood, John Caldwell**; proved November Term 1797 by **Caldwell**, Delivd. **Jno. McCauley (Irish)**.

P. 325, 24 October 1796, **William Eccles** of Orange to **John Eccles** of same, fifty pounds, 53 acres, on waters of Deep Cr., bound on the deeded land of **John Eccles**, N part of **William Eccles** deeded land, begin at a small hicory, with **John Eccles'** line W 21 ch. 25 lk. to a P. O., S 25 ch. to a small hicory near a R. O. in his former line, E 21 ch. 25 lk. to a R. O., N to first station, part of a tract from **North Carolina** to **William Eccles** in 1780; signed: **William Eccles**; witness: **Lenalhase Backer, Isaac Hall**; proved November Term 1797 by **Hall**, Delvd. **Jno. Eccles**.

P. 327, 7 August 1797, **James Patterson** of Chatham to **George Johnston** & **Samuel Hopkins** both of Orange, fifty pounds, 12 1/2 acres, on waters of Bolands Cr., begin at a black oak in **Benjamin Yeargan's** line near the Still House, W his line 78 p. to a stake, S 26 p. to a stake on line of the University lands, E with line 78 p. to a poplar on head of a branch, N 26 p. to first station; signed: **J. Patterson**; witness: **John McCauley, Stephen Gassins**; proved November Term 1797 by **McCauley**, Delivd. **Jno. McCauley (Irish)**.

P. 328, 2 May 1794, **Isaac Brackin** of Wake to **Israel Barker** of Orange, one hundred and twenty pounds, 185 acres, begin at the NE line at the creek, NE 13 ch. to a hicory, NW 60 ch. to a post oak, S35W 50 ch. to a black oak, S 22 ch. to a white oak, N52E 22 ch. to a white oak on the creek, down creek 38 ch. to first station; signed: **Isaac Brackin**; witness: **Lemuel Cox Tepson, Lasina**[?] **Boyle**; proved November Term 1797 by **Tepson**, Delivd. **Israel Barker**.

P. 329, 9 October 1797, **Obed Green** of Orange to **Joshua Pickett** [no residence given], ten pounds, 30 acres, on waters of Rock Cr., begin at a black oak his cor., S45E 15 ch. to a post oak, N45E 25 ch. to a stake, W 12 ch. to a black oak, 10 ch. to a black oak **Pickett's** other cor., his line to beginning; signed: **Obed Green**; witness: **Edmund Green**, *John P Albright* **Albright**; proved November Term 1797 by **Edmund Green**, Delivd. **Obed Green**.

P. 330, 27 May 1797, **Henry Horton** of Orange to **Thomas McFarlin** of same, one hundred pounds, 77 1/2 acres, on S side of Dyals Cr. a branch of Flat R., begin at a white oak the E side of Flat R. a cor. of **Julius King**, W with **King's** line to a stake **Archer Harris'** cor. and **King's**, N with **Harris'** line to a black oak saplin a cor. of **Harris** & **James Walker** on Dyals Cr., down creek to first station; signed: **Henry (O) Horton**; witness: **Alex McMullan, John (X) McFarlin**; proved November Term 1797 by **John McFarlin**.

P. 332, 20 December 1796, **John G. Rencher** of Orange by power of attorney from **John Hogan**, Esq., late of same to **Baxter King** of same, sufficient compensation having been paid to **John Hogan** before his removal from this state, 100 acres, on waters of Morgans Cr., adjoins **John King** & orphans of **Stephen Loyd**, begin at a hicory & red oak on **Loyd's** line, W 24 p. to a spanish oak cor. of **Loyd** on **Griffin's** line, S his line & by his cor. 218 p. to a black jack & post oak, E 74 p. to a stake on **John King's** line, N his line 218 p. to first station; signed: **Jno. G. Rencher** atty. for **John Hogan**; witness: **John Faddis**; proved November Term 1797 by **Faddis**, Delivd. **Baxter King**.

P. 333, 13 January 1797, **George Johnston** of Orange, planter, to **Mathew McCauley** of same, planter, one hundred pounds, 132 acres, begin at a black oak in the Old Field, E 30 ch. to a stake, N forty thirty five ch. to a hicory, W 36 ch. to a stake, S 46 ch. to a red oak **Henderson's** cor., E 6 ch. to **Connally's** line, N along line to beginning, **North Carolina** to **Austin Hightower**, **Hightower** to **James Blackwood**, **Blackwood** to **Johnston**; signed: **Geo. Johnston**; witness: **John Caldwell, Willm. H. Haywood**; proved November Term 1797 by **Caldwell**, Delvd. **Jno. McCauley (Irish)**.

P. 335, 25 August 1786, **North Carolina** to **John Estes** [no residence given], eight hundred and one pounds, 300 acres, on W of Hillsborough, adjoins on both sides of Eno R., begin at a pine on the side of the Occoneechy Mountain, N 67 ch. to a black jack on line of Town of Hillsborough, W 45 ch. to a black oak on **Courtney's** line, S 67 ch. to a stake on side of the mountain, E 45 ch. to first station, sold as confiscated property of **Edmund Fanning**, sale includes right & title which **Fanning** held in property as of 4 July 1776; signed: **R. Caswell**; witness: **J. Glasgow**; [no probate record], Delivd. **Jas. Whitted**.

P. 336, 13 January 1796, **Henry McClure** of Orange, planter, to **Sarah Ross** of same, fifty pounds, 100 acres, on E side of Haw R., begin on N side at a white oak at the beginning cor., E to a water oak 16 ch. 3 p., S 60 ch. to a black oak, W 16 ch. 3 p. to a red oak, N 60 ch. to a white oak; signed: **Henry McClure**; witness: **Joseph Romley**; proved November Term 1797 by **Romley**, Delivd. **Wm. Hatchett**.

P. 337, 29 September 1786, **James Freeland** High Sheriff of Orange to **William Courtney** of same, thirteen pounds eighteen shillings, 142 acres, sale of land of **Mark Patterson** to recover thirty three pounds eighteen shillings six pence awarded **Temple Powk** May 1786, sold 28 August 1786 at Market House in Hillsborough, on waters of New Hope, adjoins **John Hart** & others, **North Carolina** to **Patterson** & [blank] **Cobb**, begin at a white oak, E 40 ch. to a black jack, S 30 1/2 ch. to a stake, E 53 ch. to a white oak, S 5 ch. to a walnut, W 83 ch. to a stake, N 23 1/2 ch. to a post oak, W 10 ch. to a black jack, N 12 ch. to first station; signed: **Jas. Freeland**; witness: **Hugh Mulhollen Junr., Joseph Freeland**; proved November Term 1797 by **Mulhollen**, Delivd. **Geo. Johnston**.

P. 339, 19 August 1796, **Susannah Smothers** of Orange to **John Smothers** of same, five pounds seven shillings six pence paid by **John Smothers** to **Thomas Smothers** Decd., 100 acres, out of tract where he did live, **Susannah** his wife invested by last will and testament in right to said tract, one hundred acres confirmed to **John Smothers** their son out of SE cor. of tract, begin at a white oak cor., with boundary linwe N, then W, then S to bounded line, E to beginning, includes the cleared land adjoining where **John Smothers** now lives; signed: **Susannah (O) Smothers**; witness: **William Hatchell, Edmund Hatchell**; proved November Term 1797 by **William Hatchell**, Delivd. **Wm. Hatchett.**

P. 340, 29 September 1794, **William Smothers** of Orange to **John Smothers** of same, forty pounds, 100 acres, begin at a stake near henry **McClure's** boundary, W 24 ch. to a stake, S 41 3/4 ch. to a post oak, E 24 ch. to a post oak, N 41 3/4 ch. to first station; signed: **William (X) Smothers, Nancy (X) Smothers**; witness: **George House[?], William Hatchell**; proved November Term 1797 by **Hatchell**, Delivd. **Wm. Hatchett.**

P. 341, 23 August 1797, **Samuel Shaw Senr.** of Orange to **William Rogers** of same, fifty six pounds, 57 acres, on waters of Mill Cr., bounded all around with **Gott, Hodge, Galbreath** & Back Cr., begin at a branch, N40E 10 ch. to a black oak, N25E 10 ch. to a black oak, N58E 18 ch. to a hicory, NW 11 ch. to an ash, W 4 ch. to a black oak, S 2 ch. to a post oak, S27W 8 ch. to a post oak, S63W 8 ch. to a stake, S77W 19 ch. to a black oak on Back Cr., down creek to first station, granted to **Thomas Strain**[?} 3 September 1780; signed: **Samuel Shaw**; witness: **Thos Bradford, Moses Cate**; proved November Term 1797 by **Bradford**, Delivd. **Young Rogers.**

P. 343, 18 May 1789, **North Carolina** to **Andrew Borland** [no residence given], ten pounds per hundred acres, 184 acres, on waters of the North East of Newhope, bounded by **Abercrombie** & **Marcom** on N, **William Marcom** on W, **Thomas Hall** on S, **John Barbee** on E, begin on **Thomas Hall's** cor. black jack, N 46 ch. to a pine, E 40 ch. to a red oak, S 46 ch. to a stake, W 40 ch. to first station; signed: **Sam: Johnston**; witness: **J. Glasgow**; [no probate record].

P. 344, 2 December 1797, **North Carolina** to **Joseph Allison** [no residence given], fifty shillings per hundred acres, 550 acres, on waters of Eno, adjoins **Thomas Person** & **Henry Campbell**, begin at a white oak **Person's** cor., W 39 ch. to a gum, N 141 ch. to a stake in **Henry Campbell's** line, E 33 ch. to a pine in **Person's** line, S along line 141 ch. to first station; signed: **Saml. Ashe**; witness: **J. Glasgow**; [no probate record], Delivd. **J. Allison.**

P. 345, 15 January 1798, **North Carolina** to **Jacob Allen** [no residence given], fifty shillings per hundred acres, 34 1/2 acres, on waters of Eno, adjoins four other tracts of his own land, begin at a black oak & sassafras the SE cor. of his 100 acre tract, S 15 3/4 ch. to a stake, E 8 ch. 40 lk. to a black oak, S 5 3/4 ch. to a stake in his old line, W with line 22 ch. 15 lk. to a stake, N 21 1/2 ch. to a stake in the line of the 100 acre tract, with line E 13 3/4 ch. to first station, entered 26 May 1797; signed: **Saml. Ashe**; witness: **Wm. Hill**; [no probate record], Delivd. **Jacob Allen.**

P. 346, 15 January 1798, **North Carolina** to **Jacob Allen** [no residence given], fifty shillings per hundred acres, 25 acres, on waters of Eno, between other tracts of his own land, begin at a post oak saplin in his old line, N 21 ch. 50 lk. to a black oak & hicory in his line of 100 acre tract, with line E 11 ch. 75 lk. to a stake in line, S 21 ch. 50 lk. to a stake in his line, with line W 11 ch. 75 lk. to first station, entered 8 July 1796; signed: **Saml. Ashe**; witness: **Wm. Hill**; [no probate record], Delivd. **Jacob Allen**.

P. 347, 8 December 1797, **North Carolina** to **John Henry Hesse** [no residence given], fifty shillings per hundred acres, 40 acres, on waters of Newhope, adjoins **Joseph Hastings, John Boyles,** & "his other other",begin at apost oak his old cor. **Reeves** line, along line N 12 ch. 50 lk. to a red oak, W 2 ch. 50 lk. to a stake, N 8 ch. to a post oak on **Martin's** line, along same E 4 ch. 50 lk. to **Hastin's** cor. post oak, the same course on his line in all 21 ch. 25 lk. to a red oak bush on **Boyles'** line, along line S 20 ch. 50 lk. to his cor. white oak, W to beginning, surveyed 17 January 1797; signed: **Saml. Ashe**; witness: **J. Glasgow**; [no probate record], Delivd. **Henry Hesse**.

P. 348, 17 January 1798, **North Carolina** to **Thomas Horn** [no residence given], fifty shillings per hundred acres, 41 1/2 acres, on Pee Cr. of Eno, begin on **Jacob Allen's** line **Thomas Holloway's** cor., N 11 ch. to a small black oak, W with **Horn's** line 75 1/2 ch. to a post oak **Holloway's** cor., S81 1/2E 76 1/2 ch. **Holloway's** line to beginning, entered 5 March 1796; signed: **Saml. Ashe**; witness: **Wm. Hill**; [no probate record], Delivd. **Thomas Horn**.

P. 349, [blank day, blank month] 1798, **North Carolina** to **James Latta Junr.** [no residence given], thirty shillings per hundred acres, 47 3/4 acres, adjoins **John Kelley Cain, William Clack, William Montgomery**, and his own land, begin at a white oak **Kelley's** cor. on **Latta's** line, with **Kelley's** line E 20 ch. 50 lk. to a P. O., N 2 ch. 75 lk. to a B. O. saplin, S 38 ch. to a B. O. on **Cain's** line, with line E 1 ch. 50 lk. to a stake, N5E a part with **Clack's** & Do. **Cain's** line 83 ch. to a stake, W 7 ch. 50 lk. to a dogwood on **Montgomery's** line, along line S 44 ch. 50 lk. to his cor. a spanish oak, with another of his lines W 65 ch. to a stake, S 3 ch. to beginning, warrant dated 10 July 1794; signed: **Saml. Ashe**; witness: **Wm. Hill**; [no probate record], Delivd. **James Latta Junr.**

P. 350, 8 December 1797, **North Carolina** to **Andrew McCulloh** [no residence given], fifty shillings per hundred acres, 72 acres, on waters of Stoney Cr., begin at a black oak **Joseph McCulloh's** cor., W with his own former boundary 57 ch. 10 lk. to a stake, S by land claimed by **John Dunnagan** 19 ch. to a post oak joseph **McCulloh's** cor., along his line N60E to first station, warrant dated 10 July 1796; signed: **Saml. Ashe**; witness: **J. Glasgow**; [no probate record], Delivd. **Hardy Hurdle**.

P. 351, 8 December 1797, **North Carolina** to **Joseph McCulloh** [no residence given], fifty shillings per hundred acres, 45 acres, on waters of Stoney Cr., begin at a black oak by a branch, N with **Andrew McCulloh's** line 12 ch. 75 lk. to a black oak, E with **John Browning's** line 20 ch. 50 lk. to a white oak, S with **Thomas McCulloh's** line 60 ch. to pointers, W with his own boundary 5 ch. to a stake, N with his own boundary 54 ch. to a stake, S60W with his own boundary to first station, warrant dated 10 July 1796; signed: **Saml. Ashe**; witness: **J. Glasgow**; [no probate record], Delivd. **Hardy Hurdle**.

P. 352, 10 August 1797, **North Carolina** to **Thomas McCulley** [no residence given], fifty shillings per hundred acres, 33 1/2 acres, on waters of Owins Cr., adjoins his own land, begin at a W. O. a cor. of **Griffis** & **Ector**, S60E 43 ch. 75

lk. to a W. O., N37E 15 ch. 50 lk. to a stake on **Griffis'** line, along same to beginning, warrant dated 4 December 1796; signed: **Saml. Ashe**; witness: J. **Glasgow**; [no probate record], Delivd. **Hardy Hurdle.**

P. 353, 15 January 1798, **North Carolina** to **William Dossett** [no residence given], fifty shillings per hundred acres, 31 acres, on Eno, bounded on S & E by Eno and land of **Ansley**, on N by **Dossett**, on W by **Clinton**, begin at eno in **Ansley's** line, N with line 15 ch. to a heap of stones, with line E 32 ch. to a stake in line of **Ansley**, N 4 ch. to a red oak saplin, W 32 1/2 ch. to a stake, S 3 1/2 ch. to a stake, W 14 1/2 ch. to a cluster of dogwoods in **Clinton's** line, S with line 11 1/4 ch. to an ash on Eno, down river to first station, entered 18 February 1796; signed: **Saml. Ashe**; witness: **Wm. Hill**; [no probate record], Delivd. **Wm. Dossett.**

P. 354, 10 August 1797, **North Carolina** to **John Barnhill** [no residence given], fifty shillings per hundred acres, 137 acres, on waters of Quaker Cr., begin at a B. O. a cor. of **Robert Barnhill**, S 52 ch. to a stake on **Murry's** line, W 25 ch. to a stake, N 48 ch. to a B. O. **William Dorris'** cor., E 4 ch. to a stake, N 37 ch. to a stake, E 2 ch. 75 lk. to a stake in **Robert Barnhill's** line, S 33 ch. 50 lk. to a stake, E 14 ch. to beginning, warrant dated 27 November 1796; signed: **Saml. Ashe**; witness: **J. Glasgow**; [no probate record], Delivd. **Jno. Barnhill.**

P. 355, 10 August 1797, **North Carolina** to **John Barnhill** [no residence given], fifty shillings per hundred acres, 85 acres, on waters of Quaker Cr., begin at a stake on **Dixon's** line, with same E 18 ch. 50 lk. to a P. O., S 36 ch. 50 lk. to a P. O., W 6 ch. to a poplar on a branch, down branch S13W 5 ch. 50 lk. to a sweet gum cor. of **Robert Barnhill**, N83E 11 ch. to a P. O., N4 1/2E 65 ch. to a stake, W 27 ch. to 4 pointers, S 23 ch. to beginning, warrant dated 29 November 1796; signed: **Saml. Ashe**; witness: **J. Glasgow**; [no probate record], Delivd. **John Barnhill.**

P. 356, 2 December 1797, **North Carolina** to **William Trousdale** [no residence given], fifty shillings per hundred acres, 125 acres, adjoins land of **Sharpe & McCullock**, begin at a stake **Sharpe's** cor., sd. line N60W 12 ch. to a post oak, N 50 ch. to a post oak, S45E 45 ch. to a hicory, S13E 24 ch. to a post oak, W 27 ch. to beginning, warrant dated 8 November 1795; signed: **Saml. Ashe**; witness: **J. Glasgow**; [no probate record], Delivd. **William Trousdale.**

P. 357, 15 January 1798, **North Carolina** to **John Hunt** [no residence given], thirty shillings per hundred acres, 65 1/2 acres, on both sides the Great Road leading from Hillsborough to Halifax, begin at a stone **John Cain's** cor., his line E 12 1/2 ch. to a P. O. saplin, S with Alvis' line 52 1/2 ch. to a stake, W with **Bermilial Holloway's** line 12 1/2 ch. to a pine, N with a line formerly **McCullock's** 52 1/2 ch. to first station, warrant dated 5 February 1792; signed: **Saml. Ashe**; witness: **Wm. Hill**; [no probate record], Delivd. **Henry Hunt.**

P. 358, 15 January 1798, **North Carolina** to **Henry Hunt** [no residence given], fifty shillings per hundred acres, 45 acres, on Crooked Run waters of Eno, bounded on N by **William Dunnagan**, on W by **James Fulton**, on S by **John Latta Senr.**, on E by his own land, begin at a stake in **Latta's** line, W 53 1/4 ch.

to a white oak, N with **Fulton's** line 8 1/2 ch. to a small black oak, E with **Dunnagan's** line 53 1/4 ch. to a spanish oak, S 8 1/2 ch. to first station, warrant dated 1 August 1796; signed: **Saml. Ashe;** witness: **Wm. Hill;** [no probate record], Delivd. **Henry Hunt.**

P. 359, 16 July 1795, **North Carolina** to **Henry Morris** [no residence given], thirty shillings per hundred acres, 100 acres, on waters of Morgans Cr., begin at a large red oak on Raibons Br. **William Loyd's** cor., E 124 p. to a spanish oak in **Samuel Creather's** line, N his line 52 p. to a spanish oak **Benjamin Howell's** cor., W his line 124 p. to a sweet gum, S 52 p. to first station; signed: **Richd. Dobbs Spaight**; witness: **J. Glasgow**; [no probate record], Delivd. **Thos. Lloyd.**

P. 360, 10 August 1797, **North Carolina** to **Hugh Rea** [no residence given], fifty shillings per hundred acres, 150 acres, on waters of Haw R., begin at a W. O., N85W 15 ch. to a W. O., N5W 35 ch. to a R. O., E 30 ch. to a R. O., N 5 ch. to a P. O., E "twenty twenty five" ch. to a R. O., S 11 ch. to a W. O., W 20 ch. to a W. O., S 28 ch. to a R. O., S34E 6 ch. to beginning, warrant dated 26 October 1779; signed: **Saml. Ashe**; witness: **J. Glasgow;** [no probate record], Delivd. **John Thompson.**

P. 361, 16 July 1795, **North Carolina** to **James Dickey** [no residence given], ten pounds per hundred acres, 14 acres, on waters of DeeP Cr., adjoins **Henry White** & his own land, begin at a hicory at the Road a cor of **Mr. White**, his old line W 5 ch. to a white oak his old cor., N 6 1/2 ch. to a black oak, W to Deep Cr., down meanders 6 ch. to a poplar, S13E 22 ch. to a P. O., N22E 17 to first station; signed: **Richd. Dobbs Spaight**; witness: **J. Glasgow**; [no probate record], Delivd. **Hardy Hurdle.**

P. 362, 18 August 1797, **North Carolina** to **James Patterson** [no residence given], thirty shillings per hundred acres, 25 acres, on waters of Bolans Cr., adjoins **Benjamin Yeargan** & the University, begin at a black oak in **Yeargan's** line near the Still House, W his line 156 p. to a hicory his cor., S his line 26 p. to a post oak & red oak on line of the University lands, E with line 156 p. to a poplar on head of a branch, N 26 p. to first station, warrant dated 28 February 1795; signed: **Saml. Ashe**; witness: **J. Glasgow**; [no probate record], Delivd. **Saml. Hopkins.**

P. 363, 30 June 1797, **North Carolina** to **James Kirk** Esq. assignee of **Soloman Cole** [no residence given], thirty shillings per hundred acres, 17 1/2 acres, on waters of Little Cain Cr., adjoins **Sackfield Brewer** & others, begin at a stake on **Strudwick's** line, E 10 ch. to a hicory a cor. to **Brewer**, his line S 16 ch. to a post oak, W 15 ch. to a stake on **Strudwick's** line, with line N27E 18 1/2 chh. to beginning, warrant dated 10 July 1794; signed: **Saml. Ashe**; witness: **J. Glasgow**; [no probate record], Delivd. **Jas. Kirk.**

P. 364, 3 November 1797, **North Carolina** to **Joseph Woody** [no residence given], thirty shillings per hundred acres, 100 acres, on S side of Haw R., adjoins **Thomas Mulhollan** & **Samuel McMullin**, begin at a post oak a cor. to **Mulhollan**, W 45 ch. to a post oak on his line, S 22 ch. 20 lk. to a P. oak, E 45 ch. to a P. oak, N 22 ch. 20 lk. to beginning, warrant dated 1 October 1793; signed: **Saml. Ashe**; witness: **J. Glasgow**; [no probate record].

P. 365, 16 November 1797, **North Carolina** to **James Crawford** [no residence given], thirty shillings per hundred acres, 200 acres, on waters of Collins Cr., begin at a red oak a cor. of **Thomas Cole**, his line due S 8 ch. to a W. O. & B. oak **Samuel Baildin's** cor., with **Baildin's** line due E 18 ch. to a red oak & cor. to **Henry Edwards**, with **Edward's** line due N 47 ch. to a B. jack on sd. line, W 21 1/2 ch. to a P. Oak & cor. to **Jesse Cate**, his line due S 34 ch. to his cor. P. oak, W 27 ch. to a P. oak, N 5 ch. to a P. O. **Charles Melican's** line, due S 67 1/2 ch. to a stake, due E 12 ch. to a stake on **Thomas Cate's** line, with line due N 60 ch. to his cor. B. jack, due E with his line 37 ch. to beginning, warrant dated 30 May 1794; signed: **Saml. Ashe**; witness: **J. Glasgow**; [no probate record], Delivd. **Henry ODaniel**.

P. 366, 5 December 1794, **North Carolina** to **Alexander Hatch** [no residence given, thirty shillings per hundred acres, 50 acres, on W side of Collins Cr., begin at a spanish oak **Loyd's** line, due W 22 ch. 37 lk. to a hicory, due N 22 ch. 37 lk. to a red oak, due E 22 ch. 27 lk. to a white oak on Collins Cr., down creek 24 ch. to beginning; signed: **Richd. Dobbs Spaight**; witness: **J. Glasgow**; [no probate record], Delivd. **Thos. Lloyd**.

P. 367, 9 February 1798, **Bryson Dobbins** of Hillsborough, innkeeper, to **John Casey** & **Thomas Scott** of same, 5 shillings, three negroe slaves: **Sarah Esther**, & **Jack**, mortgage deed to cover debts due **Cattell Campbell** of Hillsborough, merchant, bond for ten shillings ten pence dated 11 January 1798, **William Cain** & **David Ray** of same, merchants, carrying on trade under the firm name of **Cain & Ray** bond for sixty three pounds nineteen shillings dated 8 January 1798, and **William Kirkland**, **Archibald Gracie**, & **Daniel Anderson**, merchants, carrying on trade in Hillsborough under the firm name of **William Kirkland & Company** bond for forty seven pounds seven shillings seven pence dated 8 January 1798, mortgage to be canceled if paid by 1 January 1799, if not paid slaves to be sold at the Market House in Hillsborough, sd. **Bryson** not to be charged with the cost of any deed made for sale of slaves; signed: **Bryson Dobbins, John Casey, Thomas Scott**; witness: **William Duffy**; proved February Term 1798 by **Duffy**, Delivd. **Catt. Campbell**.

P. 369, 22 January 1798, **Gabriel Murphey** of Caswell to **Baswell Worren** of same, fifty pounds, 200 acres, on waters of North Hico, begin at a white oak **John Breeze** cor., S 40 ch. to a post oak, E 50 ch. to a post oak, N 40 ch. to pointers, W 50 ch. to first station; signed: **Gabriel Murphey**; witness: **Willm. Muzzell, William Murphey**; proved February Term 1798 by **Muzzell**, Delivd. **Boswell Warrin**.

P. 370, 12 October 1797, **John Noey** of Orange to **James Rivers** of Guuilford, forty five pounds, 62 acres, formerly land of **Joseph Noey**, on N side of Ulias Cr., adjoins **Phillip Ulias** & **Betsey Mangum's** entry, begin on bank of creek on a ash, on **Ulias'** line N45W 50 p. to a stake or black gum grub nearly at one spot cor. of **Mangum's** entry, S 200 p. to a hicory, S45E 45 p. to a white oak, E 5 p. to creek, down creek to beginning; signed: **John Noe**; witness: **Thomas**

(T) **Dixon, James Patterson**; proved February Term 1798 by **Patterson**, Delivd. **James Rivers**.

P. 372, 10 October 1797, **Nathaniel Christmas** of Orange to **Augustus Benton** of same, fifty pounds, 2 acres, one lot in town adjacent ot the buildings of the University, on Franklin Stree, Lot # 15; signed: **Nathaniel Christmas**; witness: **Jas. Dixon, J. Scott**; provved February Term 1798 by **Jos. Dixon**, Delivd. **A. Benton**.

P. 373, 22 February 1798, **William Love** of Orange to **William Fossett** of same, fifty pounds, 14 acres, begin at a hicory by a path, N31E 12 ch. to a black oak, E 1 3/4 ch. to a post oak on **Fossett's** old line, S 21 ch. to a post oak, W 3 3/4 ch. to a black oak, N8E 6 1/2 ch. to beginning; signed: **William Love**; witness: **William Boyle, Benj. Ragsdale**; prove February Term 1798 by **Boyle**, Delivd. **Wm. Fossett**.

P. 374, 21 August 1797, **Joseph Hodge** late Sheriff of Orange to **Samuel Benton** of Hillsborough, Esq., two hundred five pounds eighteen shillings ten pence, Lot # 21, 1 acre, bounded on S by Kings Street, on W by Wake Street, on N by Lot # 31, on E by Lot # 22, levy on lands of **John Fegiman {Fairman}** for one hundred eighty seven pounds four shillings recovered by **James W. Lackey**, sheriff levied on three lots in Hillsborough that were not sold for want of time, lots sold 12 August 1795; signed: **Joseph Hodge**; witness: **Bryson Dobbins, Francis McKamey**; proved February Term 1798 by **Dobbins**, Delivd. **Wm. Duffy**.

P. 376, 13 November 1797, **James Carrington** of Orange to **Matthew McCauley** of same, sixty pounds, 2 acres, lot in town adjacent to the buildings of the University, on Franklin Street, Lot # 8, joins lot of **Daniel Boothe** on E; signed: **Jas. Carrington**; witness: **John Faddis, John McCauley**, acknowledged February Term 1798, Delivd. **Mathew McCauley**.

P. 377, 4 December 1792, **William Halliburton** of Orange to **John OKelly** of Wake, two hundred pounds, 639 1/2 acres, on W side of North East Fork of Newhope Cr., begin at a gum in bank of creek, N by a line of marked trees to a red oak saplin, W by a line of marked trees to **Richard Hobson's** cor. a blase white oak, S by a line of marked trees to a red oak on creek bank, up creek to beginning, 140 acres, another tract, On Long Branch a branch of North East Cr. of Newhope, begin at a pine in **Richard Hobson's** line, E on line 54 ch. to a white oak on **Thomas Hobson's** line, N on line 92 1/2 ch. to a pine, W 54 ch. to a pine, S 92 1/2 ch. to first station, 499 1/2 acres; signed: **William Holliburton**; witness: **J. Kinnon, William OKelly, B. Peake**; proved February Term 1798 by **William OKelly**.

P. 378, 29 February 1796, **Jacob Flowers Junr.** of Orange to **John Sparrow** of same, three hundred fifty pounds, 545 acres, on waters of Morgans Cr., begin at a post oak **Nicholas Quesenberry's** cor. on the NW line, E his line by his cor. taking along the Chatham Line 51 ch. to a post oak & **Henry Christopher Barbee's** cor., N his line 107 ch. to a pine **Barbee's** cor., W 51 ch. to a stake, passing by **Mark & John Morgan's** cor. post oak 107 ch. to first station; signed:

Jacob Flowers, Mary Flowers; witness: Christo Barbee, W. Pendergrass, Mathew Coulter; proved February Term 1798 by Barbee, Delivd. Jno. Sparrow.

P. 379, 27 February 1798, **Michael Robinson** of Orange to **James Robinson** of same, five pounds, 200 acres, on SE side of North Fork of Little R., begin at a hicory, W 65 ch. to a black oak, S 30 ch. 75 lk. to two black oak saplins & stake, E 65 ch. to black oak saplin, N 30 ch. 75 lk. to first station, part of 419 acres granted to **William Bogan** by deed dated 15 June 1754, **Bogan** to **James McCallister** 20 January 1769, **McCallister** to **Michael Robinson** 23 January 1769; signed: **Michael Robinson**; witness: **David Ray**; proved February Term 1798 by **Ray**, Delivd. to **David Ray**.

P. 381, 22 January 1798, **William Burns Senr.** of Orange to my affectionate son **Andrew Burns** of same, fifty pounds, 100 acres, on waters of Newhope, begin at a post oak on bank of Newhope Cr. on **James Burros'** line, up creek W to a red oak 68 p., N to a stake on **John Strayhorn's** line 233 p., E along **John Strayhorn's** line to **James Burroughs'** cor. white oak 68 p., S along **Burrows'** line 233 p. to first station; signed: **William Burns**; witness: **James Burns, Wm. F. Thompson**; proved February Term 1798 by **James Burns**, Delivd. to **Andrew Burns**.

P. 382, 16 August 1797, **William Lewis** of Orange, planter, to **Frederick Peck** of same, one hundred thirty pounds, 188 acres, on Buck Water Cr., begin at a post oak **James Faucet's** & **William Wood's** cor, E 22 1/2 ch. to a red oak saplin, N6E 9 ch. to a post oak **Copeland's** cor., N25E 5 1/4 ch. to a black oak, N10E 1 ch. to a maple, N67E 6 ch. to a white oak, S32 1/2E 26 1/4 ch. to a hicory, S 24 3/4 ch. to a red oak **Copeland's** cor. W 42 1/4 ch. to a hicory, S45W 13 ch. to a white oak saplin, N with **William Whitehead's** line 24 ch. to a white oak, with James **Faucet's** line 18 1/4 ch. to first station; signed: **William Lewis**; witness: **Thomas Bunch, William (X) Williams**; proved February Term 1798 by **Williams**, Delivd. **Fred. Peck.**

P. 384, 18 November 1797, **Jarrett Burrow** of Guilford, farmer, to **David Thornbury** of same, blacksmith, twelve pounds ten shillings, 32 acres, adjoins land of **David Thornbury**, begin at a hicory in Guilford County Line also a cor. of **John Clark**, N 92 p. to the Guilford County line to a ash in a pond, E 56 p. to a persimmon in **John Patterson's** line, S 92 p. to a hicory in **John Clark's** line, W 56 p. along **John Clark's** line to beginning, part of a tract from **Thomas Mulhollan** to **Jarrell Burrow**; signed: **Jarrell Burrow**; witness: **J. Patterson**; proved February Term 1798 by **J. S. Patterson**.

P. 385, 27 February 1798, **John Puckett** of Orange to **Samuel Hopkins** of same, fifty pounds, 180 acres, in State of Virginia, on waters of Chesnut & Town Cr, formerly Pittsylvania County, surveyed November 1772, granted by Virginia to **Francis & Jane Hopkins** 1 February 1781, begin at **David Haley's** cor. pointers, new line S88W 254 p. crossing a branch to pointers, N25W 34 p. to pointers on **Turners** Road, N 236 p. crossing 3 branches to a white oak, N39E 142 p. crossing a branch to a white oak, N12 1/2W 206 p. crossing a branch to a white oak, N27E 154 p. crossing Chesnut Cr. to a red oak saplin, S28E 340 p. to

ORANGE COUNTY (NC) DEED BOOK 6

David Haley's cor. pointers, along his line S65W 166 p. crossing Chesnut Cr. to a red oak, S12E 149 p. to beginning; signed: **John Puckett, Jane Puckett**; witness: **Joseph Dixon**; proved February Term 1798 by **Dixon**, Delivd. **Saml. Hopkins**.

P. 386, 10 November 1797, **John Noe** of Orange to **Henry Kime** of same, four hundred twenty three silver dollars, 170 acres, on E side of Ulias Cr., adjoins **Ulias, David Patterson & Jarrell Burrow**, begin on a white oak, 5 p. to creek, down creek to a ash, E 25 ch. to a black oak, S10W 51 ch. to a stake, S 20 ch. to a black oak, to first station; signed: **John (X) Noe**; witness: **J. S. Patterson, David Patterson**; proved February Term 1798 by **J. S. Patterson**, Delivd. **Jno. Bullock**.

P. 387, 22 February 1798, **David Hall** of Orange to **James Herndon** of same, one hundred pounds, 120 acres, begin at a pine, S 139 p. to a pine, W 130 p. to a white oak on the branch, down branch 44 p. to a pine, W 20 p. to a red oak, N 95 p. to a stake, E 140 p. to beginning; signed: **David Hall**; witness: **John Leigh, Sullivan Leigh, Leonard Carlton**; proved February Term 1798 by **Sullivan Leigh**.

P. 389, 28 February 1798, **Samuel Thompson** of Orange to **James Bailey** [no residence given], one hundred pounds, 100 acres, part of grant from **North Carolina** to **William Kennedy** 1780 Grant #319 for 300 acres, begin at a post oak the SE cor. of the 300 acre tract, N 26 ch. 32 lk. to a red oak, W 38 ch. to a black jack, S 26 ch. 32 lk. to a whitee oak, E 38 ch. to beginning; signed: **Samuel Thompson**; witness: **Charles Christmas, Hugh Mulhollan**; acknowledged February Term 1798, Delivd. **Mrs. Baley**.

P. 390, 25 August 1786, **North Carolina** to **William Watters** [no residence given], five hundred thirty five pounds, 1 acre, Lot # 15, in Hillsborough, fronting King Street, 400 lk. in length, 250 lk. in breadth, sold as confiscated property of **Edmund Fanning**; signed: **Rd. Caswell**; witness: **J. Glasgow**; [no probate record], Delivd. **Wm. Duffy**.

P. 391, 17 April 1794, **William Hays** of Wake to **George Daniel** of Orange, twelve pounds eleven shillings three pence, 1 acre, one fourth part of Lot # 4, in village adjoining the buildings of the University, on N side of the Narrow Street on the N side of Franklin Street, begin at a stake on the street a cor. of **Gray Barbee's** acre, with street E to a stake on **William Hays'** cor., along **Hays'** line to a stake, W to **Gray Barbey's** cor., S with **Barbee's** line to beginning; signed: **Wm. Hays**; witness: **Wm. Cain, William Courtney**; proved February Term 1798 by **Courtney**, Delivd. **Bennet Watson**.

P. 392, 20 September 1796, **Joseph Hart** of Orange to **James Herndon** of Wake, seventy pounds, 68 acres, begin at a pine cor. of **Robert Campbell**, N to Wattery Br., with branch to **David Hall's** line, his line to a red oak, S to a red oak bush, E to a gum bush, S to a white oak, W to beginning; signed: **Joseph Hart, Ann (X) Hart**; witness: **Thomas Gray, John Hust**; proved February Term 1798 by **Gray**.

P. 393, 28 November 1793, **William Pendergrass** of Orange to **John Walker** of same, twenty five pounds, 40 acres, on Obeds Cr. a branch of Morgans Cr., part of a tract surveyed by **Henry Beasley**, sold to **Mark Morgan,** begin at a ash cor. of **John Cannon** the old line, E along old line to a poplar cor. of **Henson Coulter** on the creek, down creek to a persimmon cor. on mouth of a branch, W up branch to a black gum cor. on **John Fann's** line, S to first station; signed: **Wm. Pendergrass**; witness: **John (X) Fann, Abijah Moses**; acknowledged February Term 1798.

P. 394, 22 February 1796, **John Leigh** of Orange to **David Hall** of same, five pounds, 20 acres, begin at a black jack cor. of **David Hall's** line, N 23 p. to a post oak, W 140 p. to a pine, S 23 p. to a red oak, E 140 p. to beginning; signed: **John Leigh**; witness: **Thomas Hall, Joseph Hust, Richd. (X) Marcom**; proved February Term 1798 by **Marcom**.

P. 395, 12 March 1792, **Michael Shoffner** of Orange to **Frederick Shoffner** of same, twenty five pounds, 51 acres, on waters of Stinking Quarter, begin at a stake near a branch, S28W 59 p. to a st., N45W 11 p. to a B. J., S63W 12 p. to a B. J., N17W 21 p. to a st. on side of the Trading Road, N45E 120 p. to a st., S45E 7 p. to a st., S26W 8 p. to a st., N68E 21 p. to a stake, S45E 44 p. to a stake in a pond, S45W 74 p. to a small hicory, N40W to beginning; signed: **Michael Shoffner**; witness: **Jacob** *Jacob Gernt* *breed zkerlar*, **Mychael Shoftner**; proved February Term 1798 by **Michael Shoftner**, Delivd. **Michl. Holt.**

P. 396, 31 December 1796, **John Fann** of Orange to **John Walker** of same, fifteen pounds, 30 acres, on S side & part of tract I now live on purchased of **John Sparrow**, begin at a black gum a cor. of **William Pendergrass** & **Walker** on side of a branch, W 60 p. up branch to a post oak, S 80 p. to a white oak & hicory **George Brown's** line, E with **Brown's** line 60 p. to a ash **Walker's** cor., along **Walker's** line to beginning; signed: **John (X) Fann**; witness: **William Dodd, Rebekah (+) Fann, Mark Fann**; proved February Term 1798 by **Mark Fann**, Delivd. **Mathew McCauley**.

P. 397, 13 september 1797, **James Coglin** of Hillsborough, merchant, to **William Duffy** of same, attorney, four hundred nintey five dollars twelve cents, 1 acre, Lot # 21 in Town of Hillsborough, bounded on S by Kings Street, on W by Wake Street, on N by Lot # 31, on E by Lot # 22; signed: **James Coglin**; witness: **R. Bell**; proved February Term 1798 by **Robert Bell**, Delivd. **Wm. Duffy.**

P. 399, 13 June 1797, **Andrew Murdock** Sheriff of Orange to **William Duffy** of Hillsborough, attorney, one hundred fifty five pounds, 1 acre, Lot # 18, bounded by King Street, Wake Street, & Margaret Lane, house & lot in Hillsborough where **William Watters** formerly resided, levy on **William Watters Senr**. Esq. deceased for two hundred fifty four pounds four shillings three pence recovered by **William Kirkland & Company**, four hundred one pounds eighteen shillings ten pence recovered by **William Cain & Company**, one hundred seven pounds eleven shillings sixx pence recovered by **John Cabe**; signed: **Andrew Murdock**; witness: **Wil Kirkland, David Ray**; acknowledged February Term 1798, Delivd.

Wm. Duffy.

P. 401, 11 September 1797, **Samuel Benton** Esq. of Hillsborough to **James Coglin** of same, two hundred five pounds eighteen shillings ten pence, 1 acre, Lot # 21 in town of Hillsborough, bounded on S by King Street, on W by Wake Street, on N by Lot # 31, on E by Lot # 22, purchased at a Sheriff's Sale on an execution against **John Fairman** at the instance of **James W. Lackey**; signed: **S. Benton**; witness: **R. Bell**; acknowledged February Term 1798, Delivd. **Wm. Duffy.**

P. 402, 24 January 1769, **John Dennis** & wife **Mary** of Orange, tanner, to **Isaac Dennis** of same, shoemaker, five pounds, 98 acres, on Buck Quarter Cr., begin at a post oak, S7 1/2E 20 p. to a white oak, S51E 22 p. 6 lk. to a red oak, S39E 13 p. 7 lk. to a Hicory, S87E 10 p. to a white oak, S38 1/2E 32 p. 12 lk. to a post oak, S9 1/2E 82 p. to a red oak, E 56 p. to a black oak, N 162 p. 94 lk. to a dogwood & sweet gum on **Thomas Jackson's** line, W along line & continuing same course to beginning at **Edward Dennis'** cor. post oak distant 151 p. 19 lk.; signed: **John Dennis, Mary** (X) **Dennis**; witness: **Ralph McNair, John Hogan**; acknowledged 18 December 1797 in Hancock County, Georgia, before **Zephanah Harvey** & **Davis Long** Esquires at the instance of **Morgan Hart** Clerk; acknowledgement recorded February Term 1798.

P. 404, 22 April 1772, **Isaac Dennis**, tanner, of Orange to **Robert Marley** of same, sixty pounds, 90 acres & 8 perch, part of tract from **Granville** to **John Dennis, John Dennis** to **Isaac Dennis** 27 April 1768, on Buck Quarter Cr., begin at a post oak, S17 1/2E 20 perches, S89E 32 perches, S53E , S36E, S87E, S37E, S9E, E 256 perches to a black oak, N 162.19 to a dogwood & sweet gum, W 142.76 to a black oak, W 7.68 to beginning; signed: **Isaac Dennis, Rebecca** (X) **Dennis** [his wife]; witness: **William Coupland, Jacob Benton**; order from **Morgan Hart**, clerk, to **Zephenah Harvey** & **Davis Long** of Hancock County, Georgia, to have **Isaac Dennis** acknowledge deed; acknowledged by **Isaac Dennis** 15 December 1797 before **Harvey** & **Long** in Hancock County, Georgia; acknowledgement recorded February Term 1798, Delivd. **John Kelley.**

P. 406, 15 December 1795, **Robert Trotter**, planter, of Orange to **Jesse Nevill** [no residence given], one hundred twenty pounds, 262 acres, on both sides of Caswells Cr. a fork of Morgans Cr., bounded on E by **Nevill**, on W by **Willm. Forsyth**, begin at **Nevill's** cor. red oak, E 9 ch. to a spanish oak, N 22 ch. to a black jack, W 42 1/2 ch. to a white oak, S 72 1/2 ch. to a red oak, E 33 1/2 ch. to a red oak, N 50 1/2 ch. to first station; signed: **Robert Trotter**; witness: **John Wilson, William** (X) **Trotter**; proved February Term 1798 by **Wilson**, Delivd. **J. Nevill Jn.**

P. 407, 20 February 1797, **Francis Baldridge** of Orange to **William Roark** of same, three hundred pounds, 216 acres, on waters of Little R., adjoins **James Watson** & **John Brown**, begin at a black oak, N 23 1/4 ch. to a stake, W 61 1/2 ch. to a run, S 63 ch. to a post oak, E 18 1/2 ch. to a post oak, N 39 3/4 ch. to a stake, E 43 ch. to first station; signed: **Francis Baldridge**; witness: **Archalus Wilson, James Torringtine**; proved February Term 1798 by **Torringtine**,

Delivd. **Wm. Roark.**

P. 409, 31 March 1797, **Philemon Hodges** of Cumberland to **Samuel Hayes** of Orange, three hundred fourty two pounds, 342 acres, on waters of Newhope, begin at a white oak on E side of Main Road, S50W 160 p. to W end of a rock, S23W 52 p. to a white oak, S55W 18 p. to a pine, S25W 62 p. to a stake in the Old Field, S9W 73 p. to a hicory, S19W 18 p. to a pine, S30W 58 p. to a stake, post oak & black jack pointers, S16E 24 p. to a pine with pointers, E with **Morgan's** line 49 p. to a pine, NB with a variation of 8 1/2 degrees in all 237 p. to a white oak, N to beginning; signed: **P. Hodges**; witness: **John Daniel, H. McAllister**; proved February Term by **Daniel**, Delivd. **Asa Benton.**

P. 410, 5 September 1797, **James Coglin** of Orange to **Joseph Dixon** of same, fifteen pounds, 111 acres, on waters of Newhope, begin at **Elmore Henley's** cor. black jack, S 20 ch. to a red oak, W 28 ch. to a post oak, N 7 ch. to a post oak, W 42 ch. to a spanish oak, N 23 ch. to a post oak, E 5 ch. to a stake, S 10 ch. to a hicory, E 65 ch. to first station; signed: **James Coghlen**; witness: **A. Benton, John Couch**; proved February Term 1798 by **Benton**, Delivd. **Jo. Dixon.**

P. 411, 29 February 1796, **Jacob Flowers** of Orange to **Christopher Barbee** of same, two hundred pounds, 100 acres, part of the tract he sold to **John Sparrow**, begin at a pine on Chatham County Line, N 66 p. to a pine cor. of **John Morgan**, continuing the same in all 443 p. with **Morgan's** line to a pine, W 35 3/4 p. to a pine, S 443 p. to a post oak & boundary of the County Line, E with same 35 3/4 p. to first station; signed: **Jacob Flowers, Mary Flowers**; witness: **John (X) Sparrow, Willm. Pendergrass, Mathew Colter**; proved February Term 1798 by **Sparrow**, Delivd. **Mr. Barbee.**

P. 412, 26 February 1798, **Andrew Murdock** & wife **Margaret** of Orange to **Amos Phillips** of same, one hundred pounds, 95 acres, on waters of Mill Cr., bounded all round by lands of **Allen, Fruit, White, & Duncan**, begin at a W. O., S20W 11 ch. to a W. O., S6W 14 ch. to a B. J., N35W 11 ch. to a [blank], N60E 6 ch. to a stump, N35W 17 ch. to a post oak, N32E 12 ch. to a black oak, E 19 ch. to a B. O., S34E 14 ch. to a post oak, S 12 ch. to first station, part of a tract from **North Carolina** to **Murdock** 3 September 1779; signed: **Andrew Murdock, Margaret Murdock**; witness: **John (X) Cradick**; acknowledged February Term 1798, Delivd. **Amos Phelps.**

P. 414, 28 February 1798, **Absalom Tatum** of Hillsborough to **Barnabus O. Ferrill** of same, one hundred seventy six pounds tem shillings, part of Lot # 25 in Hillsborough, begin on N side of King Street at the SW cor. of that part of Lot # 25 where the house that formerly belonged to **Young Miller & Company** known as the Blue House stands, N along line of the Blue House lot 55 feet to the NW cor. of Blue House lot, same course continued 25 feet along property of tatum which he purchased from **George Doherty** to a point in **Casey's** line (formerly **George Doherty**), W parralell with King Street to a point 85 feet W from Churton Street & 80 feet N from King Street, N 20 feet to a point, W to a point on E side of Lot # 24 the property of **William Lytle**, S along E side of Lot # 24 100 feet to King Street, E along N side of King Street to beginning, part of

Lot # 25 sold by **John Nichols Sheriff** to **Memucan Hunt, William Lytle, & Absalom Tatum** 29 October 1785, the part belonging to **Hunt & Lytle** conveyed to **Tatum** April 1797, part of lot sold by **George Doherty** to **Tatum** May 1790; signed: **A. Tatum**; witness: **John McKerall, Ca. Campbell, C. Dixon**; acknowledged February Term 1798, Delivd. **B. OFarlll**.

P. 416, 21 April 1797, **John Taylor** of Orange to **William Cain & David Ray** of Hillsborough, deed of trust, **Taylor** owes **William Cain & David Ray** Merchants of Hillsborough trading as **Cain & Ray** two hundred seventeen pounds eight shillings ten pence, seven certain Negroes: **Simon** about age 25 years, **Stephey** about 17, **Phillis** about 21, **Black Tom** between 30 & 40, **Molley** between 30 & 40, **Dilee** about 15, **Luce** about 12, & daughter of **Molley**, Negores can be sold if **Cain & Ray** not paid by 1 January 1798; signed: **John Taylor**; witness: **John McCauley, Archibald Reaves**; proved May Term 1797 by **Reaves**, Delivd. to **David Ray**.

P. 417, 27 December 1797, **James Watson** of Orange to **Andrew Watson** of same, one hundred pounds, 100 acres, on fork of Seven Mile Cr., adjoins **Alfred Moore**, begin at a post oak near a fel down red oak a cor. of **James Watson's** old tract, with **Moore's** line N 56 ch. to a rock in a meadow, with another of **Moore's** lines W 18 ch. to a post oak, S 56 ch. to a red oak on **Williams'** line, along same E 18 ch. to beginning, part of an old tract to **James Watson** Esq. from **Granville** 17 June 1754, conveyed to his son **James Watson** by deed 2 May 1760, then to his son **James Watson** by deed 18 April 1772; signed: **James Watson**; witness: **Hugh Mulhollan Snr., Hugh Mulhollan Junr.**; proved February Term 1798 by **Hugh Mulhollan Junr**, Delivd. **Andrew Watson**.

P. 419, 1 July 1797, **William Lewis** of Orange to **William Whitted Senr.** of same, one hundred twenty five pounds, 106 acres, begin at a post oak **James Faucet's** cor., his line S85W 14 1/2 ch. to a small black oak formerly a hicory, his line N10W 37 ch. to a black oak saplin **Faucett's** cor., E by land of **Brooks** 20 1/2 ch. to a white oak saplin formerly a post oak **Copland's** cor. S with line 6 3/4 ch. to a red oak, with his line S45E 17 1/4 ch. to a stump on the side of the Greatt Road leading from Hillsborough to Halifax, with road 5 1/4 ch. to a persimmon tree, S38E 11 1/4 ch. to a post oak, S6W 9 ch. to a red oak saplin, W 22 1/2 ch. to first station; signed: **William Lewis**; witness: **John Holden, Thomas Holden, David Copeland**; acknowledged February Term 1798, Delivd. **Wm. Whitted Senr.**

P. 420, 15 January 1798, **North Carolina** to **Joseph Townsand** [no residence given], fifty shillings per hundred acres, 53 acres, on N side of Eno R., begin at a hicory on bank of Eno **Townsand's** old cor., N his line 176 p. tto a black oak his cor., E 46 p. to a red oak on **John Daniel's** line, his line S 80 p. to a red oak his cor., E 10 p. to a spanish oak **Matthew Clinton's** cor., S his line 80 p. to a post oak on bank of Eno, up same to first station, warrant dated 1 July 1795; signed: **Saml. Ashe**; witness: **Wm. Hill**; [no probate record], Delivd. **Joseph Toundson**.

P. 421, 17 April 1797, **North Carolina** to **Lazarus Cates** [no residence given], thirty shillings per hundred acres, 150 acres, on waters of Eno, adjoins **William**

Laycock, begin at a white oak bush on **Laycock's** line, N 109 p. to a black jack, E 121 p. to a hicory & red oak, S 109 p. to a post & red oak, W 160 p. to **Laycock's** cor. & continuing same course through **Cates'** Corner Field in all 221 p. to first station; signed: **Saml. Ashe**; witness: **J. Glasgow**; [no probate record], Delivd. **Lazarus Cate.**

P. 422, 12 January 1796, **James Lea** [no residence given] to **Absalom Lea** of Caswell, one hundred pounds, 127 acres, on waters of Linches Cr. of North Hico, begin at a red oak on the dividing line between Caswell & Orange County, S 40 ch. to a white oak, S70 1/2W 47 ch. to red oak saplin, N 10 ch. to a pine **Elisha Weel's** cor., E his line 10 ch. 80 lk. to pointers **Weel's** cor., N 44 ch. 16 lk. to a hicory on County Line, E on line 37 ch. 50 lk. to beginning; signed: **James Lea**; witness: **Gabriel Murphey, W. Muzzell**; proved February Term 1798 by **William Muzzell**, Delivd. **Miles Wells.**

P. 424, 14 November 1797, **Joseph Stubbs** of Columbia County, Georgia, **Deborah Cox,** & **Rachel Cox** surviving heirs of **Thomas Stubbs** deceased to **Robert Thompson** of Orange, one hundred fifty pounds, 250 acres, on a branch of the Eno, surveyed 9 December 1751, begin at a black oak, E 50 ch. to a hicory, N 50 ch. to a black jack oak, W 50 ch. to a black oak by a large rock stone, S 50 ch. to first station; signed: **Joseph Stubbs, Zilpah (X) Stubbs, Rachl. (X) Cox, Deborah Cox**; witness: **Isaac Stubbs, Richd. Woods**; proved February Term 1798 by **Richard Woods**, Delivd. **Martin Partin.**

P. 425, 17 May 1797, **Philemon Hodges** of Cumberland to **William Edwards** of Orange, ninety pounds, 90 acres, begin at a pine on **Haises** cor., to a W branch, with branch to the head to a gum, W to a white oak, N to a pine, E to a red oak, N to a red oak, E to **Haises** line, along line to beginning; signed: **P. Hodges**; witness: **Samuel Hopkins, John Puckett**; proved February Term 1798, by **Hopkins.**

P. 426, 16 July 1795, **North Carolina** to **Isaac Reynolds** [no residence given] fifty shillings per hundred acres, 207 acres, on S side of Haw R., adjoins river, **George Sheridan,** & **Thomas Mason**, begin at a sassafras on side of Haw R., S28W 16 1/2 ch. to a post oak, S65W 11 ch. to a black oak, S 12 ch. to a spanish oak, W 54 ch. to a spanish oak, N 20 ch. to a white oak, E 20 ch. to a stake, N 13 ch. to a black oak, E 15 ch. to a black oak, N 14 ch. to a hicory, E 6 ch. to a black oak, N 5 ch. to a black oak on river, down river to first station; signed: **Richd. Dobbs Spaight**; witness: **J. Glasgow**; [no probate record].

P. 427, 25 April 1785, **North Carolina** to **Thomas Hardy Perkins** [no residence given], one hundred thirteen pounds, 325 acres, on waters of Gun Cr. & Little Allamance including the Chappel, begin at a post oak, W 50 ch. to red oak, N 65 ch. to a black jack, E 50 ch. to a stake, S 65 ch. to first station, sold as confiscated property of **Henry Eustace McCulloh**; signed: **Alex Martin**; witness: **W. Williams**; [no probate record], Delivd. **Thos. H. Perkins.**

P. 428, 8 February 1798, **James Warran** of Caswell to **Bossell Warran** of same, one hundred pounds, 200 acres, on waters of Linches Cr. of North Hico, bounded on E by **Bossell Warran**, on N by **John Bruse** & Caswell County Line, begin at **John Bruse's** cor. white oak on **Warren's** line, S his line 40 ch. tto his cor. post oak continued 18 ch. to a post oak, W 15 1/2 ch. to a pine, N 42 ch. to a red oak saplin **Miles Willis'** cor, E 37 ch. 50 lk. to first station; signed: **James Warran**; witness: **W. Muzzell, William Murphey**; proved February Term by **Muzzell**, Delivd. **Boswell Warren.**

P. 429, 28 September 1797, **Frederick Peck** of Orange to **William Whitted Senr.** of same, sixteen and three quarter dollars, 10 3/4 acres, begin at a hicory an old cor., S45W 13 ch. to a white oak, N 24 ch. to a white oak **Whitted's** cor., a straight line to first station; signed: **Frederick (X) Peck**; witness: **Sherod Allen, David Copeland**; acknowledged February Term 1798, Delivd. **Wm. Whitted Senr.**

P. 431, 2 December 1797, **William Ray Short, William Ray Long, & Rachel Chance** legatees of **Hugh Ray** deceased all of Orange to **James Thompson** of same, one hundred pounds, 150 acres, on waters of Haw R., begin at a white oak, N85W 15 to a white oak, N5W 35 ch. to a red oak, E 30 ch. to a red oak, N 5 ch. to a post oak, E 25 ch. to a red oak, S 11 ch. to a white oak, W 20 ch. to a white oak, S28W 28 ch. to a red oak, S34E 6 ch. to beginning; signed: **William Ray Short, William Ray Long, Rachel (+) Chance**; witness: **Reuben Smith, James Clindenin**; proved February Term 1798 by **Clendenin**, Delivd. **John Thompson.**

P. 432, 28 February 1798, **George Daniel** of Orange to **James Trice** of same, 25 pounds, 1 acre, 1/4 part of Lot # 4 in village adjoining the buildings of the University, on the Narrow Street on the N side of Franklin Street, begin at a stake on the street a cor. of **Gray Barbee**, with street E to a stake on **William Hays'** cor., along **Hayes** line to a stake, W to **Gray Barbee's** cor., S with **Barbee's** line to beginning; signed: **Geo. Daniel**; witness: **Robert T. Daniel, Penney Daniel**; proved February Term 1798 by **Robert T. Daniel.**

P. 433, 5 October 1797, **Samuel Daniel** of Orange to **Robert T. Daniel** of same, one hundred fifty pounds, 250 acres, on E side of Newhope Cr., bounded on S by **Charles Trice**, on E by **Robert Campbell**, on W by **William Wills Green**, begin at a pine on **Green's** line, N his line 256 p. to a hicory **Green's** cor., E 156 p. to a white oak **Robert Campbell's** cor., his line S 256 p. to a post oak on **Charles Trice's** line, W his line 156 p. to beginning; signed: **Saml. Daniel**; witness: **John Daniel, Samuel Daniel Junr., Thomas Gray**; proved February Term 1798 by **John Daniel.**

P. 435, 11 May 1797, **Edward Harris** of Orangwe to **John Phips** of Wake, fifty pounds, 100 acres, on waters of Ellebees Cr., begin at a pine on the Dutchmans Br., S75E 156 p. to a stake in the County Line, N15E 106 p. to a white oak, N50W 19 p. to a pine, N15W 50 p. to a black jack, by a line of marked trees to beginning; signed: **Edward Harris**; witness: **Elias Turner, Charles Kennon**, proved February Term 1798 by **Turner**

P. 436, 16 October 1793, **Alfred Moore, John Haywood, William Richardson Davie, & Alexr. Mebane** Esquires Commissioners & **Trustees of the University of North Carolina** to **William Hays** of Wake, fifty pounds five shillings, 4 acres,

Lot # 4 in village adjacentt ot the buildings of the University, to the N of Franklin Street; signed: **A. Moore, John Haywood, W. R. Davie, Alex Mebane**; witness: **W. Watters**; peroved February Term 1798 by **Samuel Benton** who proved the signature of **William Watters** deceased.

P. 438, 19 October 1793, **Alfred Moore, John Haywood, William Richardson Davie, & Alexr. Mebane** Esquires Commissioners & **Trustees of the University of North Carolina** to **Christopher Barbee** of Orange, one hundred five pounds ten shillings, 4 acres, Lot # 2 in village adjacent to the buildings of the University; signed: **A. Moore, Alexr. Mebane, W. R. Davie, Jno. Haywood**; witness: **W. Watters**; proved February Term 1798 by **Samuel Benton** who proved signature of **William Watters** deceased.

P. 440, 8 January 1797, **North Carolina** to **Walter Alves** [no residence given], fifty shillings per hundred acres, 28 1/2 acres, on Little R., between lines of **John Cain, Thomas Sutton**, & his own, begin at a persimmon & an iron wood on bank of river at mouth of a branch near **John Cain's** cqr., his line N59W 11 ch. to a white oak & sassafras, S31W 9 ch. 25 lk. to a pine, N59W 18 1/4 ch. to a pine **Cain's** cor., the same course continued in all 21 ch. to a pine on a line of **Sutton's** tract, along same S4W 13 ch. 25 lk. to a post oak, E 30 ch. 50 lk. to Little R., up same to beginning, warrant dated 14 January 1796; signedd: **Saml. Ashe**; witness: **J. Glasgow**; [no probate record].

P. 441, 28 February 1798, **Joseph Moore** of Orange to **William F. Strudwick** of same, one hundred pounds, 100 acres, begin at a white oak on a small branch of Haw Cr., N 20 ch. to a post oak, E 30 ch. to a red oak, S 20 ch. to a hicory in **Jonathon Jones'** line, W to beginning; signed: **Jo. Moore**; witness: **Ca. Campbell, Jo. Casey**; acknowledged February Term 1798, Delivd. **Wm. F. Strudwick**.

P. 442, 23 February 1798, **James Andrew** of Orange to **William McAnless** of same, 50 acres, on waters of Flat R. & Little R., bounded by **John McCulloh** #583, begin at a black oak, W 16 ch. to a post oak, N 31 1/4 ch. to a stake, E 16 ch. to a stake, S 31 1/4 ch. to first station, No. 324, **John McCulloh** to **James Andrew** 4 March 1783; signed: **James Andrew**; witness: **Malcomb Baldridge, James Baldridge**; proved February Term 1798 by **James Baldridge**, Delivd. **Wm. McCanless**.

P. 443, 25 November 1797, **David Thornbury** of Guilford to **James Wire** of Randolph, sixteen pounds, 77 acres, on waters of Stinking Quarter, begin at a tract containing 77 acres from **North Carolina** to **David Thornbury** 10 March 1797 & beginning on Chatham & Orange cor., N 68 p. to a black jack **Springer's** cor., E 182 p. to a persimmon, S 68 p. to Chatham Line, W to beginning; signed: **David Thornbury**; witness: **Jesse Patterson, Lewis Mcmasters**; proved February Term by **Patterson**, Delivd. **Nicholas Coble**.

P. 444, 24 September 1796, **George Charles** of Orange to **Conrod Farmer** of same, eighty pounds, 150 acres, on waters of Haw R. S side, **North Caroliina** to **Jesse Phillips** 9 November 1784, begin at a stake on **Jacob Ball's**[?] line, S 45 ch. to a post oak, W 41 ch. to a post oak, N 26 ch. to 3 white oaks on side of

Dry Cr., down meanders to a black oak, N 13 ch. to a stake, E 25 ch. to first station; signed: "something in dutch"; witness: **Lannad Farmer, Jacob Cable**; proved February Term 1798 by **Lenard Carlton** "a subscibing witness", Delivd. **Saml. James**.

P. 446, 26 December 1787, **John Hogan** of Orange to **Mathew McCauley** of same, one hundred pounds, on waters of Newhope Bolings Cr., begin at **Thomas Loyd's** cor. hicory, E 205 p. to a white oak in **Thomas Loyd's** line commonly callled **Barbee's** Tract, S his line 279 p. to a hicory his cor., along **McCauley's** own line 205 p. to a black jack **Thomas Loyd's** cor., N 279 p. to first station; signed: **John Hogan**; witness: **Anderson Stroud, William Andrews**; proved February Term 1798 by **Andrews**, Delivd. **Mathew McCauley**.

P. 447, 2 December 1797, **North Carolina** to **James Mebane** [no residence given], fifty shillings per hundred acres, 200 acres, on waters of Mill Cr., adjoins **Alexr. Mebane** deceaseed, begin at a stake **Mebane's** cor., N50E 25 ch. to a stake in **Mallett's** line, N 31 ch. to a stake **Thomas Linches** cor., S80W 5 1/2 ch. to a stake in **Mebane's** line, S 1 1/2 ch. to a black oak **Mebane's** cor., W 25 ch. to a hicory, S 7 ch. to a stake, W 25 ch. to a stake in **Mebane's** line, S with line to first station, warrant dated 28 November 1797; signed: **Saml. Ashe**; witness: **J. Glasgow**; [no probate record], Delivd. **James Mebane**.

P. 448, 20 November 1797, **Samuel Thompson** of Orange to **Caleb Simmons** of same, one hundred fifteen dollars, 100 acres, on Toms Cr., begin at a hixcory cor. bounded by **John Dunnavan**, W his line 19 ch. to pointers a path, S10W 37 ch. to a white oak by a branch, up branch S12E 7 ch. 50 lk. to a maple in branch, E 23 ch. 25 lk. to a black oak in **William Lovel's** line, N along **Lovel's** line to first station; signed: **Samuel (X) Thompson**; witness: **Allen Barber, William Fossett**; proved February Term 1798 by **Fossett**, Delivd. **Wm. Fossett**.

P. 449, 3 December 1796, **John Barnwell** of Orange to **Horatia Cope** of same, forty eight pounds, 200 acres, on waters of Quaker Cr., begin on the W by land of **Swanney** including the improvementt where **William Hopper** once lived at a stake, N 43 ch. to a black jack, W 46 1/2 ch. to a stake, S 43 ch. to a stake, E 46 1/2 to first station; signed: **John Barnwell**;; witness: **Walter Murray, Richd. Cope**; proved February Term 1798 by **Cope**, Delivd. **Richard Coop**.

P. 451, 20 January 1797, **William Hargess** [no residence given] to **William Muzzell** of Caswell, fifty pounds, 100 acres, on waters of Hico, begin at a black jack, W 27 ch. to a post oak, N 36 ch. to a black oak, E 27 ch. to a black oak, S 36 ch. to beginning; signed: **W. Hargis**; witness: **Thos. Compton, Susanah (X) Hargis**; proved February Term 1798, Delivd. **Thos. Compton**.

P. 452, 19 January 1798, **Absalom Lea** [no residence given] to **Mills Wells** of Person, seventy five pounds, 177 acres, on waters of Linches Cr. of North Hico, begin at a red oak on the dividing line between Caswell & Orange County, S70 1/2W 47 ch. to a red oak saplin, N 10 ch. to a pine **Elisha Wells'** cor., E his line 10 ch. 80 lk. to pointers **Wells'** cor. N 44 ch. 16 lk. to a hicory on County Line, E on line 37 ch. 50 lk. to beginning; signed: **Absalom Lea**; witness: **William Muzzell, Benjamin Bowles**; proved February Term 1798 by **Muzzell**, Delivd.

Miles Wells.

P. 453, 22 June 1797, **Thomas Linch** of Orange to **David Linch** of same, fifty pounds, 230 acres, on waters of Back Cr., begin at a P. oak **Thompson's** cor., S 60 1/2 ch. to a P. oak, W 38 ch. to a black jack, N4E 60 1/2 ch. to a black oak, E to first station; signed: **Thomas Linch**; witness: **Moses Lynch**; proved February Term 1798 by **Moses Lynch**, Delivd. **John Forrest.**

P. 454, 10 December 1797, **John Nichols** of Davidson County, Tennessee, to **James Ray** of Orange, four hundred fifty dollars, 436 acres, two tracts, on both sides of Forresters Cr., begin at **Robert Davis'** cor. black oak saplin, N 10 ch. to a black jack oak, W 60 ch. to a hicory saplin, S crossing Forresters Cr. 40 ch. to a white oak, E 60 ch. to a black jack on **Davis'** line, N 40 ch. to beginning, 240 acres, **Alfred Moore** Executor of **Genl. Nash** to **John Taylor**, second tract, on waters of Little R., begin at a B. O., E 25 ch. to a P. O., N 55 ch. to a P. O., W 9 ch. to a post oak, S 5 ch. to a post oak, W 49 ch. to a B. J., S 20 ch. to a P. O., E 43 ch. to a B. J., S 22 ch. to beginning, adjoins first tract & **Davis**, 196 acres, **James Bryant** to **Lebious Whitney**; signed: **John Nichols**; witness: **James Hart**; proved february Term 1798 by affirmation of **James Hart**, Delivd. **James Ray.**

P. 456, 21 February 1798, **James Love** of Orange to **William Faucett** of same, forty five pounds, 93 acres, begin at a hicory on the Hillsborough Road, N10E 4 ch. 50 lk. to a P. O., N21 9 ch. 75 lk. to a stake on **William Boyl's** line, his line N 20 ch. 75 lk. to a P. O. his cor., E 2 ch. to a P. O., N 10 ch. to a P. O. on a path **William Love's** cor., along windings thereof S60E 33 ch. to a hicory, S25E 4 ch. to a black oak on **William Faucett's** Old Line, his line W 5 ch. 85 lk. to a P. O. his cor., his line 25 ch. crossing the Hillsborough Road continued in all 33 ch. to a stake on **Harvey's** line, his line W 8 ch. 50 lk. to a P. O. on line, N 11 ch. to a B. J. on the Road, windings of road to beginning; signed: **James Love**; witness: **William Boyle, Benj. Ragsdale**; proved February Term 1798 by **Boyle**, Delivd. **Wm. Fossett.**

P. 457, 10 March 1797, **Lodwick Albright** of Orange to **Daniel Albright** son of **Ludwick** of same, fiftty pounds, 210 acres, begin at a stone, N45W 30 ch. to a stone, S45W 38 ch. to a hicory, N45W 7 ch. to a stone, S45W 7 ch. to a red oak, S45E 5 1/2 ch. to a stone, S45W 5 ch. to a stone, S45E 5 ch. to a red oak, S45W 32 ch. to a stone, E 43 ch. to a stone, N 5 ch. to a stone, N45E 50 ch. to beginning, part of a larger tract; signed: **Ludwick Albright**; witness: **Benja. Rainey, Wm. Rainey**; proved February Term 1798 by **Benj. Rainey**, Delivd. **J. Holt.**

P. 459, 15 January 1793, **Thomas Hall** of Orange to **David Hall** of same, fifty five pounds, 188 acres, begin at a post oak saplin cor. of **Thomas Marcom**, N 102 p. to a pine, E 268 p. to a pine, S 130 p. to a pine, W 90 p., N 28 p. to a black jack, W 168 p. to beginning; signed: **Thomas Hall, Nancy Hall**; witness: **John Hust, Harris (X) Tuder**; proved February Term 1798 by **Hust**, Delivd. **Saml. Couch.**

P. 460, 15 January 1794, **Thomas Hall** of Orange to **David Hall** of same, twenty pounds, 62 acres, begin at a red oak, W 34 1/2 ch. to a red oak, N 18 ch. to a hicory, E 34 1/2 ch. to a black jack, S 18 ch. to beginning; signed: **Thomas Hall, Nancy Hall**; witness: **John Hust, Harris (X) Tuder**; proved February Term 1798 by **Hust**.

P. 461, 19 February 1798, **Christopher Barbee** of Orange to **Samuel A. Holmes** Esq. of same, one hundred thirty pounds, 4 acres, Lot # 2 in the village of the University, **Trustees of the University** to **Christopher Barbee**; signed: **Christopher Barbee**; witness: **J. Dixon, John Daniel**; proved February Term 1798 by **Daniel**, Delivd. **Edwin Orsbon**.

P. 462, 21 November 1797, **Nathaniel Christmas** & wife **Mary** of Orange to **Thomas Durham** of same, twenty pounds, 47 acres, on waters of Little Cain Cr., adjoins lands of **Durham** & **Charles Christmas**, begin on a post oak stump & a black jack on **Charles Christmas'** line, S27E 13 1/2 ch. to a post oak on **Durham's** line, his line W 26 1/2 ch. to a spanish oak **Durham's** cor., S along **Durham's** line 5 ch. to a red oak another cor. of **Durham** standing on N bank of a branch, up branch N35W 32 ch. to a stake a cor. of **Charles Christmas**, with **Christmas'** line to beginning, part of a tract from **William F. Strudwick** to **Nathaniel Christmas**; signed: **Nathaniel Christmas, Mary Christmas**; witness: **Henry O. Daniel, Sarah (X) Smith**; proved February Term 1798 by **Daniel**, Delivd. **Thos. Durham**.

P. 463, 8 December 1797, **John Boughton** & wife **Ann** of King & Queen County, Virginia to **Thomas Trice** of Orange, one hundred pounds, 213 acres, begin at a red oak & large rock on Watery Br. adjoining **James Herndon's** land, N 156 p. to a poplar on Rocky Br., down branch to the Third Fork Cr. to a sassafras, up creek to 2 white oaks on **Robert Campbell's** line, W 77 p. to a pine **Campbell's** cor., S his line 224 p. to an elm on **William Sheperd's** line, E his line 50 p. to a persimmon, S 12 p. to a maple at the Watery Br., up branch to beginning; signed: **John Boughton, Ann (X) Boughton**; witness: **Leonard Carlton, Thomas Boughton, Susanah J. Boughton**; proved February Term 1798 by **Carlton**.

P. 464, 10 March 1797, **Ludwick Albright** of Orange to **George Albright** his son [no residence given], fifty pounds, 225 acres, on waters of Gun Cr., begin at a stone a cor. of **Daniel Albright**, N 47 ch. to a stake, N45W 5 ch. to a hicory, N45E 50 ch. to a stone, S45E 36 ch. to a stone, S45W 38 ch. to a hicory, N45W 7 ch. to a stone, S45W 7 ch. to a red oak, S45E 5 1/2 ch. to a stone, S45W 5 ch. to a stone, S45E 5 ch. to a red oak, S45W 32 ch. to beginning; signed: **Ludwick Albright**; witness: **Benj. Rainey, Wm. Rainey**; proved February Term 1798 by **Benj. Rainey**, Delivd. **Jeremiah Holt**.

P. 465, 5 September 1797, **James Coglin** of Orange to **Joseph Dixon** of same, nineteen pounds, 1 acre, Lot # 31 in Hillsborough, a cor. lot of Wake Street & Tryon Street, 400lk. in length, 250 in breadth; signed: **James Coghlin**; witness: **A. Benton, John Couch**; proved February Term 1798 by **Benton**, Delvd. **Jo Dixon**.

P. 466, 13 January 1798, **Thomas Trice** of Orange to **Leonard Carlton** of same, one hundred pounds, 213 acres, on both sides of Third Fork of Newhope, begin at a red oak & large rock on Watery Br. joining **James Herndon**, N 156 p. to a poplar on Rocky Br., down branch to the Third Fork to a sassafras, up Third Fork to 2 white oaks **Robert Campbell's** cor., W 77 p. to a pine **Campbell's** cor., S his line 224 p. to an elm **William Shepperd's** line, E his line 50 p. to a persimmon, S with line 12 p. to an iron wood & maple at Watery Br., up branch to beginning; signed: **Thomas Trice**; witness: **John Meacham, Peter House, Willm. Woroon**; acknowledged February Term 1798.

P. 467, 21 November 1797, **Nathaniel Christmas** & wife **Mary** of Orange to **Thomas Durham** of same, twenty five pounds, 10 acres, on waters of Little Cain Cr., begin at a post oak on **Charles Christmas'** line, with line E 10 ch. to a red oak, S50E 5 1/2 ch. to an ash on the creek, down creek 2 1/2 ch. to a white oak, S85W 13 1/2 ch. to a hicory, to beginning; signed: **Nathl. Christmas, Mary Christmas**; witness: **Henry O. Daniel, Sarah (X) Smith**; proved February Term 1798 by **Daniel**, Delivd. **Thos. Durham**.

P. 469, 18 february 1798, **William Adams** of Surry to **Peter Stout** of Orange, one hundred pounds, 200 acres, on waters of Fousts Cr., **North Carolina** to **Thomas Mulhollan, Mulhollan** to **Adams, Adams** to **Peter Stout**, deed was lost without being registered therefore this second deed, begin at a white oak, S 60 ch. to a post oak, W 33 ch. to a black oak, N 60 ch. to a stake, E 33 ch. to first station; signed: **William Adams, Susanah Adams**; witness: **William Adams Junr., James Neal**; proved February Term 1789 by affirmation of **Neal**, Delivd. **Jno. Morrow**.

Ended April 24th 1798, **J. Estes**, P. Register

ORANGE COUNTY (NC) DEED BOOK 7

P. 1, 13 August 1796, **Alston Jones** of Orange to **Edward Jones** of same, two hundred pounds, 89 1/2 acres, on Morgans Cr., begin at a hicory a cor. of the University Land, E 98 p. to a hicory joining the land I now live on, S my line 60 p. to Banks Br., down branch to a stake a cor. **Willm. Merritt's** Mill Seat, W along Mill Seat line 40 p. to a red oak cor. of the Mill Seat, S 20 p. to bank of Morgans Cr., up creek to the Banks Cabbin line on a walnut, W with line 33 p. to a red oak **Willm. Merritt's** cor., N 158 p. to first station; signed: **Alston Jones**; witness: **Wm. H. Haywood, Edmund Jones;** proved February Term 1798 by **Edmund Jones**, Delivd. **Edwd. Jones.**

P. 2, 22 February 1796, **Joseph Hust** of Orange to **David Hall** of same, ten pounds, 30 acres, begin at a red oak cor. of **Joseph Hust's** line, S 44 p. to a pine, W 130 p. to a white oak on a branch, down branch 44 p. to a pine, E 110 p. to beginning; signed: **Joseph Hust**; witness: **Thomas Hall, John Leigh, Richd. (X) Marcom**; proved February Term 1798 by **Marcom.**

P. 3, 2 March 1798, **William Hall** of Orange to **Joseph Hodge** of same, two hundred pounds, 343 acres, on waters of Back Cr. a branch of Haw R. (except 100 acres which was sold by **Griffeth Thomas** to **John Thomas**), adjoins **David Henly, James McAdams, William Raney, Alexander Kilpatrick, John Baldridge, & Sothberry**, begin at a white oak James **McAdams'** & John **Beson's** cor., S 14 1/2 ch. to a hicory, E 4 1/2 ch. to a black oak, S 8 ch. to a B., S25W 16 1/2 ch. to a black oak, W 5 ch. to a post oak, down meanders to a water oak, N22W 22 ch. rto a hicory, down meanders to a poplar, N 10 ch. to Pt., N82W 10 ch. to a stake, W 5 ch. to a B. O.; N 32 ch. to a P. O., N40E 9 ch. to a hicory, S20E 5 ch. to a B. O., S 14 ch. to a B. O., E 60 ch. to first station; signed: **Wm. Hall**; witness: **Wm. Norwood**; acknowledged February Term 1798, delivered to **Jo Hodge.**

P. 5, 9 July 1790, **James Elliott** of Orange to **Enoch Bradley** of same, forty pounds, 31 acres, on S side of Haw R., adjoins **Charles Kelly** & **George Sheridin**, begin at a beach at the mouth of a branch emptying into Haw R., down river to a black oak, S 5 ch. to a black oak, W 6 ch. to a hicory, S 14 ch. to a black oak, W 19 ch. to a black oak on bank of creek, down meanders to first station; signed: **James Elliott**; witness: **John Allison, William Cain**; proved February Term 1798 by **Allison**, delivd. **William Jackson.**

P. 6, 15 February 1791, **William Watters** Esq. of Orange to **Alexander Duncan Moore**, attorney at law, of same, eighty pounds, 1 acre, Lot # 15 in Hillsborough, fronting King Street 400 lk. in length & 250 lk. in breadth; signed: **W. Watters**; witness: **S. Benton, A. Benton**; proved February Term 1798 by **S. Benton.**

P. 7, 2 February 1796, **Samuel Stephens** of Orange to **Jesse Nevill** of same, eighty pounds, 80 acres, begin at Chatham Line at **Pomfret Herndon's** Old Waggon Road, along Old Road nearly a N course to the Meadow Fork of Prices Cr., up creek to **Nevill's** line, S his line to Chatham Line, E along Chatham Line to beginning; signed: **Daniel (X) Stephens**; witness: **John Willson, Benjamin**

Nevill; proved February Term 1798 by **John Wilson**, deld. **J. Nevill Junr.**

P. 8, 11 May 1797, **Edward Harris** of Orange to **John Phips** of Wake, eighty three dollars, 83 1/2 acres, on waters of Ellibees Cr., begin at a pine on the County Line on the sizde of a branch, N75W 188 p. to a hicory, S15W 77 p. to 2 black jacks, S75E 180 p. to a hicory in the County Line, along same N15E 77 p. to beginning; signed: **Edward Harris**; witness: **Elias Turner, Chs. Kennon**; proved February Term 1798 by **Turner**, delvd. **Elias Turner.**

P. 9, 19 February 1797, **William Courtney** of Hillsborough to **James Christmas** of Orange, five shillings to be paid first day of April in this and every year during Courtney's natural life,, 300 acres, on waters of Eno, adjoins **Edward Turner, John Caragan, Thomas Crabtree, William Watters** deceased, **William Whitted, Thomas Watts, & William Lockheart**, with these restrictions, on the road leading from the Town of Hillsborough passing through the land to **Benton's** Mill **James** shall not be at liberty to cut, sell, or dispose of any timber on the N side of Road but shall be at liberty to use of any **James** shall think necessary for fire wood for his own family, rales [rails] for fences, building his own house, etc., & shall be at liberty to clear the N side of the Road as he shall want to cultivate, but not lease, employ hand or hands to cultivate on N side of Road, but on S side of Road shall be at full liberty to clear any land, to cut timber for rales to fence 2 cultivated fields and apply all profits to his own use & be at liberty to employ hands to work the S side of road in numbers not to exceed ten, if **James** rents any part of the land he keep the benefits for his & his family's use, on S side of Road he shall be at liberty to sell & dispose of any timber for firrewood that he thinks will not make rales, shingles,plank,staves, lumber, etc., **William** shall not be prohibited from the privileges of the land, if **James** leaves the land before the death of **William** the land reverts to **William,** if the land is sold to satisfy any debt of **William, James** shall have no claim to it by virtue of this lease; signed: **William Courtney**; witness: **Jo. Courtney, Henry Thompson Junr.**; proved February Term 1798 by **Thompson**, Delivered **James Christmas.**

P. 11, 10 December 1797, **Peter Hamlin** of Surry to **Gabriel Murphey** of Caswell, twenty five, 200 acres, on waters of Hico, begin at a white oak **John Bruses** cor., S 40 ch. to a post oak, E 50 ch. to a post oak, N 40 ch. to pointers, W 50 ch. to first station, part of 400 acres from **North Carolina** to **Stephen Hamlin** 18 May 1769, recorded Book M, Folio 145; signed: **Peter (X) Hamlin**; witness: **Stephen Hamlin, William Hamlin, William Murphey**; proved February Term 1798 by **William Murphey.**

P. 12, 26 April 1797, **Chesley Page Patterson** of Orange to **John Moore** of same, ninety seven pounds, 121 3/4 acres, on SW side of Newhope, begin at a pine at **Moore's** fence, E 164 p. to a hicory on the bank of Newhope Cr., up creek agreeable to plat hereunto annexed to a spanish oak in **Man Patterson's** line, his line S passing by his cor. taking along **Moor's** line in all 205 p. to beginning; signed: **C. P. Patterson, Nancy Patterson**; witness: **Thomas Trice, William Trice**; ackknowleedged February Term 1798, delvd. **Jno. Moore.**

P. 14, 28 February 1798, **John Thompson** Esq. of Orange to **James Blair** of same, forty pounds, 223 acres, on S side of Haw R., adjoins **John Patton & Eli McDaniel**, begin at a black oak, S 11 ch. to a post oak, W 2 ch. to a hicory, S12E 63 ch. to a post oak, S60E 32 1/2 ch. to a post oak, S68E 9 ch. to a white oak on bank of Haw R., up meanders to first station; signed: **John Thompson**; witness: **John Ray, Thomas Whithead**; acknowledged February Term 1798, delvd. **John Thompson**.

P. 15, [blank] August 1794, **John Taylor** of Hillsborough to **William Lytle** of Orange, two pounds, 217 acres, on waters of Eno, addjoins **James Watson, William Crabtree, John Estes, & Patrick McCulloh**, begin at a hicory stump **Watson's & Estes'** cor. along **Watson's** line S 30 ch. to a stake, E along **Crabtree's** line 66 ch. to a post oak **Newman's** cor., N 33 ch. to a post oak **Estes'** cor., W 66 ch. to first station, **North Carolina** to **Taylor** 10 July 1788; signed: **John Taylor**; witness: **Henry Fossett, William Lytle Junr.**; acknowledged February Term 1798, delvd. **Capt. Lytle**.

P. 17, 28 May 1798, **Joseph Hodge** late Sheriff of Orange to **Hardy Hurdle** of same, thirty pounds, 50 acres, levy against **Stephen Conger** for eighty seven pounds four shillings, on Deep & Stoney Cr., sold 12 November 1795, begin at a hicory near Stoney Cr. **William Stalcup's** line, northwardly along line to a post oak 3 ch., southwardly bounded by **James Gamblin's** land to a black walnut near his spring, along line to **Adam Marley's** line, down line to Deep Cr. crossing to a hicory on the mouth of Deep Cr., up Stoney Cr. to beginning, **Joseph Dorris** to **Stephen Conger**; signed: **Joseph Hodge**, Sheriff;; witness: **L. Benton**; acknowledged February Term 1798, delivd. **Hardy Hurdle**.

P. 18, 8 January 1798, **North Carolina** to **Thomas Rhodes** [no residence given], five pounds per hundred acres, 50 acres, on waters of Eno, begin at a white oak, S 36 ch. 50 lk. to a gum, N 36 ch. 50 lk. to a stake in the **Widow McVinch's** line, W to beginnig, warrant dated 15 November 1788; signed: **Saml. Ashe**; witness: **Wm. Hill**; [no probate record].

P. 19, 15 January 1798, **North Carolina** to **Thomas Rhodes** [no residence given], fifty shillings per hundred acres, 135 acres, on waters of Eno, begin at a white oak on **Lazarrus Cate's** line, N 87 p. to a hicory on **McVinch's** line **Daniels** cor., W 141 p. to a black oak on **Rhodes'** line, S his line 114 p. to a gum his cor., his line N 154 p. to a hicory his cor., W 17 p. to a hicory **Culberson's** cor., his line S 244 p. to a black oak on the side of a Road, E with **Laycock's** line 82 p. to a white oak **Cate's** cor., his line N 109 p. to a black jack **Cate's** cor., E his line 135 p. to beginning, warrant dated 23 May 1796; signed: **Saml. Ashe**; witness: **Wm. Hill**; [no probate record], delivvd. **Thomas Rhodes**.

P. 20, 7 March 1794, **James Latta** of Orange to **James H. Ray** [no residence given], nineteen pounds one shilling seven pence, 40 acres, on N side of Great Allamance Cr., begin at a hicory saplin, N17W 22 p. to a post oak **John Trousdale's** Old Cor., E 92 p. to a hicory saplin **William Ray's** Old Cor., S 110 p. to a post oak, W 39 p. to an elm on bank of creek, up creek to first station; signed: **James Latta**; witness: **William Ray, Robert Ray**; acknowledged February Term 1798, Delivd. **James H. Ray**.

P. 22, 8 June 1797, **North Carolina** to **William Ray** [no residence given], fifty shillings per hundred acres, 37 acres, begin at a white oak on the side of a branch, S58W 74 ch. a black jack, N70E 73 ch. a white oak, to first station, entered 6 June 1796; signed: **Saml. Ashe**; witness: **J. Glasgow**; [no probate record], delvd. **John Bullock**.

P. 23, 16 July 1795, **North Carolina** to **William Cabe** [no residence given], ten pounds per hundred acres, 400 acres, on waters of Eno, begin at a post oak on **Jane Borland's** line & cor. to **Alexander Borland**, his line due W 59 ch. to a hicory, due N 19 1/2 ch. to a red oak, E 36 ch. to a hicory, N 24 1/2 ch. to a post oak, W 14 ch. to a post oak, N 44 ch. to a hicory near a highland pond, E 11 1/2 ch. to a post oak, N 27 ch. to a post oak, E 20 ch. to a red oak, S 20 ch. to a red oak & hicory, E 5 ch. to a post oak, S8W 37 ch. to a post oak, E 28 ch. to 2 post oaks, S10E 16 ch. to a black oak, W 24 ch. to a red oak, S 42 ch. to beginning; signeed: **Richd. Dobbs Spaight**; witness: **J. Glasgow**; [no probate record], delivd. **Wm. Cabe**.

P. 24, 5 April 1797, **North Carolina** to **John Campbell** [no residence given], thirty shillings per hundred acres, 100 acres, on waters of Back Cr., adjoins his own land, begin at a black jack his own cor., W 42 ch. to a black oak his cor., S50E 20 ch. to a white oak, N40E 16 ch. to aa stake, E 20 ch. to a black gum, S 20 ch. to a stake, E 10 ch. to a stake, N25E 32 ch. to a black oak, E 2 1/2 ch. to a black oak **Stephen Maddon's** cor., N 12 1/2 ch. to a hicory **John Walker's** cor., W 28 ch. to a black oak **Walker's** cor., S 4 1/2 ch. to a black jack, his line to first station; signed: **Saml. Ashe**; witness: **Wm. Hill**; [no probate record], delivd. **John Campbell**.

P. 25, 15 January 1798, **North Carolina** to **William Partin** [no residence given], thirty shillings per hundred acres, 50 acres, on waters of Bolands Cr., begin at a black jack **Mathew Colther's** cor., W 146 p. to a black jack, N 28 p. to a stake in **Partin's** line, his line E 60 p. to a white oak his cor., N his line 47 p. to a stake, E 86 p. to a stake in **Mathew Colther's** line, his line S 75 p. to first station, warrant datedd 1 October 1793; signed: **Saml. Ashe**; witness: **J. Glasgow**; [no probate record].

P. 26, 21 April 1798, **Burras Estes** of Orange to **Henry Hessa** of same, one hundred pounds, 140 acres, on waters of Newhope Cr., begin at a black oak a dividing cor. of original tract, N 19 ch. to a post oak, E 65 1/2 ch. to a black oak stump near a wild crabapple tree, S 24 1/2 ch., N85W 65 ch.; signed: **Burrows (X) Estes**; witness: **William McCauley, George Long**; proved May term 1798 by **Long**, delivd. **Henry Hessa**.

P. 27, 29 May 1798, **John Adams & Margaret** his wife of Orange to **Thomas Lewellin Lechmear Wall** of same, eighty pounds, 222 acres, on head of Grays Cr. of Seven Mile Cr., bounded on N by **Moore's** land, on E by **Elmore Hanley's** land, on S by **James Baley's** land, on W by **Joseph Clack's** land, begin at a black jack on **Moore's** line, E with his line 43 ch. to **Hanley's** cor. a red oak, S 23 ch. to **Bailey's** cor. black jack, W 10 ch. to a post oak, S 15 ch. to a white oak, W 20 ch. to a black jack, S 5 ch. to a hicory, W 29 ch. to a post oak on **Clack's** line, N 16 1/2 ch. to his cor. post oak, N30E 33 ch. to first station;

signed: **John Adams, Margaret (+) Adams**; witness: **Henry Thomson Junr., Joseph Hastings**; proved May Term 1798 by **Henry Thompson Junr.**, delivd. **Thos. L. L. Wall**.

P. 30, 29 May 1798, **Joseph Hastings** of Orange to **Thomas Lewellin Lechmear [Lechmere] Wall** of same, thirteen pounds, 222 acres, **North Carolina** to **Joseph Hastings** 10 July 1788, on head of Grays Cr. of Seven Mile Cr., bounded on N by **Moor**, on E by **Elmore Hanley**, on S by **James Bailey**, on W by **Joseph Clack**, begin at a black jack on **Moor's** line, E with his line 43 ch. to **Hasting's** cor. a red oak, S 23 ch. to **Bailey's** cor. black jack, W 10 ch. to a post oak, S 15 ch. to a white oak, W 20 ch. to a black jack, S 5 ch. to a hicory, W 29 ch. to a post oak on **Clack's** line, N 16 1/2 ch. to his cor. post oak, N30E 33 ch. to first station; signed: **Joseph Hastings**; witness: **Henry Thompson, Henry Thomson Junr.**, acknowledged May Term 1798, delivd. **Thos. L. L. Wall**.

P. 32, 5 March 1798, **Levan [Leaven] Rhodes** of Orange to **Thomas Bradshaw** of same, one hundred twenty five pounds, Nego Boy, named **Will**, between age of thirteen and fourteen; signed: **Leaven Rhodes**; witness: **Jno. Thompson, Charles Christmas**; proved May Term 1798 by **Thompson**.

P. 33, 10 February 1798, **David Linch** of Orange to **John Foust Junr.** of same, one hundred fifty pounds, 230 acres, on waters of Back Cr., begin at a post oak **Thompson's** cor., S 60 1/2 ch. to a post oak, W 38 ch. to a black jack, N4E 60 1/2 ch. to a black oak, E to first station; signed: **David Linch**; witness: **Hugh Shaw, Alexr. Russell**; proved May Term 1798 by **Alexander Russell**, delvd. **John Forrest**.

P. 34, 20 April 1798, **Abraham Piper** of Orange to **Mathew McCauley** of same, one hundred fifty pounds, 100 acres, begin at a sweet gum tree a cor. of land lately sold by **Abraham Piper** to **Brewer**, a line of marked trees W to a hicory on Morgans Cr., down creek to **Mathew McCauley's** line, along **McCauley's** line to creek, down creek tto **William Brewer's** cor. hicory, along **Brewer's** line to a hicory bush on a branch, up branch to first station; signed: **Abraham Piper, Rebekah (X) Piper**; witness: **John Burrow, Callam Parish**; proved May Term 1798 by **Parish**, delvd. **Mathew McCauley**.

P. 35, 23 March 1798, **Richard Cate** of Orange to **Samuel Holliway [Hollaway]** of same, hundred pounds, 150 acres, on Cabbin Branch & Crooked Run Cr., waters of Eno & Little R., begin at a post oak standing on W side of Road from **William Ansley's** to **John Carrington's** & on **John Cain's** line formerly line of **Henry Eustace McCulloh**, W 30 p. to a cor. pine, S 50 p. to a black oak on **Meremons Coales**, E 30 p. to a post oak standing on **William Cain's** line & on E side of road, N 50 p. to first station; signed: **Richd. (X) Cate**; witness: **Stephen Foust, John Holt**; proved May Term 1798 by **Holt**, delvd. **Tho. Holloway**.

P. 37, 14 December 1797, **Conrod Farmer** of Orange to **Anthony Cable** of same, twenty five pounds, 27 1/2 acres, on waters of Haw R. S side, part of a tract from **North Carolina** to **Jesse Phillips** 9 November 1784, begin at a stake

Cable's cor., S 9 ch. to a white oak, S76E 25 ch. to a black oak, N 4 ch. to a black oak stump cor. of another tract, same course continued in all 14 ch. 50 lk. to a black oak, W 25 ch. to beginning; signed: **Conrad Farmer**; witness: **John Coble**, *Lu Jan goble* ; proved May Term 1798 by **John Coble**, delvd. **Abner James**.

P. 38, 16 April 1798, **John G. Rencher** of Wake to **Revd. Joseph Caldwell** of Orange, fifty pounds, 2 acres, in village adjoining the University, Lot # 19; signed: **John Grant Rencher**; witness: **P. Henderson, Jno. Couch**; proved May Term 1798 by **John Couch**.

P. 39, 3 June 1797, **George Pratt** of Orange to **James Pratt** of same, seventy eight pounds ten shillings, 225 acres, on both sidees of Cates Cr., begin at a black jack, N 30 ch. crossing Cates Cr. continued in all 69 ch. to a hicory J. **Pratt's** Old Tract, along a line of tract W 50 ch. 50 lk. to cor. of tract, N 5 ch. to 2 red oaks, W 18 ch. 25 lk. to a post oak, S 2 ch. 50 lk. to a stake, to beginning; signed: **George Pratt**; witness: **J. Christmas, Saml. Turringtine**; proved May Term 1798 by **Turringtine**, delvd. **Jas. Pratt**.

P. 41, 27 January 1798, **Benjamin Rainey** of Orange to **Anthony Cable** of same, thirteen pounds, 26 acres, on waters of Traveses Cr., begin at a red oak, W 32 p. to a post oak, S 130 p. to a red oak, E 32 p. to a red oak, N 130 p. to beginning; signed: **Benj. Rainey**; witness: **William Rainey, Henry Strader,**; proved May Term 1798 by **Strader**, delvd. **Abner James**.

P. 42, 16 May 1798, **William F. Strudwick** [no residence given] to **James Johnston** [no residence given], three hundred pounds, 165 acres, begin at an ash on Kennedys Br. cor. to **John Pugh**, his line N69E 22 ch. 50 llk. to a white oak, S46E 7 ch. to a hicory, N70E 2 ch. 50 lk. to an ash on Mulberry Br., up branch N80E 11 ch. to a poplar, N78E 7 ch. to a black oak, N35W 6 ch. 50 lk. to a red oak cor. of **Gordon**, his line S75E 26 ch. 50 lk. to 2 post oak bushes, S30W 35 ch. to a sassafras, S85W crossing the New Road at 12 ch. continued in all 36 ch. to a hicory cor. to **Sterling Moore**, his line N47W 9 ch. 50 lk. to a white oak on a branch, S86W 3 ch. 25 lk. to a hicory bush, N4W 5 ch. 40 lk. to a spanish oak on Kenedays Br., down meanders to first station; signed: **W. F. Strudwick**; witness: **Henry Shepperd, John Justus**; proved May Term 1798 by **Justus**, delvd. **Jas. Johnston**.

P. 43, 4 July 1797, **Andrew Murdock** Sheriff of Orange to **Samuel Benton** of same, twenty five pounds, 4 acres in Hillsborough, bounded on E by Wake Street, on W by Lot # 135, on N by Margaret Lane, on S by the Mill Pond, Lots # 136, 137, 138, & 139, decrees of foreclosure obtained by the **Governor** agianst **James Williams** on four deeds of mortgage dated 5 June 1784, for twenty seven pounds thirteen shillingas four pence, twelve pounds one shilling four pence, nine pounds four pence, and six pounds one shillings four pence, 1 acre on lower side of Margaret Lane to W of Wake Street 250 lk. in breadth & 400 lk. in length, Lot # 136, 1 other acre, on lower side of Margaret Lane to W of Wake Street 250 lk. in breadth & 400 lk. in length, Lot # 137, 1 other acre, on lower side of Margaret Lane to W side of Wake Street 250 lk. in breadth & 400 lk. in length, Lot # 138, 1 other acre, a cor. lot of Wake Street & Margaret Lane the cor. side of Lane 250 lk. in breadth & 400 lk. in length, Lot # 139, fifty pounds nine shillings one farthing principal & interest & seventeen pounds six pence costs due on Lot # 136, twenty two pounds eight shillings ten pence three farthings principal & interest & six pounds fourteen shillings ten pence costs due on Lot # 137, Sixteen pounds fifteen shillings three pence one farthing principal & interest & sixteen pounds thirteen shillings ten pence costs due on Lot # 138, eleven pounds five shillings four pence half penny principal & interest & sixteen pounds twelve shillings nine pence costs due on Lot # 139, sold 3 July 1797; signed: **Andrew Murdock**; witness: **Jno. Taylor, Jas. Green**; acknowledged May Term 1798, delvd. **Morgan Hart.**

P. 47, 10 May 1798, **William F. Strudwick** of Orange to **Joseph Thompson** of same, one hundred pounds, 300 acres, on Meadow Cr., begin at a spanish oak on S bank of creek, S 69 ch. crossing Hillsborough Road to a hicory, S71W 16 ch. 50 lk. to a stake on **Josiah Thompson's** line, N 3 ch. to his cor. a post oak, S85W 20 ch. 50 lk. to a post oak a cor. to **Eubank's** Tract, along a line of that tract N 15 ch. to a hicory, N60W 46 ch. crossing Meadow Cr. to a post oak, to beginning; signed: **W. F. Strudwick**; witness: **David Mebane, H. Shepperd**; acknowledged May Term 1798, delvd. **Jno. Thompson.**

P. 48, 28 November 1797, **Thomas Cole** of Orange to **John Hufman** of same, six hundred dollars, 300 acres, on Haw R., begin at a hicory a cor. of **Henry Suver[?]** land, his line S 29 ch. to a post oak cor. of **James Murray**, W 28 ch. to a post oak, S 10 ch. to a post oak, W 10 ch. to a stake, N 20 ch. to a red oak, W 30 ch. to a post oak, N7E 20 ch. to a white oak & red oak on S bank of Haw R., down river to beginning, **North Carolina** to **William Mebane**; signed: **Thomas Cole**; witness: **James Hutcherson, James Murray, William (X) Dixon**; proved May Term 1798 by **Dixon**, delvd. **Robert Dixon.**

P. 49, 16 September 1797, **John Cook & Henry Cook** of Orange to **Peter Gortner** of same, one hundred twenty five pounds, 102 acres, on water course called Stinking Quarter, begin at a post oak adjoining **Gortner**, his own line S48 1/2W 50 ch. to a hicory, S45E 16 1/2 ch. to a red oak, N58E 2 ch. to a poplar on bank of Stinking Quarter Cr., down creek 43 1/2 ch. to a forked white oak, N34E 34 ch. to a gum, N45W 23 1/2 ch. to beginning; signed: **John Cook, H. Cook Junr.**; witness: **Michl. Holt Junr., David Gortner**; proved May Term 1798 by **Holt**, delvd. **Michl. Holt Junr.**

P. 51, 16 September 1797, **John Cook & Henry Cook** of Orange to **Michael Shoftner** of same, four hundred pounds, 167 acres, on branches of Stinking Quarter Cr., begin at a black oak a cor. of 4 tracts, N45W 23 1/2 ch. to a gum **Peter Gortner's** cor., S34W 34 ch. crossing Stinking Quarter Cr. continuing a piece on side of creek to a forked W. O. oak on bank of creek, up creek 43 1/2 ch. to a poplar, leaving creek S58W 2 ch. to a red oak **Henry Smith's** cor., S45W 4 ch. to a stake, S45E crossing Stinking Quarter 36 ch. to a W. O., N45E 50 ch. to beginning; signed: **John Cook, H. Cook Junr.**; witness: **Michael Holt Junr., David Gortner**; proved May Term 1798 by **Holt**, delvd. **Michl. Holt Junr.**

P. 52, 6 December 1797, **Israel Barker** of Orange to **Robert Moore** of same, forty five dollars, 30 acres, on Laughlins Cr. a branch of Stoney Cr., begin on

ORANGE COUNTY (NC) DEED BOOK 7

creek at a white oak, S52W 22 1/2 ch. white oak, along **Moore's** line to a black oak N 18 1/2 ch., N35E 13 1/2 ch. to creek, down creek to first station; signed: **Israel Barker**; witness: **George Barker, Robert Moore Junr.**; acknowledged May Term 1798, delvd. **James Moore.**

P. 53, 4 January 1798, **John Graves** of Orange to **Jacob Graves** of same, one hundred dollars, 19 1/2 acres, on Stinking Quarter Cr., begin on bank of creek at a sassafras, S45W 64 p. to a white oak, N25W 56 p. to a black oak **Jacob Graves'** cor., his line N45E 50 p. to a red oak, S45E 52 p. to beginning; signed: **John Graves**; witness: **Joshua Holt, Michl. Holt**; proved May Term 1798 by Holt, delvd. **Michl. Holt Junr.**

P. 55, 28 October 1783, **Joseph Pevey** of Orange to **William O'Neil** of same, one hundred thirty pounds, 150 acres, on S side of Haw R., on waters of Little Allamance, begin at a post oak on **Henry Eustace McCulloh's** line, N 52 ch. to a post oak, E 12 ch. to a hicory, S45E 13 1/2 ch. to a post oak **Edward Gwinn's** cor., his line S 70 ch. to a hicory another cor. of **Gwinn**, N45W 34 ch. to first station, **North Carolina** to **William Rainey**; signed: Joseph (+) **Peavey**; witness: **John Harden,**   , **John Jouett**; proved May Term 1798 by **Hardin**, delvd. **Thos. H. Perkins.**

P. 56, 27 January 1798, **Benjamin Rainey** of Orange to **Christopher Huffhines** of same, fifty pounds, 100 acres, on waters of Traveses Cr., begin at a post oak, E 21 p. to a post oak, N 25 p. to a post oak, E 61 p. to a red oak, S 197 p. to a red oak, W 82 p. to a post oak, N 175 p. to a post oak, N 175 p. to beginning; signed: **Benjamin Rainey**; witness: **Wm. Rainey, Anthony Coble**; proved May Term 1798 by **Coble**, delvd. **Jno. Strader.**

P. 57, 27 May 1798, **Daniel Cotner** of Orange to **John Holstead** of same, fifty pounds, 50 acres, on waters of Rock Cr., begin at a post oak, E 18 ch. to a hicory bush, N20E 15 ch. to a sweet gum, N15E 22 ch. to a post oak, N65W 3 ch. to a hicory, S45W 75 ch. to a post oak, S70W 18 1/2 ch. to first station; signed: **Daniel (X) Cotner**; witness: **John Wheeler**; acknowledged May Term 1798, delvd. **Jno. Hornaday.**

P. 58, 10 April 1798, **Thomas Hallaway** of Orange to **Thomas Horn** of same, in exchange for twenty seven acres and a half, 27 1/2 acres, begin at a post oak **Hallaway's** cor., S81 1/2E 20 ch. to a black oak in **Horn's** line of a new tract, S 13 3/4 ch. to a black oak, N31 1/2W 20 ch. to a post oak saplin in the old line, with line N 13 3/4 ch. to first station; signed: **Thomas Hallaway**; witness: **S. Harris**; proved May Term 1798 by **Sterling Harris**, delvd. **Thos. Horn.**

P. 59, 17 August 1797, **Malachi Man** [no residence given] to **Mary Byrns** [no residence given], one hundred pounds five shillings, 394 acres, on Vernals Cr., begin at a hicory on the mountain, N 17 ch. to a post oak **Nicholas Hobbs'** ine, E 3 1/2 ch. to a white oak his cor., N 5 ch. to a red oak, S45E 7 ch. to a black jack **John Holt's** cor., N45E 60 ch. to a white oak his other cor., S 3 ch. to a black jack, E to **Elias Smith's** line, his line to his other cor., W to beginning; signed: **Malachi (X) Man**; witness: **Lewis Wood, Thos. Byrn**; proved May Term 1798 by **Thomas Byrn**, delvd. **Jas. Patterson.**

ORANGE COUNTY (NC) DEED BOOK 7

P. 60, 13 February 1798, **Richard Tate** of Davidson Co., Tennessee, to **John Tate** of Orange, three hundred four and one half dollars, 203 acres, on a branch of Stoney Cr., begin at a stake, W 84 p. to a black oak, S 4 p. to a stake, W 51 p. to a stake, S 73 rods to a black jack, W 78 p. to a black oak, N 55 p. to a black jack, W 136 p. to a post oak, S 110 p. to a black oak, E 148 p. to a post oak, N 36 p. to a white oak, E 80 p. to pointers, S 25 p. to a black oak, E 121 p. to a spanish oak, N 120 p. to first station; signed: **Richard Tate**; witness: **Jo. Hart, William Brackin**; proved May Term 1798 by **Joseph Hart**.

P. 62, 9 December 1797, **General Benjamin Smith** of Belvidere in Brunswick County and wife **Sarah** the only daughter & heir at law of **William Dry** to **James Hogg** of Orange, [consideration not given], one undivided sixty fourth and one undivided one hundred and twenty eighth part of the Indian purchase, being the part purchased by **William Dry** from **John Williams**, by 2 deeds dated 17 March 1775 the Cherokee Nation of Indians sold to **Richard Henderson, John Williams, Thomas Hart, Nathaniel Hart, John Luttrell, William Johnston, James Hogg, David Hart, & Leonard Henly Bullock** a tract on waters of Kentucky, Green R., Cumberland, Powels, & Clinch R. & other branches of the Ohio, one eighth part each to **Richard Henderson, John Williams, Thomas Hart, John Luttrell, William Johnston, & James Hogg** and one sixteenth part to **David Hart & Leonard Henly Bullock**, on 22 August 1777 **John Williams** sold **Colo. William Dry** of Brunswick County one fourth part of his one eighth, on 30 April 1778 **John Williams** sold **William Dry** another one fourth of his one eighth, being a total of one half of the one eighth part; signed: **Benjamin Smith, Sarah Smith**; witness: [none listed]; acknowledged 9 December 1797 in Raleigh before **John Williams** Judge of Superior Court of Law & Equity.

P. 64, 22 June 1778, **William Dry** of Brunswick to **Daniel Tucker** of George Town, South Carolina, merchant, eight hundred thirtyb three pounds, 1/12 part of **William Dry's** share in **Henderson & Co.** lands (one three hundred & eighty fourth part of whole), [see preceding deed], on 27 August 1777 **James Hogg** sold **William Dry** Esq. of Brunswick 1/4 part of his 1/8 share (1/32 part of the whole); signed: **Willm Dry**; witness: **Jas. Brown, Wilson Dalzell**; received 23 September 1797 a memo dated 16 September 1778 that **Daniel Tucker** sold a moiety of the land to **Mr. Henry Ebouch**, merchant, of Charles Town; also dated 24 March 1796, **Daniel Tucker** of George Town, Esq., to **Benjamin Smith** [no residence given], forty two dollars nineteen cents, a moiety of the within lands; signed: **Danl. Tucker**; witness: **George Harlot, James Carson**; proved before J. Haywood JSCL&E 19 May 1798 by **James Carson**; George Town District, South Carolina, recorded in Book D, folio 98 to 100 23 Sept. 1793; affidavit of **George Heriot**, George Town District that **William Heriot** swore that signature of **Jas. Brown** was a valid signature dated 23 September 1793.

P. 68, 19 August 1797, **Joseph Holmes** of Orange to **Levin Wood** of same, one hundred ten pounds, 120 acres, begin at a persimmon a cor. of **Edmund Green**, S45W 31 ch. 25 lk. to a white oak, N45W 33 ch. to a red oak, N45E 20 ch. to a black oak, N45W 12 ch. a P. oak, N45E 11 ch. 25 lk. to a black oak cor. of **Green**, with **Green** S45E 45 ch. to beginning; signed: **Joseph Holmes**; witness: **Obed Green, Thomas Byrn**; proved May Term 1798 by **Obed Green**, delvd. **Jacob Rich**.

P. 69, 29 May 1798, **William McCauley** Esq. High Sheriff of Orange to **Thomas Watts** of same, twenty one pounds thirteen shillings six pence, 195 acres, levy on lands of **Josiah Watts** adjoining lands of **William Courtney & William Johnston** to satisfy execution at instance of **John Haywood** vs **Watts & Jno. Steel** vs **Watts** & others [amount of execution not given], sold 17 July 1798[?], begin at a black jack on line of Town land, W 19 ch. to a post oak, N 55 ch. to a black jack, E 60 ch. to a hicory, S 22 ch. to a black oak, W 41 ch. to a black jack, S 28 ch. to first station; signed: **Wm. McCauley**; witness: [none listed]; acknowledged May Term 1798, delivered **Thomas Watts**.

P. 71, 15 May 1798, **John Pugh** of Orange to **Elizabeth** now wife of **Robert Cate Junr.**, natural love & affection, a Negro girl, named **Else,** about nine years of age; signed: **John Pugh**; witness: **William Moore, Charles Kelley, Robert Cate Senr.**; proved May Term 1798 by **Moore**, delivd. **Robert Cate Junr.**

P. 72, 9 March 1798, **John Wilkinson** of Orange to **Daniel Wilkinson** of same, one hundred sixty four pounds, 164 acres, **John Riley** to **John Wilkinson,** begin at a rock in the creek below the Walnut Ford, N72E 19 ch. to the Great Road, N 14 1/2 ch. to a pewrsimmon in **Nelson's** line, E 6 1/2 ch. to a black oak **Nelson's** cor., N10E 22 1/2 ch. to a white oak, N25E 17 ch. to a post oak, W 22 ch. to a red oak, S60W 6 1/2 ch. to creek, down creek to beginning; signed: **John Wilkinson**; witness: **William Wilkinson**; acknowledged May Term 1798, delvd. **Danl. Wilkinson.**

P. 74, 29 may 1798, **Thomas Horn Senr.** of Orange to **Thomas Holloway** of same, twenty seven pounds ten shillings, 27 1/2 acres, begin at holloway's old cor. in **Jacob Allen's** line near Eno R., N 11 ch. to a small black oak in **Allen's** line, W part with **Horn's** line 34 1/2 ch. to a spanish oak, S 6 ch. to a black oak, S 81 1/2E 35 ch. to first station; signed: **Thomas (T) Horn**; witness: **Sterling Harris**; proved May Term 1798 by **Harris.**

P. 75, 25 October 1796, **Richard Cate**, planter, of Orange to **Bremelion Holloway**, planter, of same, eighty pounds, 150 acres, begin at a post oak, W to a post oak on the W side of the road that leads from **John Carrington's** to **William Ansley's** Mill, S to a white oak on E side of road, E to a stake, N to first station; signed: **Richard (X) Cate**; witness: **Henry Bunch, John (X) Riley**; proved May Term 1798 by **Riley**, delvd. **Thos. Holloway.**

P. 76, 4 July 1797, **Conrod Pile** of Orange to **Daniel Albright** of same, three hundred pounds, 205 acres, on S side of Haw R., begin on **James Williams'** line, E crossing Gun Cr. 58 ch. to a post oak, N 44 ch. to a black jack, W 23 ch. to a stake, S 14 ch. to a black oak, W 35 ch. crossinfg Gun Cr. to a black oak, S 30 ch. to beginning; signed: **Conrod Pile**; witness: **Jacob Rich, Obed Green**; proved May Term 1798 by **Rich**, Delvd. **Robt. Dixon.**

P. 77, 28 May 1798, **Andrew Murdock** High Sheriff of Orange to **William Lytle** of same, sixty nine pounds nine shillings, 430 acres, levy on **Thomas O. Neill [O'Neill]** for thirty pounds eighteen shillings eight pence recovered by **Robert Eagan**, sold 20 August 1796, begin at a post oak, N 102 ch. 50 lk. to a black oak near **Lytle's** cor. white oak, W 22 ch. 50 lk. to a black jack, S 27 ch. to a black jack, E to beginning; signed: **Andrew Murdock**; witness: **James Carson, Reuben Smith**; acknowledged May Term 1798, delvd. **Wm. Lytle**.

P. 79, 26 december 1794, **Joseph Clark** [no residence given] to **Malichi Man** [no residence given], sixty five pounds, 394 acres, on Vernals Cr., begin at a hicory on the mountain, N 17 ch. to a post oak **Nicholas Holt's** cor., E 3 1/2 ch. to a white oak his cor., N 5 ch. to a red oak, S45E 7 ch. to a black jack John **Holt's** cor., N45E 60 ch. to a white oak his other cor., S 3 ch. to a black jack, E to **Elias Smith's** line, along line to his cor., W to beginning; signed: **John (X) Clark**; witness: **Obed Green, Nicholas (+) Holt**; proved May Term 1798 by **Green**.

P. 80, 6 April 1797, **Malachi Hatmaker** and wife **Mary** of Orange to **Jeremiah Holt** of same, ninety two pounds, 100 acres, on waters of Gun Cr., begin at a red oak, S 46 ch. 50 lk. to a stake on **Dixon's** line, E 21 ch. 50 lk. to a stake, N 46 ch. 50 lk. to a red oak, W to beginning, purchased from the **Trustees of the University of North Carolina** as confiscated property; signed: **Malicia (X) Hatmaker, Mary (+) Hatmaker**; witness: **Benja. Rainey, William Phillips**; proved May Term 1798 by **Phillips**, delvd. **Robt. Dixon**.

P. 82, 22 February 1794, **John Grant Rencher** of Orange to **James Vaughan** of same, one hundred thirty three pounds six shillings eight pence, 406 acres, begin at a black oak on **Samuel Shepperd's** line, S 256 perches to a black oak, W 250 perches to a hicory, N 256 p. to a black oak, E 250 p. to first station; signed: **Jno. G. Rencher**; wittness: **James Nelson, Arch Nelson**;; proved May Term 1798 by **Arch Nelson**, delvd. **Jas. Vaughan**.

P. 83, 1 May 1796, **Trustees of the University of North Carolina** to **Conrod Pile Junr.** of Orange, sixty pounds, 100 acres, on waters of Haw R., begin at a hicory **James Williams'** line, E crossing Gun Cr. 35 ch. to a stake, N 30 ch. to a black oak, W 35 ch. crossing creek to a black oak, S to beginning; signed: **W. Shepperd**, Attorney; witness: **Andrew Gibson, Robert Dixon**; proved May Term 1798 by **Dixon**, delvd. **Danl. Albright**.

P. 84, 8 May 1798, **Michael Charles** of Orange to **Samuel James** of same, fifty pounds, 123 acres, on W side of Haw R., begin at a white oak on bank of river, S14W 46 ch. to a black jack, S 10 ch. to a post oak, E 13 ch. to 3 white oaks on Dog Cr., down creek 17 ch. to a black oak, N 35 ch. to a hicory on Haw R., up meanders to beginning; signed: **Michael Charles**; witness: **William Ray, Martin Seley**[?]; proved May Term 1798 by **Ray**, delvd. **Saml. James**.

P. 85, [blank] [blank] 1796, **Moses Hutchins** of Orange to **William Herndon** of same, thirty two pounds, 80 acres, on waters of Newhope between First & Second Cr., part of a tract from **North Carolina** to **Hutchins**, begin at a pine **Page Patterson's** cor. on **Willm. Rhodes** line, E his line 162 p. to 3 pines his cor. on **William Pickett's** line, his line S 73 p. to a hicory & pine saplin, W 162 p. to a pine on **Page Patterson's** line, N his line 69 p. to beginning; signed: **Moses (+) Hutchins**; witness: **Edward Trice, Thos. Hutchins**; proved May Term 1798 by **Thomas Hutchins**, delvd. **Mr. Trice**.

P. 87, 10 August 1797, **North Carolina** to **James Freeland Junr.** [no residence given], fifty shillings per hundred acres, 80 acres, on waters of Boyds Cr. of Haw R., begin at a black oak a cor. of his own, S38E 38 1/2 ch. to a black oak, NE 44 ch. to a post oak, N10E 2 1/2 ch. to a post oak, W 55 ch. to beginning; signed: **Saml. Ashe**; witness: **J. Glasgow**; [no probate record], delvd. **Jno. Freeland**.

P. 88, 10 December 1797, **William Francis Strudwick** of Orange to **William Crutchfield** of same, two hundred pounds, 280 acres, on Meadow Cr., begin at a post oak on E side of creek, S7E crossing the University & Hillsborough Roads 75 ch. to a red oak on **Benard Lasley's** line. along line N73W 8 ch. 75 lk. to his cor. a spanish oak, S71W 38 ch. to a hicory, N crossing Hillsborough Road at 3 ch. continued in all 69 ch. to a spanish oak on bank of creek, up meanders to beginning; signed: **W. F. Strudwick**; witness: **Dd. Mebane, H. Shepperd**; acknowleddged May Term 1798, delvd. **Jno. Thompson**.

P. 89, 10 April 1797, **Samuel Daniel** of Orange to **John Daniel** of same, one hundred pounds, one Negroe man, named **Mingo**, about thirty eight years of age; signed: **Saml. Daniel**; witness: **Thomas Trice**; [notation following deed] forty pounds received 3 Sept. 1796, forty two pounds nineteen shillings paid **Sheriff Hall**, six pounds paid **James Coglin**, eleven pounds four pence given on note this day for ballance; proved May Term 1798 by **Trice**.

P. 90, 8 February 1787, **William Galbreath** of Orange, planter, to **Andrew Mitchell** of same, two hundred pounds, 150 acres, on S side of Haw R., adjoins **Daniel Hanley, James McAdams, William Rainey, & John Albright**, begin at a stake, S 35 ch. 75 lk. to a stake, W 41 ch. 75 lk. to a black oak near the Great Road leading to Hillsborough, N across the Great Road 35 ch. 75 lk. to a stake, E 41 ch. 75 lk. to first station; signed: **William Galbreaith, Catherine (X) Galbreaith**; witness: **James Freeland**; proved May Term 1798 by **Freeland**.

P. 91, 28 May 1798, **Andrew Murdock** Sheriff of Orange to **James Jackson** of same, eight pounds eight shillings, 94 acres, on S side of Foresters Cr., adjoins **James Jackson Junr., Jonathon Nichols Senr., & William Jackson Senr.**, begin at the SE cor. of **McCool's** tract at a black jack, N 5 ch. to a black jack, E 5 ch. to a post oak, N 34 ch. to a post oak, E 32 1/2 ch. to a post oak, S 11 ch. to a black jack, S 28 ch. to a stake, W 25 ch. to beginning, levy against **William Jackson Junr.** for six pounds five shillings five pence recovered by **William Cain & Company**; signed: **Andrew Murdock**; witness: **Saml. Hill, Wm. Nunn**; acknowledgedd May Term 1798, delvd. **James Jackson**.

P. 92, 17 July 1790, **Samuel Parkes** [no residence given] to **Rainey Phillips** [no residence given], eighty pounds, 100 acres, on N side of Haw R., part of a larger tract of 400 acres granted **Samuel Parkes** by deed dated 13 March 1780, begin at a red oak on Haw R., up river to a gum at mouth of a branch, N15W 12 ch. to a W. oak, N30E 5 ch. to a W. oak, N 5 ch. to a B. oak, E 12 ch. to a B. jack; signed: **Samuel Parkes**; witness: **Alexr. Parkes, Rachel Phillips**; proved May Term 1798 by **Alexander Parkes**, delvd. **An Phillips**.

P. 93, 4 March 1797, **Mary Parkes** of Orange to **Rainey Phillips** of same, forty pounds, 100 acres, on N side of Haw R., part of a larger tract of 400 acres granted to **Samuel Parkes** 13 March 1780, begin at a gum bush on bank of Haw R., N 42 ch. to a black jack, E 40 ch. to a black jack, S 10 ch. to a black oak, W on **Baldwin's** line to a white oak **Baldwin's** cor., S 38 ch. to a hicory on bank of river, up river to beginning; signed: **Mary (+) Parkes**; witness: **Henry Johnston, Nancy Parks**; proved May Term 1798 by **Johnston**, delvd. **Ann Phillips.**

P. 95, 18 November 1797, **Frederick Shofner** & **Michael Shofner** of Orange to **Michael Shofner Junr.** of same, two dollars, 1 acre, on branches of Stinking Quarter Cr., begin at a gum bush near a pond, S70E 8 ch. to a hicory, with **Michael Shofner's** line N45W 7 ch. to a stake, S45W 4 1/2 ch. to beginning; signed: **Frederick Shofner, Michaeel (X) Shofner**; witneess: **Michael Holt**, "something in dutch"; proved May Term 1798 by **Holt**, delvd. **Michael Holt Junr.**

P. 96, 24 May 1798, **John Umstead** of Orange to **Joseph Moore** of same, three hundred pounds, 400 acres, three tracts, on headwaters of Forresters Cr. & on the Hico Road leading to Hillsborough, begin at a white oak, W 55 ch. to a hicory, S 45 ch. to a white oak, E 55 ch. to a black jack, N 45 ch. to first station, 240 acres, another tract, adjoins first tract on Forresters Cr., begin at a spanish oak, 19 ch. to a black, W 28 ch. to a black oak, S 19 ch. to a post oak, E 28 ch. to first station, 50 acres, 2 tracts sold & disposed of by **Issac Gaddis** & wife **Hannah** to **Andrew Burke** Esq., third tract, on waters of Eno, begin at a post oak, W 25 ch. to a black oak, N 46 ch. to a black oak, E 25 ch. to a white oak, S 46 ch. to first station, bounded on S & W by **Robert Smith**, on E by **Gaddis** Old Place, 110 acres, **Jane Anderson** & son **James** to **Andrew Burke**; signed: **Jno. Umstead**; witness: **H. Shepperd**; acknowledged May Term 1798, delvd. **Joseph Moore.**

P. 97, 10 May 1798, **William Francis Strudwick** of Orange to **Thomas Thompson** of same, one hundreed pounds, 265 acres, adjoins **Barnard Lasley, Benjamin Dixon, John Thomspon, & Simon Thompson**, begin at a spanish oak a cor. of **Barnard Lasley**, his line S5W 33 ch. 25 lk. to a hicory, S25E 18 ch. 25 lk. to a black oak a cor. of **Lasley & Dixon**, along **Dixon's** line S74W 36 ch. to his cor. a black gum, S 13 ch. 75 lk. to a persimmon, along **John Thompson's** line, N84W 20 ch. to a black oak a cor. to **Thompson's** Old Tract, along a line of that tract N crossing the Hillsborough Road at 51 1/2 ch. continued in all 52 ch. 50 lk. to a stake, N71E crossing road 54 1/2 ch. to beginning; signed: **William F. Strudwick**; witness: **Dd. Mebane, H. Shepperd**; acknowledged May Term 1798, delvd. **Thos. Thompson.**

P. 98, 5 Eighth Month 1797, **William Clarke** & wife **Sarah** of Orange, farmer, to **Thomas Lindly** of Chatham, farmer, three hundred fifty pounds, 200 acres, joining on Eno R. & E side of Haw R., begin at a forked water white oak on bank of Eno R. on W side, W 27 ch. to a black oak saplin, S 15 ch. to 2 hicorys, W 32 1/4 ch. to a stake in **Armstrong's** line, S 23 1/2 ch. to a hicory in "bones" line, E 69 ch. to a red oak on bank of Eno R., up river to beginning, part of a tract bequeathed to **William Clark** by his father **William Clark** deceased; signed: **William Clarke, Sarah (+) Clarke**; witness: **Owen Lindly, Patrick McGuire**;

ORANGE COUNTY (NC) DEED BOOK 7

proved May Term 1798 by **Owen Lindly**, delvd. **Owen Lindley**.

P. 100, 27 January 1798, **Jacob Holt** of Orange to **William Dixon** of same, one hundred pounds, 200 acres, on waters of Little Allamance, begin at **Michael Holt's** cor., his line S45E 38 ch. to a red oak near the Allamance, S45W 70 ch. to a black jack, N 645 ch. to a stone, E 24 ch. to a black walnut, N 10 ch. to beginning; signedd:: **Jacob Holt**; witness: **Robert Dickson, Wm. Rainey, Benj. Rainey**; proved May Term 1798 by **Robert Dixon**, delvd. **Robert Dixon**.

[Page numbers 101 through 200 omitted. It appears no records are missing.]

P. 201, 27 January 1798, **Benjamin Rainey** of Orange to **Henry Strader** of same, fifty pounds, 100 acres, on waters of Traveses Cr., begin at a spanish oak, N 175 p. to a red oak, E 93 p. to a post oak, S 175 p., W to beginning; signed: **Benjn. Rainey**; witness: **Wm. Rainey, Anthony Cable**; proved May Term 1798 by **Cable**, delvd. **Abner James**.

P. 202, 26 May 1798, **John Shaddy [Senr.]**, planter, of Orange to **John Shaddy Junior** of same, one hundred fifty pounds, 100 acres, on North Fork of Stinking Quarter Cr., begin at a stump on bank of creek, S45E 29 ch. to a stone on **Frederick Kimbroe's** line, N45E with **Peter Poor's** line 62 1/2 ch. to a black oak, N45W 3 1/2 ch. to a white oak on the creek, up creek to beginning; signed: **John Shaddy Senr.**; witness: **Michael Holt, Joshua Holt**; proved May Term 1798 by **Michael Holt**, delvd. **Michl. Holt Junr.**

P. 203, 9 February 1798, **William Wolf** & wife **Ann** of Orange to **John Bullack** of same, eighty one pounds five shillings, 128 acrees, **North Carolina** to **John Rudolph** 17 November 1790, adjoins **David Coble** & **William Wood**, begin at a post oak on **David Coble's** line, E 33 1/2 ch. to a black oak, S 42 ch. to a post oak, W 28 ch. to a black oak **Graves'** line, N20W 41 1/2 ch. to first stattion; signed: **William Wolf, Ann (X) Wolf**; witness: **Benjamin Jackson**; proved May Term 1798 by **Jackson**, delvd. **Jno. Bullock**.

P. 205, 22 November 1797, **John Millikin** of Orange to **Robert Cates** of same, five pounds, 10 acres, begin at a black oak at **Jesse Cates'** cor. & **Robert Cates'** line, W 4 outs to a white oak on the branch, up branch 1 out to a hicory, E 4 outs to a post oak on **Jesse Cates'** line, N with line 1 out to beginning; signed: **John Millikin**; witness: **Charles Riley, Robert Cates Junr**; proved May Term 1798 by **Riley & Robert Cates**, delvd. **Robert Cates**.

P. 205, 12 January 1798, **James Vaughan** of Orange to **John Strayhorn** of same, one hundred pounds, 254 acres, begin at a pine **John Edwards'** cor., N 302 p. to a red oak & black jack, W with **Shepperd's** line 122 p. to a sweet gum standing on **Marcom Bairies** Branch, up branch to a poplar & white oak, S 154 p. to a stake on **Meacham's** line, E to first station; signed: **James vaughan**; witness: **Jas. Nelson, James Hart**; acknowledged May Term 1798, delvd. **Wm. Strayhorn**.

P. 207, 27 October 1795, **Adam Coble**, planter, of Orange to **John Hornaday** [no residence given], one hundred fifty pounds, 280 acres, adjoins **William**

Ward & **John Coble**, begin at a sweet gum, S 28 ch. to a black oak, E 14 ch. to a post oak, S 14 ch. to a post oak, W 47 ch. to a hicory, S 22 ch. to a white oak, E 8 ch. to a persimmon, S55W 15 ch. to a hicory on side of a branch, up meanders to a gum, N 30 ch. to a hicory, N13E 9 1/2 ch. to a black oak, N50E 9 ch. to a hicory, N 13 ch. to a black oak, N50E 16 ch. to a post oak, S85E 30 ch. to a post oak, E 18 ch. to a hicory, N20E 15 ch. to first station, **North Carolina** to **Adam Coble** in 1790; signed: **Adam Coble, Margaret (+) Coble**; witness: **Stephen Ward, Christopher Hornaday**; proved May Term 1798 by **Ward**, delvd. **Jno. Hornaday**.

P. 208, 27 October 1795, **Adam Coble**, planter, of Orange to **John Hornaday** [no residence given], one hundred fifty pounds, 107 acres, on **Henry McCulloh's** boundary, on S side of Haw R. & Cain Cr., begin at a hicory **Robert Stout's** cor., his line W 190 p. to a small white oak saplin, N 90 p. to a hicory saplin, E 190 p. to a white oak, S to beginning, **Henry McCulloh's** agent to **Adam Coble** 20 March 1750; signed: **Adam Coble, Margaret (X) Coble**; witness: **Stephen Ward, Christopher Hornaday**; proved May Term 1798 by **Ward**, delvd. **John Hornaday**.

P. 210, 25 August 1786, **North Carolina** to **William Shepperd** [no residence given], five hundred fifty pounds, 1 acre, Lot # 33 in Hillsborough, fronting Tryon Street 400 lk. in length & 250 lk. in breadth, sold as confiscated property of **Edmund Fanning**; signed: **Rd. Caswell**; witness: **J. Glasgow**; [no probate record], delvd. **Wm. Lytle**.

P. 211, 2 April 1798, **Peter Mallett** of New Hanover to **James Davis** of Orange, one hundredd fifty pounds, 200 acres, part of 5,000 acres purchased by **Mallett** from **Roger Moore** deceased in 1777 recorded in Register's Book of Orange County Book K2 page 87, begin at a hicory **Joseph Hamilton's** cor., N10W 44 ch. to a stake at **Strudwick's** Old Cor., N80E 45 1/2 ch. to a red oak bush, S10E 44 ch. to a stake on **Patten's** line in an Old Field, S80W 45 1/2 ch. to first station, surveyed 24 January 1798 by **John Ray**; signed: **Peter Mallett**; witness: **J. Estes, Thomas McCracken**; proved May Term 1798 by **John Estes**, delvd. **James Davis**.

P. 212, 31 May 1798, **William Partin** of Orange to **John McCauley** of same, fifty pounds, 50 acres, on waters of Borlands Cr., begin at a black jack **Matthew Cother's** cor., W 146 p. to a black jack, N 28 p. to a stake in **William Partin's** line, his line E 60 p. to a white oak his cor., N his line 47 p. to a stake, E 86 p. to a stake in **Mathew Cother's** line, his line S 75 p. to first station; signed: **William (X) Partin**; witness: **John Caldwell, William Peace**; acknowledged May Term 1798, delvd. **Jno. McCauley**.

P. 213, 31 May 1798, **John McCauley** of Orange to **John Caldwell** of same, thirty pounds, 1 acre, one half of Lot # 9 in the village adjoining the University, the lot formerly purchased by **John Carrington** from the **Trustees of the University**, on S side of Franklin Street adjoins a lot formerly purchased by **Alexr. Mebane** on W, adjoins other half of lot on E, begin at **Mebane's** lower cor. on Franklin Street, S with line of lot to SE cor. of **Mebane's** lot near to an Old Sand Pit, E with line of lot as far as will be sufficient to incude one half of the 2 acre lot to a stake, N along a line of chopped trees to a stake on Franklin Street so as to divide the 2 acre Lot # 9 equally in 2, W with Franklin Street to beginning; signed: **John McCauley**; witness: **T. H. Phillips, Robert Campbell**; acknowledged May Term 1798, delvd. **John Caldwell**.

P. 214, 15 March 1798, **John Jenkins & Ephriam Jenkins** of Orange to **John Jenkins** of same, sixty pounds, all title, claim, interest, or demand to estate of our late father **Samuel Jenkins** deceased real or personal; signed: **John (X) Jenkins, Ephriam (X) Jenkins**; witness: **Thomas Bunch**; proved May Term 1798 by **Bunch**.

P. 215, 30 November 1797, **James Carrington** of Orange to **John McCauley** of same, sixty pounds, 2 acres, lot in town adjoininf the buildings of the University, on S side of Franklin Street, Lot # 9, adjoins Lot # 11 on E & Lot # 6 on E, **Trustees of the University of North Carolina** to his father **John Carrington**, sold by **Sheriff** to satisfy an execution to **James Carrington**; signed: **Jas. Carrington**; witness: **John Faddis, Matthew McCauley, John Caldwell**; proved May Term 1798 by **Faddis**.

P. 216, 3 June 1793, **Tilman Dixon** of Caswell to **John Flintom [Flintham]** of Orange, one hundred pounds, 183 acres, on Eno R., begin at 3 red oaks a cor. of **Flintom**, N77E 192 p. to a maple on bank of Eno R., down river to a hicory on the bank, S77W 134 p. to a white oak in **Borland's** line, N13W 188 p. to first station; signed: **Tilmon Dixon**; witness: **Will. Lytle, Joseph Dixon, Spencer Vaughan**; proved May Term 1798 by **Lytle**.

P. 218, 27 May 1793, **Gilbert Strayhorn** of Orange to **David Strayhorn** of same, twenty pounds, 182 acres, on waters of Eno R., adjoins **John Connor & Thomas Crabtree**, begin at a post oak his own deeded cor., N 26 ch. to a spanish oak, W 70 ch. to a white oak, S 26 ch. to a black oak, E 70 ch. to first station; signed: **Gilbert (X) Strayhorn**; witness: **John Daniel**; acknowledged May Term 1798, delvd. **D. Strayhorn**.

P. 219, 18 March 1798, **James Heflin** of Oglethorpe County, Georgia, to **John Riley** of Orange, three hundred and twenty silver dollars, 320 acres, begin at a black oak on **John Holt Senr.** line, N 33 ch. to a black jack, 16W 25 ch. to a black jack, N 7 ch. to a black jack, W 75 1/2 ch. to a white oak, S 36 ch. to a pine on side of Holt's land, E 100 1/2 ch. to first station; signed: **James (X) Heflin**; witness: **John Holt, John Cabe**; proved May Term 1798 by **Cabe**, delvd. **Jno. Riley**.

P. 220, 13 Mayy 1798, **Thomas Horn Senr.** of Orange to **James Horn Junr.** of same, thirty pounds, 118 1/2 acres, begin at a white oak on side of a road **William Horn's** cor., S 7 3/4 ch. to a black oak, W 45 1/2 ch. to a black oak, N with **White's** line 44 1/2 ch. to a post oak on side of the road, along road to beginning; signed: **Thomas (+) Horn**; witness: **John Reding, Thos. Reding**; proved May Term 1798 by **John Reding**, delvd. **Wm. Horn**.

P. 221, 16 May 1798, **Robert T. Daniel** of Orange to **Christopher Daniel** of same, two hundred pounds, 250 acres, on waters of Newhope, begin at a pine

ORANGE COUNTY (NC) DEED BOOK 7

Charle Trice's cor. on **Green's** line, N his line 256 1/2 p. to a hicory, E 156 p. to a post oak, S with **Campbell's** line 256 1/2 p. to a small post oak, W 156 p. to first station; signed: **Robert T. Daniel**; witness: **John Daniel, Penny Daniel**; acknowledged May Term 1798, delvd. **Chris Daniel.**

P. 222, 18 September 1797, **Catherine McVinch** of Orange to **William Riley** of same, "a certain sum", 250 acres, on Dry Cr. waters of Eno R., part of a tract formerly surveyd for **John McVinch**, begin at a post oak, W 38 1/2 ch. to a black oak, N 65 ch. to a post oak, E 6 1/2 ch. to a spanish oak, N 10 ch. to a hicory, E 28 ch. to a black oak, S 75 ch. to first station; signed: **Catherine (X) McVinch**; witness: **Henry Bunch, Thomas Bunch**; proved May Term 1798 by **Thomas Bunch**, delvd. **Wm. Riley.**

P. 223, 16 March 1798, **Peter Hufman** of Orange to **Barnett Clap** of same, sixty pounds, 30 acres, on waters of Great Allamance, begin at a stake on bank of Allamance, S45W 15 1/2 ch. to a red oak **Barnet May's** cor., N45W 15 ch. to a white oak **May's** cor., N45E 10 1/2 ch. to a hicory, N45W 15 1/2 ch. to a white oak, N45E 2 ch. to a beach on bank of creek, down meanders to beginning; signed: **Peter Hufman**; witness: **Jacob Wilhoit, Ancil Melton**; proved May Term 1798 by **Wilhoit**, delivered **Tobias Smith.**

P. 224, 30 May 1798, **Thomas Horn Senr.** of Orange to **William Horn Junr.** of same, thirty pounds, 167 acres, bounded by **John Cabe** on E & N, **Joseph White** on W, **James Horn Junr.** on S, begin at a hicory, W 39 1/2 ch. to a post oak, S 16 ch. to a stake, W 13 1/2 ch. to a red oak, S 4 ch. to a post oak on side of road **James Horn's** cor. with road SE to a white oak **James Horn's** other cor., N 24 1/2 ch. to a hicory, E 7 1/2 ch. to a black oak, N 30 ch. to beginning; signed: **Thos. (+) Horn**; witness: **Thomas Reding, John Reding**; proved May Term 1798 by **John Reding**, delvd. **Wm. Horn.**

P. 225, 26 May 1798, **John McManamy** of Caswell to **John Cabe & William Cabe** of Orange, two hundred twenty nine pounds, 282 acres, on waters of Ellebeys Cr., begin at a pine a cor. of **Daniel Green**, S67E 262 p. to a stake cor. of **Daniel Chandler**, N his line 232 p. to 2 pines, N76W 56 p. to a pine, W 120 p. to a stake & hicory, N 20 p. to a white oak, N40W 28 p. to a red oak, W 80 p. to a post oak a cor. of **McDaniel**, S his line 166 p. to a hicory on **Daniel Greeen's** line, E his line 64 p. to a hicory, S 12 p. to first station; signed: **John McManamy**; witness: **John Faddis, Danl. Green**; proved May Term 1798 by **Faddis**, delvd. **Jno. Cabe.**

P. 227, 30 May 1798, **Thomas Reding** of Orange to **John Reding** of same, forty pounds, 81 acres, on S side of Eno R., bounded by **Abraham Whitacre** on S, **Jacob Allen** on E, Eno R. on N, begin on bank of Eno at a stake, E 190 p. to a stake on **John Reding's** line, N 34 p. to **Allen's** line, W along **Allen's** line 90 p. to a white oak, N 112 p. to a stake, W 8 p. to a stake on bank of Eno R., up river to first station; signed: **Thomas Reding**; witness: **Stephen Reding, James Horne**; proved May Term 1798 by **Horne**, delvd. **Jno. Reding.**

P. 228, 1 June 1798, **John Riley** of Orange to **John Redman Junr.** of same, fifty five pounds, 110 acres, begin at a hicory on **John Riley's** line, N 5 1/2 ch.

to a black jack, W 25 ch. to a black jack, N 7 ch. to a black jack, W 75 1/2 ch. to a white oak, S 12 1/2 ch. to a pine on **Riley's** line, E 100 1/2 ch. to first station; signed: **John Riley**; witness: **Jno. Cabe, John Reding**; proved May Term 1798 by **John Cabe**, delvd. **Jno. Redman.**

P. 229, 21 March 1798, **John Flintham** of Orange to **Thomas Scarlett** of same, sixty pounds, 240 acres, begin at a poplar on bank of Stones Cr., S 43 ch. to a post oak, E 48 ch. to a white oak, N 49 ch. to a post oak on **Alexander Borland's** cor. along **Borland's** line S77W 36 1/2 ch. to a hicory on bank of Stones Cr., up meanders to first station; signed: **John Flintham**; witness: **Alexander Borland, Wm. Cook;** proved May Term 1798 by **Borland.**

P. 230, 1 June 1798, **Thomas Reding** of Orange to **James Crabtree** of same, eighty pounds, 163 3/4 acres, on S side of Eno R., begin at a white oak on bank of Eno, S 39 1/2 ch. to a post oak, E 50 ch. to a black oak, N 26 ch. to a post oak on bank of river, up meanders to first station; signed: **Thomas Reding**; witness: **John Reding, James Horn**; proved May Term, 1798 by **John Reding**, delvd. **Jas. Crabtree.**

. 231, 9 January 1798, **Samuel Thompson** of Orange to **Alexander Borland** of same, eleven pounds four shillings, 32 acrees, on waters of Eno, begin at a white oak on a little branch & cor. of **William Crabtree & Betty Newcomb**, his line due S 4 ch. to a stake on **Alexr. Borland's** line, his line due E 32 1/2 ch. to his cor. white oak, his line due N 41 ch. to a red oak on **Newmon's** line, his line due W 3 1/2 ch. to a hicory cor. to **William Crabtree**, his line due S 32 ch. to his cor. spanish oak on the branch, up branch to beginning; Signed: **Samuel Thompson**; witness: **John Faddis**; proved May Term 1798 by **Faddis**, delvd. **Alex Borland.**

P. 233, 26 May 1798, **William Cabe** of Orange to **Alexander Borland** of same, ten pounds, 115 acres, on waters of Eno R., begin at a post oak on **Borland's** line, W 59 ch. to a hicory, N 19 1/2 ch. to a red oak, E 59 ch. to a red oak on **Cabe's** line, S with line to beginning, **North Carolina** to **William Cabe**; signed: **William Cabe**; witness: **John Flintham;** proved May Term 1798 by **Flintham**, delivered **Alex Borland.**

P. 234, 21 April 1798, **Abraham Nelson** of Orange to **Thomas Nelson** of same, three hundred pounds, 225 acres, on both sides of Stones Cr. waters of Eno, "whereon" I now live, adjoins **Alexr. Borland, James Strayhorn, William Nunn, Christian Peeler**, & a small entry of **Thomas Nelson**, part of a larger tract entered in **Earl Granville's** Office of 450 acres & surveyed for **Abraham Nelson**, the other part now occupied by **James Strayhorn**, [no metees and bounds description]; signed: **Abraham (+) Nelson**; witness: **John G. Rencher, Ann Rencher;** proved May Term 1798 by **John G. Rencher**, delvd. **Thos. Nelson.**

P. 235, 10 June 1786, **John Reeves** of Orange to **Joseph Townsand** of same, fifty pounds, [no acreage given], on Rocky Br. of Eno, on N side of Eno R., begin at a hicory on river, N 44 1/2 ch. to a red oak, W 22 1/2 ch. to a black jack, S 44 1/2 ch. to a post oak on river, down river to first station; signed: **John**

Reeves; witness: **Benjamin Newman**; proved August Term 1789 by **Newman**.

P. 237, **North Carolina** to **Barnet Troxler** [no residence given], ten pounds per huundred acres, 162 acres, begin at a hicory, N45E 20 ch. to a dogwood, N45W 45 ch. to a post oak, S45W 29 ch. to a stake, S40E 6 ch. to a spanish oak, S45W 20 ch. to a stake, S45E 30 ch. to a white oak, N45E 23 ch. to a black oak, N45W 11 ch. to first station; signed: **Saml. Johnston**; witness: **J. Glasgow**; [no probate record], delvd. **Barnet Troxler**.

P. 238, 12 July 1785, **George Doherty** & wife **Mary** of Orange to **Archibald Lytle** & **Jesse Benton** of same, five shillings, 1/2 of all lands which he shall be possessed of at the time of his death as well those lying on the Mississippi or within the bounds of North Carolina, also the following Negore slaves: **Harry, Polley, Princess, Naney, John,** & **Abraham** & their increase, also 1 tract on Hayes Cr. waters of Duck R. entered in the land office for 5,000 acres, **George Doherty** & wife **Mary** to enjoy full use of property during their lifetime, if **George Doherty** survives his wife he is to have full use & benefit of property with power to dispose of same as though these presents had never been made, if **Mary** survives **George** she is to have the same privileges; signed: **Archd. Lytle, Jesse Benton, Geo. Doherty, Polly B. Doherty**; witness: **A. Tatum, Wm. Lytle**; proved August Term 1798 by **Absalom Tatum** & **William Lytle**, delvd. **John Whitted, Jack** & **Morgan Hart's** note.

P. 241, 12 July 1785, **George Doherty** & wife **Mary** of Orange to **Archibald Lytle** & **Jesse Benton** of same, five shillings, [repeat of previous deed]; signed: **George Doherty, Polly B. Doherty, Archibald Lytle, Jesse Benton**; witness: **A. Tatom, Wm. Lytle**; proved August Term 1798 by **Absalom Tatum** & **William Lytle**, delvd. **Mr. Whitehead, Jack** & **Morgan Hart's** note.

P. 243, 9 June 1794, **North Carolina** to **James Murry** [no residence given], fifty shillings per hundred acres, 116 acres, on waters of Owens Cr., adjoins his own land, begin at a post oak, N 26 ch. to a post oak, W 48 ch. to a black oak, E[?] 42 ch. to a stake, S 2 ch. to a white oak, E 6 ch. to first station; signed: **Alex: Martin**; witness: **James Glasgow**; [no probate record].

P. 244, 9 November 1784, **North Carolina** to **James Murry** [no residence given], fifty shillings per hundred acres, 100 acres, on waters of Owens Cr. of Haw R., adjoins his own land, begin at a post oak on his own land, E 22 1/2 ch. to a black oak, N 45 ch. to a white oak, W 22 1/2 ch. to a maple, S 45 ch. to first station; signed: **Alex: Martin**; witness: **J. Glasgow**; [no probate record].

P. 245, 9 November 1784, **North Carolina** to **James Murry** [no residenc given], fifty shillings per hundred acres, 81 acres, on Owens Cr., adjoins his own land, **James Bird**, & **Levi Hall**, begin at a post oak, S 6 ch. to a black oak, E 12 ch. to a hicory, S 13 ch. to a black oak, E 39 ch. to a hicory, N 19 ch. to a stake on his own line, W 51 ch. to first station; signed: **Alex: Martin**; witness: **J. Glasgow**; [no probate record].

P. 246, 26 August 1798, **James Watson Junr.** of Orange to **William McQuiston** of Hillsborough, one thousand dollars, 2 acres, lot where **McQuiston** now lives,

Lot # 2 & # 44, bounded on N by **William Courtney's** Tavern Lot, on E by **William Courtney's** Still House Lot, on S by **Walter Alves** & the Public Brick Spring Lot, on W by the Public Lot where the Courthouse now stands; signed: **James Watson**; witness: **Andrew Watson, John Allison**; acknowledged August Term 1798, delvd. **Wm. McQuiston.**

P. 247, 23 September 1791, **John Carrington** of Orange to **William Brown** of Person, one hundred fifty dollars, [no acreage given], on waters of Camp Cr. a branch of Nap of Reeds, adjoins **Robert Graves** line & lines of Caswell & Granville & also **McCulloh's** line, begin at a black oak 5 ch. W of **Jones'** cor., E 64 ch. along Caswell County line to a post oak a cor. of Caswell County on Granville County line, along line S 47 ch. to a black oak,W 64 ch. to a stake, N 47 ch. to first station; signed: **John Carrington**; witness: **Nathl. Clark, Willm. Bagley, Jas. H. Carrington**; proved August Term 1798 by **James H. Carrington**, delivd. **Willis Roberts.**

P. 248, 10 June 1798, **James Dickey** of Orange to **William Dickey** of same, fifty pounds, 14 acres, on W on Deep Cr., adjoins **Pennery White**, begin at a hicory at the road a cor. of **White**, his old line W 5 ch. to a white oak his Old Cor., N 6 1/2 ch. to a black oak, W to Deep Cr., down meanders 6 ch. to a poplar, S13E 22 ch. to a post oak, N22E 17 to first station, **North Carolina** to **James Dickey** 16 July 1795; signed: **James Dickey**; witness: **Hardy Hurdle, Alexander Robbs**; proved August Term 1798 by **Hurdle**, delvd. **Wm. Dickey.**

P. 250, 14 September 1797, **Stephen Tatom** & **Mourning Tatom** of Orange to **George Casey [Cary]** of Granville, twenty pounds, 50 acres, on Camp Cr. waters of Nap of Reeds, part of tract where **Stephen Tatom** deceased formerly lived, begin at a white oak on bank of Camp Cr. **Jenkin's** cor., S 70 p. to a maple on the Lick Br., down branch to Camp Cr., up creek to first station; signed: **Stephen (X) Tatom, Mourning (+) Tatom**; witness: **Samuel Cary, John Wilburn**; proved August Term 1798 by **Wilburn**, delivered Jno. **Wilbourn.**

P. 251, 20 January 1798, **George Gray** of Orange to **John Campbell** of same, twenty nine pounds, 1 feather bed bedstead & furniture, 1 cupboard with drawers, 1 pine table, 6 chairs, 1 iron pot, 1 dutch oven, 1 scillet [skillet], 6 cups & saucers, 2 bowls, 1 mug, 1 teapot, 1 ax, 1 mattock, 1 hilling hoe, 1/2 my crop of wheat now growing where **Thomas Thomas** now lives, & 1 year old sow; signed: **George Gray**; witness: **Samuel (X) Whitsell, Freeman Wood, James Tate**; receipt of **George Gray** 6 April 1798 that he had borrowed from **Campbel** within feather bed & furniture, 1 cupboard with drawers, 1 pine table, 6 chairs, 1 iron pot, 1 dutch oven, skillett &tc. with promise to return when called for; proved August Term 1798 by **Wood**, delvsd. **John Campbell.**

P. 252, 11 December 1795, **Jonathon Clower** of Orange to **Richard Holeman** of same, thrity three pounds, 1 set of smiths tools & nailing tools, 2 cows & calves, 2 hoggs, 1 cutting hoe & plough, 3 beds & furniture, 1 dutch oven, 1 pot, 2 tables, 4 pales [pails], 1 churn, 1 salt keg, 6 plates, 1 bason, 1 dozen spoons, 1 shovel, 1 ax, 20lb. iron, 56lb. slit iron, 1 tea cannister, 1 pepper box, 2 flat irons, 1 table, 2 chairs, 1 bridle, 1 case of razors & box, 4 tins, 1 Bible, 1 hymn book, 2 eartern pots, 3 cowhides, 3 barrels, 2 bushels flax seed, 10 dozen oats, 1 bushel flax seed sowing; signed: **Jonathon Clower;** witness: **Saml. Turringtine, Robert Hall**; proved August Term 1798 by **Turringtine**, delvd. **Saml. Torringtine.**

P. 253, 31 July 1798, **David Lewis** of Orange to **Jacob Troxler** of same, security for payment of forty pounds eight shillings, Negro girl, named **Rose**; signed: **David (X) Lewis**; witness: **Barnaby (X) Troxler, William Ray**; proved August term 1798 by **Troxler**, delvd. **Barney Troxler.**

P. 254, 18 April 1794, **James Murray** of Orange to **Samuel Ector** of same, four pounds, 119 acres, on waters of Owens Cr., begin at a black oak in **Ector's** former line bounded for **Henry Murray**, W along line 52 ch. 50 lk. to a post oak, S17W 16 ch. to a maple, E 23 ch. to a white oak, S 37 ch. to a white oak **Ector's** former cor., NE along his former line to first station; signed: **James Murray**; witness: **Conally Walker**; acknowledged August Term 1798, delvd. **Saml. Ector.**

P. 255, 19 June 1798, **John Tate** of Orange to **Joseph McCulley** of same, three hundred seventy five dollars, 250 acres, on both sides of Watsons Cr. a branch of Stoney Cr., begin at a B. O. in the old line, E 37 1/2 ch. to a double post oak, N 8 1/2 ch. to a hicory & W. O., E 20 ch. to pointers, S 5 ch. 70 lk. to a red oak, E 30 1/2 ch. to a red oak, E conrtinued 16 ch. 75 lk. to a stake & pointers, N crossing creek 28 ch. 35 lk. to a Great Flat Rock in center of a small branch, W 16 ch. 75 lk. to a W. O., N 1 ch. 65 lk. to pointers, W 21 ch. 30 lk. to a red oak, S 1 ch. to a stake & pointers, W 13 ch. 8 lk. to a stake in the Peach orchard, S 18 1/2 ch. to a turkey oak, W 19 ch. 60 lk. to a red oak, N 18 1/2 ch. to a black jack, W 34 ch. to a P. O., S to first station; signed: **John Tate**; witness: **Rt. Mitchell, Jo. Hart**; proved August Term 1798 by **Joseph Hart**, delivered to **Philip Walker.**

P. 257, 27 October 1797, **Andrew McBroom** of Orange to **John Ellis** of same, twenty nine pounds, 50 acres, on waters of Eno, part of 301 acres granted to **Henry McCoy**, begin at a post oak, S 37 ch. to a pine, W 13 ch. 60 lk. to a white oak on Blown Fork Br., N 37 ch. to a hicory, E 13 ch. 60 lk. to beginning; signed: **Andrew McBroom**; witness: **David Allison, Jas. Clark**; acknowledged August Term 1798, delvd. **A. McBroom.**

P. 258, 30 May 1798, **Aaron Sharp Senr.** of Orange to **George Foust** of same, one hundred thirty pounds, 185 acres, on waters of Allamance, begin at a post oak, S45W 37 ch. to a stake, S45E 7 ch. 50 lk. to a stake, S 11 ch. to a black oak, E 44 ch. to a post oak, N10E 30 ch. 50 lk. to a post oak, N 24 ch. to a stake, S50W 20 ch. to a stump, N68W to beginning, **Henry E. McCulloh** to **Sharpe** in 1764; signed: **Aaron (+) Sharp**; witness: **William Ray, James Tinnin**; proved Auugust Term 1798 by **Tinnin**, delvd. **Geo. Foust.**

P. 259, 7 August 1797, **Rebecca Reed** of Caswell to **Vincent Roberts** of Orange, eight pounds, 100 acres, right, title, or claim to tract on head of Stonn Cr. of Hico, part of tract from **North Carolina** to **John Reed** deceased, willed to **Robert's** wife & **Rebecca Reed** by **John Reed**; signed: **Rebecca (R) Reed**; witness: **Absalom (A) Night, John Coble**; proved August Term 1798 by **Night**.

P. 260, 10 April 1798, **Joseph Sharp** of Hillsborough to **Abner B. Bruce** of Orange, thirty six pounds, 1 acre, Lot # 128 in Hillsborough, bounded by King Street on N, Margaret Lane on S, adjoins **Abner Bruce** on W, begin at a cor. of **William Cumming's** lot, S 400 lk., W 250 lk., N 400 lk., E along street to beginning; signed: **Joseph Sharpe**; witness: **John McKerrall, Joshua Wittle**; proved August Term 1798 by **McKerrall**, delvd. **A. B. Bruce**.

P. 261, **Jacob Nugent** of Orange to **George Foust**, fifty two pounds twelve shillings, bill of sale, [clerk noted "Errore"], [see page 290].

P. 262, 29 August 1798, **William Courtney** of Hillsborough in behalf of **William Courtney Junr.** deceased as administrator to **Henry Hesse** of same, **Henry Hesse** purchased 140 acres from **William Courtney Junr.** for seventy one pounds, this was land purchased by **William Courtney Junr** at a Sheriff's Sale from the **Sheriff** acting for **William Courtney (Bricklayer)**, this document acknowledges that **Hesse** has paid the seventy one pounds in full; signed: **William Courtney**, Administrator; witness: **Will. Lytle, Jo. Courtney**; acknowledged August Term 1798, delvd. **H. Hesse**.

P. 263, 18 April 1798, **Henry Shepperd** of Orange Commissioner appointed by the General Assembly to sell a lot in Hillsborough known as the Blue House to **Catlett Campbell**, merchant, of Hillsborough, six hundred fifty pounds, part of Lot # 25 in Hillsborough, a cor. lot of King Street & Churton St., on N side of King Street, bounded on W by **Dr. O'Ferrill's** lot & on N by **Absalom Tatum**, sold under an act of the General SAssembly to sell the Blue House & Church dated 2 November 1797, sold 16 April 1798; signed: **H. Shepperd**, Com.; witness: **James Yarbrough, John McKarrall, James Palmer**; proved August Term 1798 by **McKerrall**, delvd. **Catlett Campbell**, sent Mr. Campbell by **John Evans**.

P. 265, 28 July 1798, **Thomas Armstrong** of Orange to **John Reeves** of same, two hundred pounds, 1,000 acres, one undivided half of tract in two parts to be divided, in Davidson County, Tennessee, on S side of Cumberland R. below a place known as **Dyer's** Camp, begin at **Capt. Hickman's** NE cor. at a cherry tree, poplar, & sassafras, W with **Hickman's** line crossing Hickmans Cr. 300 p. to a red oak & dogwood, N 500 p. to a walnut, E 320 p. to a stake, S 500 p. to beginning; signed: **Thomas Armstrong**; witness: **Wm. Norwood, Will. Lytle, Enoch Collins**; proved 8 October 1798 before **David Stone** Judge of Superior Court of Law & Equity; affidavit of **Samuel Ashe**, Gov., that **David Stone** is a Superior Court Judge 10 October 1798, delvd. **Jno. Reeves**.

P. 267, 28 July 1798, **James Armstrong** of Orange to **John Reeves** of same, two hundred pounds, 1,000 acres, the remaining half of land described in preceding deed; signed: **James Armstrong**; witness: **Will, Lytle, Wm. Norwood, Enoch Collins**; proved 8 October 1798 before **Judge David Stone**, delivd. **Jno. Reeves**.

P. 269, 15 September 1797, **Alexander Gwinn** [no residence given] to **James Wilson** [no residence given], fifty five pounds, 100 acres, on W side of Haw R., part of a larger tract of 550 acres granted to **John Pitman** 15 March 1756,

Pitman to **Mordical Gwin**, willed by **Mordical Gwinn** to **Alexander Gwin** & **James Gwin**, begin at a black oak on Haw R., W to a post oak, S to a white oak, E to a hicory on the river, up river to first station; signed: **Alexander Gwin**; witness: **Charles (+) Wood Junr., James McClary**; proved by **Charles Wood** [term of court not given], delivd. **James Wilson**.

P. 270, 8 May 1794, **Joel Moody** of Chatham to **George Brown** of "County Aforesaid", fifty pounds, 100 acres, on waters of Morgans Cr., bounded on N by **John Morgan**, on S by Chatham Couunty Line, begin at a spanish oak on the Crosscreek Road, N with road 8 ch. to a stake, E 30 ch. to **Morgan's** cor. hicory, continued E 95 ch. to a red oak, S 8 ch. to a stake on County Line, W with line 125 ch. to beginning; signed: **Joel Moody**; witness: **Collam Parish, W. Regans**; proved August Term 1798 by **Parrish**.

P. 271, 11 August 1798, **John Hastings** of Orange to **Matthias Willson** of same, eighty two dollars, 82 acres, on both sides of Little Back Cr., adjoins **William & John Bailey**, begin at a black oak **Bailey's** cor., N80W 2 ch. to a persimmon on the branch, down branch to a hicory, S27E 5 1/4 ch. to a black oak, S65E 18 1/2 ch. to a post oak on his own land, N10E 30 ch. to **Mulhollan's** cor., continuing in all 35 ch. to **Bailey's** cor., his line to first station; signed: **John (IH) Hastings**; witness: **D. Mebane, Jas. Mebane**; acknowledged August Term 1798, delivd. **Mathis Wilson**.

P. 273, 26 December 1797, **James Patterson** of Orange to **Francis Hatmaker** of same, one hundred seventy dollars, 252 acres, on waters of Stinking Quarter Cr., begin at a stake, E 60 ch. to a hicory, N 41 3/4 ch. to a white oak, W 55 ch. to a stake, S45E 10 ch. to a B. J., S45W 16 ch. to a stake, S to beginning, part of 440 acres from **North Carolina** to **James Patterson** 30 June 1797; signed: **James Patterson**; witness: , **James Freeland**; acknowledged August term 1798, delivd. **Aaron Sharp**.

P. 274, 25 August 1798, **Richard Bennehan** Esq. of Orange to **James Baxter**, planter, & wife **Rosannah** of same, five shillings, 225 acres, begin at a forked pine on **George Guess'** conditional line, with same S37E 18 ch. to a black jack in **Collins'** line, N50E 46 ch. 50 lk. to a post oak, N 22 ch. 50 lk. to a stake, W 25 ch. 50 lk. to a stake, N 20 ch. to a pine, W 21 ch. 50 lk. to a stake, S 53 ch. to beginning, part of a tract from **North Carolina** to **Rosannah** 10 July 1788, **James & Rosannah** to **Richard Bennehan** 24 August 1798, to hold lands during their natural life & life of survivor fdor all tenantly uses, wilful waste excepted, paying annually one peppercorn if demanded, if property is wasted bennehan can reclaim land, **James Baxter** to pay all taxes; signed: **Richard Bennehan**; witness: **Wm. Bennehan, John Green**; acknowledged before **Judge David Stone** 25 August 1798, delivd. **Richd. Bennehan**.

P. 276, 24 August 1798, **James Baxter**, planter, & wife **Rosannah** of Orange to **Richard Bennehan** Esq. of same, fifty six pounds fve shillings, 225 acres, begin at a forked pine on **George Gesses** conditional line, with same S37E 18 ch. to a black jack in **Collins** line, N50E 46 ch. 50 lk. to a post oak, N 22 ch. 50 lk. to a stake, W 25 ch. 50 lk. to a stake, N 20 ch. to a pine, W 21 ch. 50 lk. to a stake, S 53 ch. to beginning, part of a tract from **North Carolina** to **Rosanna Baxter**

10 July 1788; signed: **James (X) Baxter, Rosannah (O) Baxter**; witness: **Wm. Bennehan, John Green**; acknowledged before **Judge David Stone** & proved by **John Green** 25 August 1798, delivd. **Richd. Bennehan**.

P. 278, 27 Second Month 1798, **Peter Stout** of Orange to **John Morrow** of same, ten pounds, 50 acres, on waters of Fousts Cr., adjoins his own land, **North Carolina** to **Peter Stout** 18 Fifth Month 1789, begin at a cor. of the Old Deeded Land, N 20 ch. to a post oak, W 10 ch. to a hicory, S 32 ch. to a black jack, E 25 ch. to a post oak, N 12 ch. to a stake, W 15 ch. to first station; signed: **Peter (X) Stout**; witness: **Andrew Morrow, Daniel Foust**; proved by **Morrow** [term of court not given], delivd. **Richd. Thompson**.

P. 279, 30 June 1798, **Capt. John Moore** of Orange to **Thomas Robinson** of same, two hundred pounds, 121 1/2 acres, on N side of Haw R., part of 190 acres from **Granville** to **George Smith** 6 December 1761, begin at a spanish oak on bank of Haw R., E 37 ch. 75 lk. to a post oak a cor. to **Oldfield John Moore**, his line S11W 26 1/2 ch. to a poplar in fork of a branch, down branch SW 35 ch. to an ash at mouth of branch on bank of Haw R., up river to beginning; signed: **John Moore**; witness: **Nathaniel Robertson, John Moore**; proved August Term 1798 by **John Moore**, delivd. **Thos. Robinson**.

P. 281, 13 June 1798, **North Carolina** to **Thomas Mulhollan** [no residence given], fifty shillings per hundred acres, 300 acres, on waters of Little R., adjoins **William McKee**, begin at a hicory a cor. of the tract formerly **Ellimon's** now **Person's**, with a line of tract N 40 ch. to a white oak a cor. to tract the same course continued in all 81 ch. 25 lk. to a B. jack on **McKee's** line, E 37 ch. to a hicory bush, S 81 ch. 25 lk. to a stake a cor. of **Person's** 200 acre tract, W 37 ch. to beginning, warrant dated 1 July 1781; signed: **Saml. Ashe**; witness: **J. Glasgow**; [no probate record], delivd. **Thos. Person**.

P. 282, 13 June 1798, **North Carolina** to **Thomas Person** [no residence given], ten pounds per hundred acres, 300 acres, of falls & islands between banks of Haw R., begin at a stake on N bank of Haw R. & confluence of Cain Cr. with river, up N bank a northwestwardly course 900 ch. to a stake on the lower side at the mouth of Marrowbone R. or Black Cr., W crossing river 3 ch. 50 lk. to a stake on S bank in **Phillips'** land, down S bank 920 ch. to a stake in **Shy's** land & opposite mouth of Cain Cr., crossing river to beginning, warrant dated 20 October 1789; signed: **Saml. Ashe**; witness: **J. Glasgow**; [no probate record], delivd. **Thos. Person**.

P. 283, 13 June 1798, **North Carolina** to **Thomas Mulhollan** [no residence given], ten pounds per hundred acres, 200 acres, on waters of Little R., adjoins **Thomas Boyle**, begin at a black oak a cor. of **Person's** new granted land, S 19 ch. to a black oak on **Boyle's** line, on line E 13 ch. 50 lk. to his cor. a pine, S 28 ch. to a black oak **James Muurdock's** cor., his line E crossing the Hillsborough Road in all 21 ch. to a post oak, N 65 ch. 50 lk. to a stake near the road, E with **Guinn's** line 17 ch. 50 lk. to a spanish oak his cor. N 11 ch. 50 lk. to a stake on line of **Person's** 300 acre tract, with line S 30 ch. to his cor. a stake, W 14 ch. to beginning, warrant dated 17 March 1783; signed: **Saml. Ashe**; witness: **J. Glasgow**; [no probate record], delivd. **Thos. Person**.

ORANGE COUNTY (NC) DEED BOOK 7

P. 284, 10 June 1798, **William McQuiston** of Hillsborough to **James Watson Junr.** of same, two hundred dollars, 100 acres, joins **James Watson's** land where he lives, begin at a large white oak at **James Hogg's** cor. on **Watson's** line, S 46 ch. to a black oak saplin at cor. of Old Field, W 31 3/4 ch. to a black oak, N 66 ch. to a spanish oak on **Hogg's** line, E 21 3/4 to first station, **James** agrees **William** shall have liberty to cut timber on Lots # 2 & 44 in Town but if **James** has a clearing **William** is obliged to take from there if **James** feels proper; signed: **William McQuiston**; witness: **Willm. Riley, John Allison**; acknowledged August Term 1798.

P. 285, 26 Second Month 1798, **Peter Stout** of Orange to **John Morrow** of same, forty pounds, 200 acres, on waters of Fourth Cr., **Thomas Mulhollan** to **William Adams, Adams** to **Peter Stout,** begin at a white oak, S 60 ch. to a post oak, W 33 ch. to a black oak, N 60 ch. to a stake, E 33 ch. to first station; signed: **Peter (X) Stout**; witness: **Andrew Morrow, Daniel Foust**; proved by **Andrew Morrow** [term of court not given], delivd. **Richd. Thompson**.

P. 286, 20 June 1798, **John Bullock** of Orange to **Henry Cimb [Kimb]** of same, fifteen pounds, 30 acres, begin at a post oak on **David Coble's** line, S58W 60 ch. to a black jack, N70E 70 ch. to a white oak, to first station; signed: **John Bullock**; witness: **Boston (X) Graves, Thomas Whitted**; acknowledged August Term 1798, delivd. **Jno. Bullock**.

P. 287, 10 October 1787, **Joseph Allison** of Orange to **Thomas Person** of Granville, twenty pounds, 20 acres, on branches of Little R., begin at 2 black oaks **Cheek's** NW cor. tree, by a line agreed upon by **Allison & Person** 1786 & run by **Thomas Mulhollan** N 178 p. to a white oak & black oak near **Allison's** fence, W [blank] p. to a stake, S 178 p. to a white oak, E to first station, includes all land if any on W side of the first line originally granted to **David Mitchell, Mitchell** to **John Allison, John Allison** to **Joseph Allison**; signed: **Joseph Allison**; witness: **Thomas Mulhollan, Henry Mason**; proved before **Judge David Stone** by **Henry Mason** 18 October 1798, delivd. **Thos. Person**.

P. 289, 30 June 1798, **James Millikin** of Orange to **Nathaniel Robinson** of same, one hundred pounds, 100 acres, begin at a gum a cor. of **John Moore's** Old Field, W 25 ch. 50 lk. to a gum between the Race Paths a cor. of **Thomas Robinson**, his line N6 1/2E 48 ch. to a post oak, E 19 ch. to a black oak, S 48 ch. to beginning, part of 200 from **North Carolina** to **John Jenkins** 21 September 1785 No. 820, 100 acres from **Jenkins** to **James Millikin** 6 November 1789; signed: **James Millikin**; witness: **Thomas Robinson, John Moore**; proved August Term 1798 by **Thomas Robinson**, delivd. **Mark Derham**.

P. 290, 23 May 1798, **Jacob Nugent** of Orange to **George Foust** of same, fifty two pounds, 2 bay mares, 1 five year old branded "H" on the near shoulder 1 flesh mark on the hinder part of her off thigh, 2 yearling colts, 1 bay horse with a star on his face with black mane & tail, the other is a black with a star & a snip, & 2 white feet; signed: **Jacob Nugent**; witness: **William Woolfe, Peter Foust**; proved August Term 1798, delivd. **Geo. Foust**.

P. 291, 6 June 1798, **Hardy Hurdle** of Orange to **William Wallis** of same, fifty pounds, 46 acres, on Deep & Stoney Cr., begin at a hicory near Stoney Cr., formerly **William Stalcup's** line, N along line 3 ch. to a post oak, S bounded by a line formerly **James Gamblin's** now **William Wallis** to a black oak near his spring, along line to a persimmon & poplar stump, S31W 7 1/2 ch. to a stake, S20E to Deep Cr., down creek to Stoney Cr., up Stoney Cr. to first station, part of a tract to **Hardy Hurdle** from **Joseph Hodge** late Sheriff as property of **Stephen Conger**; signed: **Hardy Hurdle**; witness: **Sten. Conger, Alexander (R) Robbs**; acknowledged August Term 1798, delivd. **Hardy Hurdle**.

P. 292, 18 February 1793, **Luke Pendergrass** of Caswell to **Isham Jordan** of Isle of Wight County, Virginia, ninety [blank], 200 acres, at Rock Land, on headwaters of Quaker Cr. of Back Cr., joins line of **William Barnhill** on E, begin at a stake, E 48 ch. to a black jack, S 42 ch. to a black jack, W 48 ch. to a black oak, W 42 ch. to beginning, **North Carolina** to **Isham Jordan** 16 February 1793; signed: **Luke Pendergrass**; witness: **William Pleasant, Sampson Barlon**; proved by **Pleasant** [no term of court given], delivd **Luke Pendergrass**.

P. 293, 8 June 1798, **Hardy Hurdle** of Orange to **Robert Marley** of Guilford, fifty pounds, 4 acres, on Deep Cr., begin at 2 post oaks **William Wallace's** cor. formerly **Adam Marley's** line, N30W crossing Deep Cr. 9 1/2 ch. to a persimmon & poplar stump **William Wallace's** cor., S31W 7 1/2 ch. to a stake near the Saw Mill **Wallace's** cor., S20E to Deep Cr., N80E to beginning, includes the Saw Mill, part of a tract from **Joseph Hodge** late Sheriff to **Hurdle** sold as property of **Stephen Conger**; signed: **Hardy Hurdle**; witness: **Reaben Holt, Martin Hurdle**; acknowledged August Term 1798, delivd. **Hardy Hurdle**.

P. 295, 19 February 1798, **Augustine Willis** of Orange to **Richard Cochran** of same, two hundred sixty two dollars fifty cents, 248 1/2 acres, begin at a post oak **Frederic Kimro's** cor., N70E 21 ch. to a post oak, E 11 ch. to a white oak, S 22 ch. to a stake, N45E 42 ch. to a post oak, N45W 55 ch. to a hicory, S45W 55 ch. to a hicory **Hilton's** cor., S45E 22 ch. to first station; signed: **Augustine Willis**; witness: **Plummer Willis, John Willis**; [notation] A. the post oak at the Beginning, AB - N70E 21 to Post Oak, BC - East 11 to white oak, CD - South 22 to stake, DE - N45E 42 to postoak, EF - N45W 55 to hicory, FG - S45W 55 to hicory Hilton's cor., GA S45E 22 to beginning, 19 Feby. 1798; acknowledged 11 October 1798 before **Judge David Stone**, delivd. **Austin Willis**.

P. 296, 8 June 1798, **Martin Hurdle** of Orange to **Robert Marley** of Guilford, five pounds, 5 acres, on Deep Cr., begin at a hicory a cor. of **Martin Hurdle** on a line formerly **Adam Marley**, S80W to Deep Cr., S48E 8 1/4 ch. to a persimmon in a branch, up branch to a maple in branch, N19W 12 ch. to beginning, includes house **Stephen Conger** formerly lived in; signed: **Martin Hurdle**; witness: **Reuben Holt, Hardy Hurdle**; proved by **Hardy Hurdle** [no term of court given], delivd. **Hardy Hurdle**

P. 297, 20 June 1798, **Benjamin Rainey** of Orange to **James Wilson** of same, twenty five pounds, 55 acres, begin at a stone a cor. of **Michael Charles** land, E 21 ch. to a black jack, N 22 ch. to a stake, W 30 1/2 ch. to a hicory, S 12 1/2 ch. to a red oak, S45E 7 1/2 ch. to beginning; signed: **Benjamin Rainey**; witness: **Shadrack (X) Holt, Charles (X) Wood**; proved August Term 1798, delivd.

Jas. Wilson.

P. 298, 25 June 1798, **James Murray** of Orange to **Thomas Williams** of same, fifty pounds, 163 acres, begin at a W. O., S with **Saml. Ector's** line 37 1/2 to a small hicory, [blank] ch. to a B. O., W with **Brown's** line 26 ch. to a P. O., N his line 18 ch. to a P. O., W his line 20 1/4 ch. to a B. J., N with **Walker's** line & **Joseph Cantrell's** line 25 ch. 60 lk. to a P. O., E 26 ch. 20 lk. to a double B. J., S 6 ch. 60 lk. to a maple, E with **Saml. Ector's** line 23 ch. to beginning, **North Carolina** to **James Murray**; signed: **James Murray**; witness: **John Brown Senr. John Brown Junr.**; acknowledged August Term 1798, delivd. **Thos. Williams.**

P. 300, 28 May 1798, **Jarral Burrow** of Guilford to **William Burrow** of Orange, twenty five pounds, 43 1/2 acres, on Spoons Cr., part of a tract from **Thomas Mulhollen** to **Jarral Burrow** for 90 acres 23 November 1795 recorded in Book G folio 374, begin at a post oak, N67E 58 p. to a P. O., S 140 p. to a persimmon in the Old Field, W 54 p. to a stump in a pond, N 118 p. on County Line to beginning; signed: **Jarrel Burrow**; witness: **J. S. Patterson, Michl. Holt**; proved August Term 1798 by **Michael Holt**, delivd. **John Long.**

P. 301, 1 April 1797, **Margaret Denning** of Orange to **Colstin Lovel** of same, ninety pounds, 99 acres, on Whittel a branch of Stoney Cr., begin at a stake, W 44 ch. to a post oak, N 23 ch. to a black oak, E 34 ch. to a post oak on Denning's line, S 2 ch. to a red oak, E 10 ch. to a black oak, S 21 ch. to first station; signed: **Margaret (+) Denning**; witness: **John Denning, James Boyle**; proved August Term 1798 by **John Denning**, delivd. **Jo. Barber.**

P. 302, 18 April 1798, **John Gordon, William Gordon, & James Gordon** of the Hawfields, Orange County, to **William Wilson** of same, two hundred twenty pounds, one Negro woman named **Let**, one Negroe boy named **Key** five years old, one Negro girl named **Hannah** two years old; signed: **John Gordon, William Gordon, Jas. Gordon**; witness: **Edward Wilson, Thomas Bradford**; proved August Term 1798 by **Edward Wilson**, delivd. **Willm. Wilson.**

P. 303, 20 November 1797, **James Watson Jnr.** of Orange to **David Parker** of same, one hundred twenty five pounds, 320 acres, on S side of Flat R., begin at a turkey oak on bank of Flat R., S 80 ch. to a post oak, W 40 ch. to a white oak, N 80 ch. to a small black jack oak, E 40 ch. to first station, adjoins **Walter Alves, James Cozart** & others; signed: **Jas. Watson**; witness: **Andrew Watson, James Thompson**; acknowledged August Term 1798, delivd. **David Parker.**

P. 305, [blank] [blank] 1797, **Thomas Cate** of Orange to **George Smith** of same, fifty pounds, 100 acres, on waters of Collins Cr., begin at a post oak on **Loyd's** line on bank of Collins Cr., E with **Loyd's** line 13 ch. to a post oak, N 19 ch. to a post oak, E 10 ch. to a post oak, N 24 ch. to a hicory, S82W 16 ch. to a red oak on Crows Road, S26W 6 ch. to a white oak on Collins Cr., W 23 ch. to a red oak, S 9 ch. to a red oak, E 21 ch. to a red oak, S 7 ch. to a red oak, E 6 ch. to a post oak on bank of Collins Cr., down creek 23 ch. to first station; signed: **Thomas Cate**; witness: **Green Bowen, John Cate**; proved August Term 1798 by **Bowen**, delivd. **Geo. Smith.**

P. 306, 30 June 1798, **Captain John Moore** of Orange to **John Moore Old**

Field of same, two hundred fifty pounds, 129 1/2 acres, on N side of Haw R., begin in center between a walnut, hicory, & spanish oak on the bank of Haw R. at mouth of a branch, E 10 ch. 50 lk. to a black oak & cor. of **James Moore**, N 18 ch. 50 lk. to a hicory on a branch, up meanders northeastward 21 1/2 ch. to a post oak on a path, along same N27W 5 ch. to a black jack, N45W 20 ch. to a hicory on the Old Line, N 22 ch. to a black oak on **Millican's** line, with line W 7 ch. 75 lk. to a post oak, a cor. to **Thomas Robinson,** his line S11W 26 1/2 ch. to a poplar at confluence of 2 branches, down branch a southwestwardly course 35 ch. to an ash at mouth of branch on bank of Haw R., down river to first station, part of 2 tracts, 1 of which was 190 acres **Granville** to **George Smith** 6 December 1761, the other for 300 acres **North Carolina** to **John Moore & David McSwaine** 10 July 1788 No. 909; signed: **John Moore**; witness: **Nathaniel Robinson, Thomas Robertson**; proved by **Thomas Robinson** [no term of court given], delivd. **Jno. Moore.**

P. 308, 27 October 1795, **Martha Strudwick,** Executrix to **Samuel Strudwick,** & **William F. Strudwick** both of Orange to **John Nelson**, of same, sixty pounds, 66 acres, begin at a poplar **James Mebane's** cor., N56E 10 ch. to a stake on a branch on **Widow Holloway's** line, her line S10E 47 ch. to a P. O. **Pollock's** cor., S5W 17 ch. to a hicory a cor. of **James Mebane**, his line S60W 7 ch. to a spanish oak, N10W 62 ch. to beginning; signed: **Martha Strudwick, W. F. Strudwick**; witness: **James Tate, Eli Collins**; proved August Term 1798 by **Tate,** delivd. **Jno. Nelson.**

P. 309, 10 June 1798, **James Dickie** of Orange to **William Dickie** of same, one hundred fifty pounds, 142 acres, on both sides Deep Cr., adjoins **James Dickie** on E, **Thomas Finley** on W, begin at a stake, W 18 ch. to a post oak, N50W 16 ch. to a white oak, N40W 20 ch. to a black oak, N35E 17 ch. to a post oak, N52E 16 ch. to a black jack on side of a road, down road to a black oak, S 30 ch. to first station, **North Carolina** to **Josiah Thedford** 1784; signed: **James Dickie**; witness: **Hardy Hurdle, Alexr. (A) Robbs**; proved August Term 1798 by **Hurdle**, delivd. **Wm. Dickey.**

P. 311, 4 August 1790, **William Clendinnen,** planter, of Orange to **Joseph Clendinnen** of same, one hundred pounds, 200 acres, part of 100,000 acres granted **Henry McCulloh** 3 March 1745 known as Tract #11, begin at a red oak on Vernals Cr., N45W 160 p. to a white oak grub, S45W 200 p. to a stake, S45E 160 p. to a stake, N45E 200 p. to beginning, **William Numah** to **William Clendinnen** 30 May 1765 registered in Book I page 467 by **William Churton**; signed: **William Clendinnen**; witness: **Jeremiah McCracken, James Clendinnen**; proved August Term 1798 by **James Clendinnen**, delivd. **Jacob Rich.**

P. 313, 15 Ninth Month commonly called September 1791, **Daniel Freeman** of Orange to **Lewis Hornaday** of same, thirty two pounds, 80 acres, on waters of Wells Cr., **North Carolina** to **Daniel Freeman** 18 fifth month 1791, adjoins land late property of **Henry E. McCulloh,** begin at a hicory on line of **H. E. McCulloh** & cor. of **James Staneman**, S70E 28 ch. to a black jack, N 11 1/2 ch. to a post oak **Dale's** cor., E 7 ch. to a post oak, N 23 1/2 ch. to a hicory, S22W 29 ch. to first station; signed: **Daniel Freeman**; witness: **John Long, John Allen**; proved

ORANGE COUNTY (NC) DEED BOOK 7

August Term 1798 by **Long.**

P. 314, 16 April 1796, **Trustees of the University of North Carolina** to **Jeremiah Holt** of Orange, twenty three pounds twelve shillings six pence, 105 acres, on waters of Gun Cr., begin at a stake, W 23 ch. to a stake, N 50 ch. to a red oak, S75E 15 ch. to a gum, N64E 21 ch. to a red oak, S 35 ch. to beginning; signed: **William Shepperd**, Attorney; witness: **M. Holt Junr., Obed Green**; proved August Term 1798 by **Michael Holt Junr.**

P. 316, 13 September 1798, **North Carolina** to **John Tate** [no residence given], thirty shillings per hundred acres, 60 acres, on waters of Watsons Cr., adjoins **James Moore, John Moore, & Robert Tate**, begin at a white oak & post oak a cor. of **Thomas Moore**, with **John Moore's** line S 11 ch. to a white oak, N88W 53 ch. 50 lk. to a red oak a cor. of **Thomas Bradford**, his line N 12 ch. 50 lk. to a stake, E 20 ch. to a stake on **Moore's** line, along line S 3 ch. to his cor. a post oak, E 33 ch. 50 lk. to beginning, warrant datedd 10 March 1794; signed: **Saml. Ashe**; witness: **Wm. Hill**; [no probate record], delivd. **Thos. Bowls.**

P. 317, 17 April 1797, **North Carolina** to **Robert Cates** [no residence given], fifty shillings per hundred acres, 150 acres, on waters of Eno, begin at a red oak **James Fulton's**, S with **Latty's [Latta?]** line 152 p. to a white oak **John Daniel's** cor., his line W 158 p. to a black jack on **Daniel's** line, N 152 p. to a hicory on **Fulton's** line, his line E 158 p. to beginning; signed: **Saml. Ashe**; witness: **J. Glasgow**; [no probate record], delivd. **Jno. Cole.**

P. 318, 15 January 1798, **North Carolina** to **William Dunnagan Junr.** [no residence given], ten pounds per hundred acres, 18 1/2 acres, on waters of Little R., adjoins **William Dunnagan, Willm. Cain, & Geo. Carrington**, begin at a black jack & dogwood, N 14 1/2 ch. to a stake, W 12 ch. to a hicory, S 15 1/2 ch. to a stake, E 12 ch. to beginning, warrant dated 17 March 1788; signed: **Saml. Ashe**; witness: **W. Hill**; [no probate record], delivd. **Wm. Dunnagan Junr.**

P. 319, 24 August 1786, **North Carolina** to **George Doherty** [no residence given], three hundred seven pounds, 292 1/2 acres, on S side of Haw R. on waters of Great Allamance, nigh **Captain William Rogers**, begin at a white oak, W 45 ch. to a post oak, N 65 ch. to a stake, E 45 ch. to a stake, S 65 ch. to first station, sold as confiscated property of estate of **Henry Eustace McCulloh**; signed: **Richd. Caswell**; witness: **Ja. Glasgow**; [no probate record].

P. 320, 8 June 1797, **North Carolina** to **Moses Holmes** [no residence given], fifty shillings per hundred acres, 30 acres, begin at a stake a cor. of **Moses Holmes & Joseph Clendennin**, N45E 33 ch. to a B. O., W 33 ch. to a B. O., S 23 ch. to beginning, warrant dated 10 October 1795; signed: **Saml. Ashe**; witness: **J. Glasgow**; [no probate record], delivd. **Jacob Rich.**

P. 321, 28 November 1798, **William Courtney** of Orange to **William Cain** of same, two hundred pounds, a Negroe man slave named **Africa**, if **William Courtney** pays **William Cain** two hundred pounds before 28 February next with interest bill of sale to become void; signed: **William Courtney**; witness: **James**

Yarbrough, Reuben Smith; proved by James Yarbrough [no term of court given], delivd. Wm. Cain.

P. 322, 19 July 1797, North Carolina to George Johnston [no residence given], ten pounds per hundred acres, 40 acres, on waters of Newhope, begin at his SW cor. hicory bush of a tract originally belonging to John Young, E 160 p. along his line to a black oak, S 40 p. to a sassafras Johnston's cor. originally Andrew Patterson, W with a line of same 160 p. to a white oak, N 40 p. to first station, warrant dated 29 August 1786; signed: Saml. Ashe; witness: J. Glasgow; [no probate record].

P. 323, 19 July 1797, North Carolina to George Johnston [no residence given], thirty shillings per hundred acres, 51 acres, on Cedar Fork waters of Newhope, begin at a white oak on bank of Cedar Fork, S down creek 53 p. to a white oak on John Davis' line, W his line 71 p. to a hicory, a red oak his cor. in James Gaddis' line, N his line 20 p. to a whitee oak his cor., his line W 115 p. to a hicory his cor., N his line 39 p. to a white oak on Johnston's line, E his line 186 p. to first station, entered 27 Dec. 1792; signed: Saml. Ashe; witness: J. Glasgow; [no probate record].

P. 324, 21 March 1798, Joseph Moore, wheelright, of Orange to James Phillips, sadler, of sme, eighty pounds, 2 acres, Lots # 83 & 84 in Town of Hillsborough, bounded by Queen Street on N, on S by Lots # 102 & 103, on W by Lot # 82, on E by Town Commons; signed: Joseph Moore; witness: Ca. Campbell, James Palmer; proved November Term 1798 by Campbell, delivd. Wm. Locheart.

P. 325, 24 Octobwer 1798, William Courtney of Hillsborough to James Phillips, saddler, of same, thirty pounds, 2 acres, 2 lots in Hillsborough, Lot # 102 bounded on W by Lot # 101, on N by Lot # 83 the property of James Phillips, on E by Lot # 103, on S by Tryon Street, & Lot # 103, bounded on W by Lot # 102, on N by Lot # 84 the proeprty of James Phillips, on E by Town Commons, on S by Tryon Street; signed: William Courtney; witness: Ca. Campbell, A: Tatom; proved November Term 1798 by Catlett Campbell, delivd. Wm. Lochart.

P. 327, 24 October 1798, William Courtney of Hillsborough to William Lockhart of same, thirty pounds, 2 acres, Lot # 100 in Hillsborough, bounded on W by Lot # 99 the property of William Rider, on E by Lot # 101 the property of William Lockhart, on S by Tryon Street, 1 acre, also Lot # 101, bounded on W by Lot # 100, on N by Lot # 82 supposed to be public property, on E by Lot # 102, on S by Tryon Street, 1 acre; signed: William Courtney; witness: Ca. Campbell, A. Tatom; proved November Term 1798 by Catlett Campbell, delivd. Wm. Lochart.

P. 328, 6 October 1798, William Lytle Esq. of Orange to William Norwood of same, eight hundred dollars, 2 1/2 acres, Lot # 23 in Hillsborough, Lot # 33 in Hillsborough, & Lot # 24 to be divided by a line to run from a point on the street N to the northern line; signed: Will. Lytle; witness: Saml. Turringtine, Isham Blake; proved November Term 1798 by Samuel Turringtine, delvd. Wm.

Norwood.

P. 330, 5 June 1798, **William Eccles Senr.** of Orange to son **William Eccles Junr.** of same, natural love & affeection & better maintenance, 280 acres, granted **William Eccles Senr.** by Patent No. 269, on Quaker Cr., bounded on E by **Murray** & on other sides by vacant land, begin at a B. O., N 40 ch. to a B. O., W 75 ch. to a post oak, S 20 ch. to a B. O., E 10 ch. to a B. O., S 20 ch. to a P. O., E 65 ch. to first station; signed: **William Eccles**; witness: **Joseph Baker Pace, John King, John Barnhill**; proved November Term 1798 by **Barnhill**, delivd. **William Eccles Junr.**

P. 332, 15 February 1798, **John Baxter** of Orange to **William Linge** of same, thirty five pounds, 50 acres, **North Carolina** to **Baxter**, on waters of Nap of Reeds in NE cor. of Baxters Cr., bounded on N & E by **Baxter's** line, on W by line drawn by **James Baxter** & **William Petigrew** near the Mile Br. running S for complement, [no metes and bounds description]; signed: **James (I) Baxter, Rose (S) Baxter**; witness: **Alexr. Sample, James Sample, Reuben Baxter**; proved November Term 1798 by **James Sample**, delivd. **Jno. Goodloe** for Rd. **Bennehan**.

P. 333, 9 January 1794, **Abraham Whinney** of Orange to **Moses Holmes** of same, thirty pounds, 30 acres, on waters of Vernals Cr., begin at a stake a cor. of **Joseph Clendennen**, his line S45E [blank] p. to another stake on side of a branch, up branch to a poplar, N20W 100 p. to a stake in a field, straight to first station, part of a larger tract from **North Carolina** to **Samuel Campbell** as confiscated property 25 August 1786; signed: **Abraham Whinney, Martha (R) Whinney**; witness: **Joseph Clendennen, James Thompson**; proved November Term 1798 by **Clendennen**, delivd. **Joseph Clendennen**.

P. 335, 3 December 1798, **North Carolina** to **Moses Carson** [no residence given], fifty shillings per hundred acres, 200 acres, on waters of Hico & Eno, adjoins land formerly belonging to **Carson** including **Hugh Shannon's** Old Improvement, begin at a black oak on **Carson's** Old Line, S 50 ch. to an old black jack, witness 2 pines & a post oak, E 40 ch. to a pine & post oak, N 50 ch. to a stake in the Old Line, W along line to first station, entered 7 December 1773; signed: **W. R. Davie**; witness: **Will. Whyte**; [no probate record].

P. 336, 20 December 1798, **North Carolina** to **Thomas Cate** [no residence given], fifty shillings per hundred acres, 206 acres, on Cain Cr., adjoins **John Cate, Frederick Williams**, & his own land, begin at a post oak, N 1 ch. 75 lk. to a hicory a cor. of **Cate's** Old Tract, along line of tract W 22 ch. to a gum on Cain Cr., up creek N25E 14 ch. to a white oak **Williams'** cor., along his own E 53 ch. to a black oak on Bear Cr., N 21 ch. 50 lk. to a white oak on creek, E 38 ch. to a black jack, S 35 ch. 50 lk. to a black oak on **John Cate's** line, along same W 75 ch. to beginning; signed: **Wm. R. Davie**; witness: **Will. White**; [no probate record], delivd. **Thomas Cate**.

P. 337, 17 September 1797, **William Roach** of Orange to **Thomas Cate** of same, fifty pounds, 100 acres, on waters of Collins Cr., begin on a red oak, W 25 ch. to a red oak, S 25 ch. to a post oak cor. on **Lewis Kirk's** line, E with line 9 ch. 50 lk. to a black jack, S with line 24 ch. to a red oak, E 15 ch. 50 lk. to a red oak, N 49 ch. to beginning; signed: **William Roach;** witness: **John Cate, Martha Moore;** proved by **John Cate** [no term of court given].

P. 338, 16 November 1798, **James Stockard** of Orange to **Stephen White** of same, one hundred sixty five dollars, 332 acres, on waters of Autor[?] Cr., begin at a post oak on **Wilkins'** line,S50W 50 ch. to a black oak, S50E 8 ch. to a stake, S 18 ch. to a post oak, N50E 16 ch. to a spanish oak, S50E 34 ch. to a stake, N50E 54 ch. to a stake, N50W 60 ch. to beginning; signed: **James Stockard;** witness: **Joseph Baker, Jas. Trousdale;** acknowledged November Term 1798, delivd. **Stephen White.**

P. 339, [blank] November 1798, **Daniel Torrentine** of Orange to **Joseph Hodge & Richard Christmas** of same, one hundred pounds, 250 acres, on waters of Haw Cr., begin at a post oak **Clendennen's** cor., N54W 6 ch. to a black oak, N28W 28 1/2 ch. to a hicory, N17E 1 1/2 ch. to a white oak, S62W 29 1/2 ch. to a stake, S10E 26 ch. to a black oak, S 6 1/2 ch. to a black jack, S18E 20 ch. to a black oak, S10W 9 ch. to a branch, S62E 4 1/2 ch. to fork of branch, N30E 7 ch. to a post oak, S67E 10 ch. to a stake, S48E 9 1/2 ch. to a black oak, N14E 17 ch. to a black oak, N22E 33 ch. to beginning, **North Carolina** to **Archibald Mahon, Mahon** to **Joseph Hodge** 1789, **Hodge** to **Daniel Turrentine** 1798; signed: **Daniel Turrentine;** witness: [none listed]; acknowledged November Term 1798, delivd. **Jo. Hodge.**

P. 341, 27 November 1798, **Joseph Hodge** of Orange to **Daniel Turrentine** of same, one hundred pounds, 250 acres, on waters of Haw Cr., begin at a post oak **Clendenin's** cor., N54W 6 ch. to a black oak, N28W 28 1/2 ch. to a hicory, N17E 1 1/2 ch. to a white oak, S62W 29 1/2 ch. to a stake, S10E 26 ch. to a black oak, S 6 1/2 ch. to a black jack, S18E 20 ch. to a black oak, S10W 9 ch. to a branch, S62E 4 1/2 ch. to fork of a branch, N30E 7 ch. to a post oak, S67E 10 ch. to a stake, S48E 9 1/2 ch. to a black oak, N14E 17 ch. to a black oak, N22E 33 ch. to beginning, **North Carolina** to **Alexander Mahon, Mahon** to **Joseph Hodge** 29 Octobeer 1789; signed: **Joseph Hodge;** witness: [none listed]; acknowledged November Term 1798, delivd. **Jo. Hodge.**

P. 343, 13 August 1798, **North Carolina** to **Sackfield Brewer** [no residence given], thirty shillings per hundred acres, 72 acres, on waters of Little Cain Cr., adjoins **Ezekiel Brewer, Thomas Cate,** & his own land, begin at a white oak on his own line, S 50 p. to a white oak, E 116 p. to a black oak on **Ezekiel Brewer's** line, N his line 122 p. to a red oak his cor., E 70 p. to a red oak, N 42 p. to a red oak, W 94 p. to a red oak on his own line, S with line 114 p. to a white oak, W 92 p. to first station, warrant dated 28 February 1795; signed: **Saml. Ashe;** witness: **J. Glasgow;** [no probate record], delivd. **Sackfield Brewer.**

P. 344, [blank] August 1798, **John Gattis** of Orange to **Edmund Shelton** [no residence given], three pounds, 4 1/2 acres, begin at a poplar on Presswoods Cr. **James Gattis'** former cor., N through the field formerly cultivated by **James Gattis** 78 p. to a stake near the corn, W 2 1/3 p. to a hicory at the fence, with fence S21W 34 p. to a stake, S 4 p. to a white oak on bank of Presswoods Cr., down creek to beginning; signed: **John Gattis**; witness: **Alexander Gattis, Bennet Watson**; proved November Term 1798 by **Bennett Watson**, delivd. **Edmd. Shelton**.

P. 345, 1 August 1798, **James Gattis** of Orange to **Edmund Shelton** of same, two hundred pounds, 300 acres, on waters of Newhope, begin at **Daniel Booth's** cor. red oak, W 142 p. to **Polly Castlebury's** cor poplar, N his line 228 p. to a white oak, E 115 p. to a white oak, S 20 p. to **Allen's** cor. hicory & continued S along his line 189 p. to first station, **North Carolina** to **Gattis** No. 273 13 March 1780; signed: **James Gattis, Ann Gattis**; witness: **Alexander Gattis, Wm. Gattis, Saml. Hopkins**; proved November Term 1798 by **Hopkins**, delivd. **Edmd. Shelton**.

P. 347, 30 August 1798, **Thomas Clark** of Orange to **John Ray** Esq. of same, six hundred fifty dollars, 378 acres, undivided one half of tract, on waters of Little R., begin at the NW cor. of **James Wilkinson's** formerly **Ralph Williams'** land, to a black oak, E to a black oak, N to a post oak on **John Ray's** formerly **James Ray's** line, W along line & along **James Clark's** line to a black oak, S to first station, **John Rutherford** to **Thomas Clarke** deceased 2 August thirtieth year of Reign of **George Second** King of England; signed: **Thomas Clark**; witness: **William Clark, Jesse Clark**; proved by **William Clark** & **Jesse Clark** [no term of court given], delivd. **Jno. Ray**.

P. 348, 30 August 1798, **William Clark** of Orange to **John Ray** Esq. of same, six hundred fifty dollars, 378 acres, one half undivided interest in tract, on waters of Little R., begin at the NW cor. of **James Wilkinson's** formerly **Ralph William's** land, to a black oak, E to a black oak, N to a post oak in **John Ray's** formerly **James Ray's** line, W along line & along **James Clark's** line to a black oak, S to first station, **John Rutherford** to **Thomas Clarke** deceased 2 August thirty first year of reign of **George the Second** King of England; signed: **William Clark**; witness: **Willm. Clark, Jesse Clark**; proved November Term 1798 by **Willm. Clark** & **Jesse Clark**, delivd. **Jno. Ray**.

P. 350, 22 July 1798, **John Daniel** of Orange to **William Pickett** of same, twenty nine shillings three pence, 49 acres, on waters of Obeds Cr., begin at a hicory **J. Morgan's**, his line N 126 p. to a white oak on the head of Haw Br. near **Morgan's** other cor., down branch N40W 30 p. to a hicory, W down branch to **Pickett's** Old Line, with same 150 p. to a stake in **Cother's** Field, E 56 p. to beginning; signed: **John Daniel**; witness: **William Pendergrass**; proved November Term 1798 by **Pendergrass**.

P. 351, [blank] November 1797, **William McCauley** Esq. late Sheriff of Orange to **Alexander Kirkpatrick**, planter, of same, sixty pounds, 150 acres, levy on estate of **George Hodge** Decd. in hands of **Margaret Hodge** Administratrix for twenty eight pounds seventeen shillings recovered by **Andrew Gibson**, land sold 26 November 1790, granted to one **Hutcheson** 13 March 1780, adjoins **Jacob Bason** & **William Mebane**, begin at a white oak near a spring about 10 p. from Otter Cr. on S side of creek in the Old Field, by a line of marked trees to **Jacob Bason's** line, along **Bason's** line & bounded by the same line til it reaches a tract of land where **George** formerly lived, by a line of marked trees marling the line or boundary formerly made between **George Hodge** when he owned the land on which **Mebane** lives & **James Hutcherson** who owned the land divided for **George** by the line to a post oak about 10 p. N of the North Spring, by a line of marked trees to Otter Cr., down creek till a S line will strike the beginning tree, subject to the widow's dower; signed: **William McCauley**; witness: **James Roberts, James Freeland**; proved November Term 1798 by **Roberts**, delivd. **James Hutcheson**.

P. 353, 22 July 1798, **John Daniel** of Orange to **William Pendergrass** of same, thirty four shillings eight pence, 86 acres, on waters of Obeds Cr., begin at a red oak **John Morgan's** NW cor., E his line & by his cor. 164 p. to a pine, N 72 p. to a stake, due E from **William Merritt's** cor. sassafras, W along **Merritt's** line 220 p. to a red oak **Pickett's** cor., S 48 p. to a stake at **Pickett's** cor. of the division on Haw Br., up meanders W to a hicory, S40E 30 p. to beginning, it being a parcel of land taken by **Daniel's** deed [land grant] that **Pendergrass** claimed as his right therefore **Daniel** relinquishes his right to **William Pendergrass**; signed: **John Daniel**; witness: **William (X) Pickett**; proved November Term 1798 by **Pickett**, delivd. **Jo. Hodge**.

P. 354, 28 November 1798, **William Hodge** of Orange to **Joseph Hodge** of same, two hundred fifty pounds, 157 acres, on Back Cr., bounded all around by **James Dixon, Benjamin Rainey, Stephen White, Robert Hodge, Robert Patten, & William Hodge**, begin at a black jack, W 35 ch. to a burch on bank, down creek 20 ch. to a gum, S6W 12 ch. to a black oak, S558E 9 ch. to a post oak, S70E 6 ch. to a persimmon, S60E 10 ch. to a black oak, S32E 11 ch. to a hicory, N72E 31 ch. to a post oak, a straight line to first station, **North Carolina** to **Alexander Kirkpatrick** 3 September 1779, **Kirkpatrick** to **Hugh Shannon** 1781, **Shannon** to **William Hodge** 1783, **Hodge** to **Thomas Holgan** 1787, **Holgan** to **William Hodge** 1791; signed: **Wm. Hodge**; witness: **John Squires, Daniel Turrentine**; acknowledged November Term 1798.

P. 356, 10 March 1798, **Thomas Atwood Senior** of Orange to **Thomas Atwood Junr.**, fifty pounds, 50 acres, on waters of Haw R., begin at a post oak **Thomas Atwood Senr.** cor., his line S 18 ch. to a post oak on side of a branch, N86W to **Hatwod** line 28 ch. to a black oak, his line N 17 ch. to a post oak, E 27 ch. to first station; signed: **Thomas (X) Atwood Senr.**; witness: **Samuel Bradford, Frederick Lloyd**; proved November Term 1798 by **Lloyd**, delivd. **Thos. Atwood Jnr.**

P. 357, 26 September 1798, **Alexander Anderson** of Orange to **William Freeman** of same, one hundred seventy five pounds, 300 acres, on waters of Quaker Cr., begin at a stake on his own line, N 15 ch. to a stake his cor., E 12 1/2 ch. to a black oak **Walter Murray's** cor. on **Anderson's** line, N 16 ch. to a black oak, W 103 ch. to a stake, S 29 1/2 ch. to a black oak, S71E 5 ch. to a stake, E to beginning; signed: **Alexander Anderson**; witness: **Thomas Anderson, William Jenkins**; proved November Term 1798 by **Jenkins**, delivd. **Mr. Cotton[?]**.

P. 358, 24 September 1798, **Alexander Anderson** of Orange to **William Freeman** of same, eighty five pounds, 140 acres, on waters of Quaker Cr., begin at a stake, S 31 ch. to a hicory, W 23 1/2 ch. to a post oak, N17W 10 1/2 ch. to a black oak, N71W 64 ch. to a stake, E to first station; signed: **Alexander Anderson**; witness: **William Jenkins, Thomas Anderson**; proved November Term 1798 by **Jenkins**, delivered to **Mr. Cotton[?]**.

P. 359, 9 September 1797, **John Trousdale** of Orange to **John Campbell** of Bartee [Bertie], four hundred pounds, 203 acres, on both sides of Main Fork of Back Cr., begin at a hicory, S 9 ch. to a black oak, S22W 24 1/2 xch. to a black oak, S50E 30 1/2 ch. to a black jack, E 37 ch. to a black jack, N 20 ch. to a black jack, N45W 34 ch. to a white oak, N70W 31 ch. to first station, **North Carolina** to **James Whitsell** November 1784, **Whitsell** to **John Trousdale**; signed: **John Trousdale**; witness: **Jno. Ray, Martha Campbell**; proved November Term 1798 by **John Ray**, delivered **John Campbell**.

P. 360, 27 November 1798, **William Ansley** of Orange to **David Hinchey** of same, fifty pounds, 175 acres, on waters of Newhope, begin at a stake on **Hart's** line now **Couch's** line, S along line 140 p. to his cor. hicory continuing same course 49 p. to a black jack, W 52 p. to **Malcom** or **Johnston's** cor. a post oak & continuing along his line 140 p. to his cor. stake on **Hall's** or **Johnston's** line, N to his line 130 p. to **Couch's** cor. red oak saplin, E on his line 140 p. to a white oak saplin his cor., N 60 p. to a post oak, E 50 p. to first station, **North Carolina** to **William Ansley**; signed: **Willm. Ansley**; witness: **Wm. Ansley Junr., John Allen Wallace, Gilbert Ansley**; proved November Term 1798 by **Gilbert Ansley**, delivd. **Davd. Hinshey**.

P. 362, 31 December 1795, **James Faucett**, planter, of Orange to **George Ress[?]** of same, ten pounds, 23 acres, 1/2 of tract on S side of Little R., begin at a black oak on **Robinson's** line, 10 ch. to **Ress'** line, S 23 ch. to a stake, W 10 ch. to a black oak on **John McMannes'** line, N 23 ch. to first station, part of a tract from **North Carolina** to **Fosett** 17 November 1790; signed: **James Faucett**; witness: **Hugh Woods, Lucy Faucett**; acknowledged [no term of court given], delivd. **Jno. Latta Senr.**

P. 363, 6 September 1798, **Barnabas O'Ferrell** of Hillsborough to **Baxter King** of Orange, one hundred ninety pounds ten shillings, 310 acres, on Morgans Cr., begin on **Baxter King's** line at a white oak saplin, N on **John Adam's** line 64 ch. 25 lk. to a stake in the Old Line, W with line 48 ch. 25 lk. to the cor. white oak, S 64 ch. 20 lk. crossing Morgans Cr. to a red oak & hicory, E crossing creek 48 ch. 25 lk. to beginning; signed: **Barnabas O'Ferrell**; witness: **Geo: Moore, Ca. Campbell, A. Tatom**; acknowledged November Term 1798, delivd. **Baxter King**.

P. 364, 28 November 1798, **William Hodge** of Orange to **Joseph Hodge** of same, one hundred pounds, 200 acres, on Boyds Cr. a branch of Haw R., bounded by **Samuel Means, Andrew Huffman, & Robert Turner**, begin at a black oak, W 25 ch. to a post oak, S 30 ch. to a black jack, W 20 ch. to a black jack, S 35 ch. to a post oak, E 35 ch. to a black jack, N 65 ch. to first station, **North Carolina** to **Andrew Huffman, Huffman** to **John Elmore, Elmore** to **William Hodge**; signed: **Wm. Hodge**; witness: **John Squires, Daniel Turringtine**; acknowledged November Term 1798.

ORANGE COUNTY (NC) DEED BOOK 7

P. 366, 28 November 1798, **Daniel Turrentine** of Orange to **William Hodge** of same, three hundred twenty pounds, 260 acres, on waters of Back Cr., bounded by **Robert Patton, Stephen White, Joseph Baker, Joseph Hodge, & James Dixon**, begin at a post oak, S46E 20 ch. to a stake, S52E 8 ch. to an ash on Mill Cr., up creek N65E 18 ch. to an ash, N48E 33 ch. to a black oak, N35W 12 ch. to a willow oak in a branch, down branch N71W 12 ch. to a poplar, S 2 ch. 75 lk. to a white oak, W 32 ch. 50 lk. to a black jack, S 15 ch. to a black jack, a straight line to beginning; signed: **Daniel Turrentine**; witness: **Joseph Hodge, John Squires**; acknowledged November Term 1798.

P. 367, 12 May 1798, **William Ansley Senr.** of Orange to **George Carrington** of samee, fifteen hundred pounds, 612 acres, on waters of Eno, begin at a pine Old **Shoemaker's** cor. formaerly, S30E 117 p. to a white oak, S running by a black jack cor. of **Grisham's** tract 263 p. crossing the road to a pine **John May's** cor., W 72 p. to a red oak saplin on line of **Wallace** tract, N with line 81 p. to a hicory a cor. of same, W 98 p. to a black jack **Warrin's**[?] cor., N his line 117 p. to a white oak his cor., W his line 217 p. to an ash on E side of Mill Cr. on **Warran's** line, down creek 40 p. to a gum on same, N with **Senate's** line across Eno at a marked willow oak 160 p. to a hicory **Sinnet's** old cor., E 206 p. to a black walnut saplin on bank of river, down river to a stake at **Forrest's** line, his line S30E 42 p. to beginning; signed: **Wm. Ansley**; witness: **Joseph Brittain, Gilbert Ansley**; proved November Term 1798 by **Joseph Brittain & Gilbert Ansley**, delivd. **Geo. Carrington**.

P. 369, 3 February 1798, **John Knight** of Orange to **George Carrington** of same, five hundred pounds, 172 acres, on both sides of Mountain Cr., adjoins **James Commons & Walter Alves**, begin at a black oak on **James Commons'** line, E 43 ch. to a black oak, N 40 ch. to a stake, W 43 ch. to a black oak on S side of a branch, S 40 ch. to first station; signed: **John Knight**; witness: **Hubert Sims, Zachariah (X) Maze, James Horton**; proved November Term 1798 by Horton, delivd. **Geo. Carrington**.

P. 370, 12 May 1798, **William Ansley** of Orange to son **Gilbert Ansley** of same, one hundred pounds, 200 acres, purchased from **William Wallace**, begin at a hicory **Willm. Ansley's** line, S268 p. to a red oak on **May's** Old Line a cor. in a Draft, up Draft 84 p. S some degrees W a conditional line to a pine on **May's** line, W some degrees N 110 p. to a pine saplin on **May's** line, N 51 p. to a white oak on Jumping Run on **Clinton's** cor., continuing N6W on **Clinton's** line 168 p. to a pine & red oak on **Warrin's** cor. or line, E across the Meadow to a stake above the Meadow Spring 84 p., N 78 p. to a pine on **William Ansley's** line, E 84 p. to first station, **William Wallis** to **William Ansley** 1 December 1794; signed: **Wm. Ansley**; witness: **Wm. Ansley Junr., David Ansley, Southerland May**; proved November Term 1798 by **Sutherland May**, delivd. **Gilbert Ansley**.

P. 371, 19 October 1797, **Thomas Rich** of Orange to **John Loy** of same, one hundred dollars, 60 acres, on S side of Great Allamance bounded on Great Allamance, adjoins **Peter Harmen**, begin at a gum on Great Allamance, S15W 42 ch. to a hicory, E 12 ch. to a post oak, S45E 18 ch. to a white oak, N 8 ch. to a black oak **Peter Hermen's** cor., S75W 2 1/2 ch. to a white oak, N15W 22 ch. to a white oak on the Allamance, on the meanders to first station; signed: **Thos.**

Rich; witness: **Jacob Rich, Peter Rich**; proved November Term 1798 by **Jacob Rich**, delivd. **Jno. Loy.**

P. 373, 23 October 1798, **Samuel Clenny** of Orange to **James Cain** of same, seven hundred pounds, 339 acres, begin at a cor. of **John Woods'** land a heap of stones formerly a red oak, S 52 ch. to 2 white oaks & a persimmon tree, Eastwardly with **William Clenney's** line of marked trees to a black oak saplin in **Stephen Carrol's** line, N 32 ch. to a walnut bush in a line of **Willm. Cain**, W 33 1/2 ch. to a hicory **John Kelley's** cor., N 82 1/2 ch. to a stake in the Old Line, W 21 1/2 ch. to the Old Cor. red oak, S 62 1/2 ch. to beginning; signed: **Samuel Clenny**; witness: **Stephen Hart, James Latta, Jnr.**; proved November Term 1798 by **Latta**, delivd. **James Cain.**

P. 374, 27 August 1798, **Charles Kelley**, planter, of Orange to **Robert Cate Senr.**, planter, of same, five pounds, 15 acres, on N side of Marshalls Br., begin at a post oak on the Meeting House Road, along road 16 ch. to a cross path on **William Moore's** line cor. a black jack, along path northwardly 16 ch. to a cor. post oak stake on **Cate's** line, S 17 ch. to a post oak on Marshalls Br., 6 ch. to beginning; signed: **Charles Kelley**; witness: **Robert Cate, Thomas (X) Cate**; proved November Term 1798 by **Robert Cate**, devd. **R. Cate Junr.**

P. 375, **North Carolina** to **John Riggs** [no residence given], thirty shillings per hundred acres, 66 acres, on waters of Little R., adjoins **John Nesley, William Jamison, & Joseph Wood**, begin at a post oak **John Nesley's** cor. **William Jamison's** cor., W 53 ch. to a black jack **Jamison's** cor., S 13 ch. to a stake **Joseph Wood's** cor., to first station; signed: **W. R. Davie**; witness: **Will: White**; [no probate record], delivd. **John Riggs.**

P. 376, 25 March 1797, **Ezekiel Boggs** of Washinfgton County, Georgia, to **John Williams** of Orange, seventy five pounds, 200 acres, on waters of Stinking Quarter of Great Allamance, adjoins **John Spoon & Phillip Ulis** including an improvement which **Ezekiel Boggs** purchased of **Andrew Boggs**, begin at a post oak, W 22 ch. to a stake, N 52 1/2 ch. to a stone, E 20 ch. to a black oak, N 5 ch. to a hicory, E 19 ch. to a post oak, S 40 ch. to a hicory, W 9 ch. to a white oak, S 10 ch. to first station, **North Carolina** to **Ezekiel Boggs**; signed: **Ezekiel (+) Boggs**; witness: **John Curry, Phillip (+) Moore, Joseph Boggs**; proved November Term 1798 by **Moore**, delivd. **Jas. Oneil.**

P. 377, 23 June 1798, **Richard Christmas** of Orange to **Andrew Gibson** of Guilford & **Thomas Hardin Perkins** of Moore, one hundred pounds, 150 acres, on S side of Haw R., begin at a hicory on S side of river in a line of the Mill Tract, S37W 37 1/2 ch. to a black oak saplin in the fork of the Road, W 21 ch. to an ash on Mill Tract in **Stockard's** line, along line S21E 12 ch. to a persimmon & dogwood, S13W 11 1/2 ch. to a walnut, S5W 7 3/4 ch. to a hicory on bank of Great Allamance, down meanders 38 1/2 ch. to confluence with Haw R., up river to beginning, where **James Patterson** now lives which was sold by **Joseph Hodge** Sheriff & purchased by **Richard Christmas**; signed: **Richard Christmas**; witness: **James Patterson**; acknowledged November Term 1798.

P. 379, 18 June 1793, **William Shepperd** of Orange to **William Hooper** of

Hillsborough, twenty two pounds, 1 acre, Lot # 32 in Hilsborough, on Tryon Street, purchased by **Shepperd** at sale of confiscated property on which he built, bounded on E by Lot # 33, on N by Tryon Street, on W by Lot # 31, on S by Lot # 22, begin at cor. of Lot # 33 on Tryon Street, W 400 lk. along Tryon Street to cor. of Lot # 31, S along line of Lot 250 lk. to cor. of Lot # 31 21 & 22, E along Lot # 22 400 lk. to cor. of Lot # 23 & 33, N along line of Lot # 33, 250 lk. to first station; signed: **Wm. Shepperd**; witness: **Andrew Burke, Wm. Watters**; receipt dated 18 June 1793 from **William Hooper** of purchase money; acknowledged November Term 1798, delivd. **Gaven Alvis**.

P. 380, 10 September 1798, **James Hogg** of Orange to **William Hooper** of New Hanover, two hundred pounds, [no acreage given], near Town of Hillsborough, begin at a gum **Henry Watters'** cor. formeerly **Shankland's**, S 16 ch. to the Old Halifax Road, S45W on N side of Old Road 12 ch. to a branch, S 16 1/2 ch. to forks of road, N86 1/2 ch. 27 lk. to **James Phillips'** cor., N 11 ch. 70 lk. along **Phillips'** line to a stake in **Henry Watters'** line, E 8 ch. 27 lk. to a stake **Henry Watters'** other cor., N along **H. Watters'** line 16 1/2 ch. to another cor. of **Henry Watters**, E along **Watters'** line formerly **Shankland's** 26 1/2 ch. to first station; signed: **James Hogg**; witness: **Walter Alvees, Gaven Alves**; proved November Term 1798 by **Gavin Alves**, deld. to **Gavil Alves**.

P. 382, 22 September 1798, **Gilbert Strayhorn**, planter, of Orange to son **James Strayhorn** of same, twenty pounds, 225 acres, on waters of Eno on both sides of Stones Cr., begin on the long North at an ash standing by Elder Spring, down branch to creek & crossing creek by **Abraham Nelson's** dividing line to the longest S line to a red oak, on line W to a hicory, S 5 ch. to a white, W 15 ch. to a red oak, N 20 ch. to a hicory, W 20 ch. to an ash, N 35 ch. to a red oak, E 26 ch. to a black oak, N 10 ch. to a white oak, E on N line to first station; signed: **Gilbert (X) Strayhorn**; witness: **David Strayhorn, W. F. Thompson**; acknowledged November Term 1798, delivd. **James Strayhorn**.

P. 383, 2 December 1797, **North Carolina** to **Edward King** [no residence given], fifty shillings per hundred acres, 47 acres, on waters of Deep Cr., adjoins his own land, begin at a white oak **John Lynch's** cor., W 5 1/2 ch. to a black gum, S 2 1/2 ch. to a white oak, S 51 ch. to a stake, E 9 ch. to a stake, N 53 1/2 ch. to first station, warrant dated 7 June 1796; signed: **Saml. Ashe**; witness: **J. Glasgow**; [no probate record], delivd. **H. Hurdle**.

P. 384, 2 December 1797, **North Carolina** to **Edward King** [no residence given], thirty shillings per hundred acres, 150 acres, on waters of Deep Cr., adjoins **John Lynch** & **Jacobs**, begin at a post oak his own cor., E 24 ch. to a black oak, N 10 ch. to a white oak **John King's** cor., S 29 ch. to a B. jack, W 2 ch. to a B. jack, S 28 1/2 ch. to a B. jack, W 38 1/2 ch. to a B. jack on **Henry Jacobs'** line, N 29 ch. to a stake, E 9 ch. to a stake, N 18 ch. to first station, warrant dated 5 June 1795; signed: **Saml. Ashe**; witness: **J. Glasgow**; [no probate record], delivd. **H. Hurdle**.

P. 385, 2 December 1797, **North Carolina** to **John King** [no residence given], fifty shillings per hundred acres, 40 acres, on waters of Deep Cr., adjoins lands of **Edward King** & his own, begin at 2 white oaks on his line, E 14 ch. to a stake on line, S 29 ch. to a stake **King's** cor., W 14 ch. to a black jack, N 29 ch. to first station, entered 7 March 1796; signed: **Saml. Ashe**; wiitness: **J. Glasgow**; [no probate record], delivd. **H. H. Hurdle.**

P. 386, 2 December 1797, **North Carolina** to **John King** [no residence given], fifty shillings per hundred acres, 100 acres, on waters of Deep Cr., adjoins **Joseph Baker Pace, Williams Eccles**, & his own land, begin at a black oak his own cor., E 11 1/2 ch. to a black jack, N 3 1/2 ch. to a black jack, E 14 ch. to a hicory in **William Eccles'** line, S 31 1/2 ch. to a black oak, W 6 ch. to a black oak, S 12 ch. to a stake, W 19 1/2 ch. to a stake **King's** cor., N 40 ch. to first station, warrant dated 31 May 1796; signed: **Saml. Ashe**; witness: **J. Glasgow**; [no probate record], delivd. **H. Hurdle.**

P. 387, 13 November 1798, **North Carolina** to **Hardy Hurdle** [no residence given], fiifty shillings per hundred acres, 202 acres, adjoins **Marley, Robert Turner, & Shanks**, includes plantation where **Hurdle** now lives, begin at a black oak at head of a branch, S20E 20 ch. to a black jack on the Great Road, W 60 lk. to **Turner's** cor., the same course continued on his line passing his other cor. at 32 1/2 ch. continued in all 45 1/2 ch. to a post oak, E 20 ch. to a persimmon on a branch, uo meanders to beginning, entered 19 December 1797; signed: **Saml. Ashe**; witness: **Will White**; [no probate record], delivd. **Hardy Hurdle.**

P. 388, 13 November 1798, **North Carolina** to **Martin Hurdle** [no residence given], fifty shillings per hundred acres, 14 1/2 acres, on waters of Stoney Cr., adjoins **Hardy Hurdle, Robert Turner, & John Cook**, begin at a P. Q. a cor. of **Hardy Hurdle**, E his line 13 ch. 50 lk. to a post oak **Turner's** cor., his line S 16 ch. to a black jack **Cook's** cor., his line N45W 19 ch. 50 lk. to a post oak **Hurdle's** cor., his line N 2 ch. 25 lk. to beginning, warrant dated 16 September 1797; signed: **Saml. Ashe**; witness: **William White**; [no probate record], delivd. **Hardy Hurdle.**

P. 389, 13 August 1798, **North Carolina** to **John Graham** [no residence given], fifty shillings per hundred acres, 466 1/2 acres, on both sides Jourdans Cr., begin at a P. O., with a conditional line made by **James Dicky** & **Thomas Bracken** N65E 37 ch. to a hicory bush, N 19 ch. 50 lk. to a B. O. **Hall's** line, his line W 5 ch. 75 lk. to his cor. a P. O., N 47 ch. 75 lk. to a R. oak in **Harvey's** line, W 30 ch. 50 lk. to a W. oak on **Tate's** line, S 6 ch. to his cor. spanish oak, N64W 43 ch. to a W. oak, S 41 ch. to a hicory & P. oak **William Bracken's** cor., S37E 68 ch. 50 lk. to beginning, warrant dated 7 December 1779; signed: **Saml. Ashe**; witness: **J. Glasgow**; [no probate record], delivd. **Jno. Graham.**

P. 390, 5 April 1798, **North Carolina** to **Man Patterson** [no residence given], fifty shillings per hundred acres, 348 acres, on W side of Newhope, begin at a white oak on edge of the Low Grounds in **Page Patterson's** line, W 406 p. to a pine on bank of Dry Cr., N 147 p. to a stake, E 340 p. to a stake on bank of Newhope, down creek to **Page Patterson's** cor. hicory, his line S 64 p. to beginning, warrant dated 1 May 1796; signed: **Saml. Ashe**; witness: **J. Glasgow**; [no probate record], delivd. **Mann Patterson.**

P. 391, 13 June 1798, **North Carolina** to **Elias Wilholt** [no residence given], fifty shillings per hundred acres, 150 acres, on waters of Cedar Cr. a branch of Great Allamance, begin at a post oak a cor. of **John Hufman,** his line S 47 1/2 ch. crossing Cedar Cr. to a hicoryy on **Barnet Troxler's** line, **Troxler's** line N45E 27 1/2 ch. crossing Cedar Cr. 3 times to a P. oak **Troxler's** cor., E 5 ch. to a stake on **Henry E. McCulloh's** line, S 42 ch. to a stake, W 36 to a white oak grub, S30W 15 ch. to a stake, E 20 ch. to beginning, warrant dated 20 November 1778; signed: **Saml. Ashe**; witness: **J. Glasgow**; [no probate record].

P. 392, 15 February 1799, **North Carolina** to **James Baldridge** [no residence given], ten pounds per hundred acres, 250 acres, on waters of Little & Flat R., adjoins **William Lockhart** & others, begin at a pine in the County Line, 43 ch. to & with **Lockhart's** line to a stake his SE cor., W his other line 50 ch. to his cor. pine on **Allison's** line, along line S 24 ch. to his cor. post oak, E with **James McCullock's** line 11 ch. 25 lk. to his cor. post oak, S 6 1/2 ch. to a red oak, along **Rugley's** line E 24 1/2 ch. to his cor. post oak, N 12 ch. to a stake **Mebane's** cor, E his line 38 ch. to a stake, N 63 1/2 ch. to a stake the NW cor. of **Baldridge's** 200 acre tract in the County Line, with same to beginning; signed: **W. R. Davie**; witness: **Will. White**; [no probate record], delivd. **Malcom Baldridge.**

P. 393, 15 February 1799, **North Carolina** to **James Baldridge** [no residence given], fifty shillings per hundred acres, 200 acres, on waters of Little R., adjoins **McCulloch**, begin at a black oak his cor., his line to & beyond his cor. 36 ch. to a spanish oak in County Line, with same W 50 ch. 70 lk. to a stake near the Big Road, S 36 ch. to a stake, E to beginning; signed: **W. R. Davie**; witness: **Will Hill**; [no probate record], delivd. **Malcomb Baldridge.**

P. 394, 13 August 1798, **North Carolina** to **Jane McCandless** [no residence given], fifty shillings per hundred acres, 101 acres, on waters of Little R., within the boundary of her own line, begin at a post oak & B. J. a cor. to **David English**, W 17 ch. to a stake, N 55 ch. to a stake, W 10 ch. to a stake, S3E 78 ch. to a B. J. on **Baldridge's** line, with line E 22 ch. 50 lk. to 2 B. jacks, N 22 ch. to beginning, entered 30 November 1795; signed: **Saml. Ashe**; witness: **J. Glasgow**; [no probate record], delivd. **Malcomb Baldridge.**

P. 395, 26 January 1799, **James Pratt** of Orange to **Daniel Cloud** of same, five hundred ninety one dollars, 209 1/2 acres, begin at a black jack cor. of **Frederick Taylor, Joseph Hastings Senr., & William Cain,** N along **Cain's** line 61 ch. 50 lk. to a stake **James Pratt's** cor., W 50 ch. to a post oak **James Pratt's** cor., N 9 ch. 50 lk. to a black oak, W 19 ch. to a post oak **Pratt's** Old Cor., S 3 ch. to a black jack **Andrew Collins' & Hasting's** cor., S45E 98 ch. to beginning; signed: **James Pratt**; witness: **Wm. Norwood**; proved February Term 1799 by **Norwood**, delivd. **Daniel Cloud.**

P. 397, 19 February 1799, **William McCandless** of Orange to **James Baldridge** of same, fifty five pounds, 50 acres, on waters of Flat R. & Little R., bounded by **John McCulloh** No. 583, begin at a black oak, W 16 ch. to a post oa, N 31 1/4 ch. to a stake, E 16 ch. to a stake, S 31 1/4 ch. to first station, No. 324, **John McCulloh** to **James Andrews** 4 March 1780, **Andrews** to **William McCandless**

23 February 1798; signed: **William (X) McCandless**; witness: **Malcom Baldridge, James Woodrow, Thomas Jourdan**; acknowledged February Term 1799, deliveered **James Baldridge** Esq.

P. 398, 25 February 1799, **James Mitchell**, planter, of Orange to **Jesse Hunter**, planter, of same, one hundred pounds, 100 acres, on waters of Morgans Cr. waters of Newhope, begin at a stake, S 25 ch. to a red oak, W 40 ch. to a stake & marked saplins, N 25 ch. to a stake, E 40 ch. to first station; signed: **James Mitchell**; witness: **M. Hart**; acknowledged February Term 1799, delivd. **Jesse Hunter**.

P. 399, 18 October 1797, **Johnston Jones** of Orange to **William Harvey** of same, one hundred thirty three pounds, 230 acres, on waters of Haw R., adjoins **John Murray & Jesse Toweln**, begin at a post oak a cor. of **John Murray**, E 33 ch. to a black oak, N 15 ch. to a black, E 43 1/2 ch. to a willow oak, S 25 ch. to a black oak, W 38 ch. to a black oak, S15W 17 ch. to a black oak, S 11 ch. to a black oak, W 39 ch. to a post oak, N 23 ch. to a black oak, N10E 16 ch. to first station, **North Carolina** to **Thomas Jones** 18 May 1789; signed: **Johnston Jones**; witness: **Eli Harvey, Jacob Nugen**; proved February Term 1799 by affirmation of **Eli Harvey**, delivd. **Thomas Lindly**.

P. 401, 4 May 1798, **Christopher Hornaday**, planter, of Cain Creek Settlement of Orange to **George Hobson** of same, twenty six pounds five shillings, 5 7/8 acres, begin at **Pike's** cor., N 10 p. to a black gum, W 94 p. to a black oak, S 10 p. to a black oak on **Marshall's** line, E 94 p. to first station; signed: **Christopher Hornaday**; witness: **Nathan Wells, John Dixon**; proved February Term 1799 by **Wells**, delivd. **Geo. Hobson**.

P. 402, 20 December 1798, **Robert Jordan** of Orange to **Thomas Jordan** of same, two hundred dollars, 360 acres, on waters of North Fork of Little R., begin at a stake, S 17 ch. to a black oak, W 10 ch. to a white oak, S 30 ch. 75 lk. to a stake, W 20 ch. to a black oak jack, S 10 ch. to a post oak, W 60 ch. to a pine, N 10 ch. to a white oak, E 20 ch. to a pine, N 47 ch. & 75 lk. to a black oak on side of the Great Road leading from Hillsborough to Dan R. a few ch. from the North Fork of Little R., E 69 ch. to first station, **North Carolina** to **Robert Jordan** 25 October 1782, warranty deed for all except so much as lies E of a line run by **James Latta** & sold by me to **Mary Clark** my daughter contaning 160 acres; signed: **Robert (X) Jordan**; witness: **James Baldridge, Elizabeth Baldridge**; proved February Term 1799 by **James Baldridge**, delivd. **Thos. Jordon**.

P. 403, 25 April 1797, **Conrad Pile** of Orange to **Jacob Rich** of same, forty pounds, 1 acre & 2 poles, on Great Allamance, begin in middle of Allamance 6 1/2 p. below a Mill Seat known as **Jacob Rich's** Mill, up middle of Allamance 13 p. W, S 12 1/2 p. to a stone, E 13 p. to a stone, N 12 1/2 p. to beginning, part of a larger tract from **North Carolina** to **Conrad Pile**; signed: **Conrad (X) Pile**; witness: **Colbe (+) Jackson, Peter (+) Rich**; proved February Term 1799 by **Colbe Jackson**, delivd. **Jno. Loy**.

P. 405, 22 September 1798, **Samuel Smith** of Orange to brother **Sampson Smith**, for divers good causes, 237 1/2 acres, part of 565 acres legated to

Saml. by his father **William Smith** in last will & Testament, begin at a hicory on **Robert Hatrick's** line, S 21 ch. to a B. O., W 6 ch. to a B. O., S 13 ch. to a P. O., W 67 ch. to a P. O., N 34 ch. to a B. O. on the Division Line between sd. land & **Robert Hatrick's**, E 67 ch. along line to a hicory, S 3 ch. to a hicory, E 6 ch. to beginning, except 100 acres including the improvements & buildings which **William Smith** willed to his wife **Mary Smith** wholly at her disposal during her life and to descend to **Sampson Smith** at her death; signed: **Samuel Smith**; witness: **Robert Hatrick, Stephen Morriss**; proved February Term 1799 by **Hatrick**, delivd. **Thos. Brandford**.

P. 406, 1 February 1798, **Ann Roach & Absalom Roach** Executors of **James Roach** Decd. of Orange to **James Crutchfield** of same, five hundred pounds, 182 acres, begin at a spanish oak on side of a branch, S15W 14 ch. to a post oak, S21W 15 ch. to a black oak, S31E 40 ch. to a black oak, E 18 ch. to a black jack, N 41 1/2 ch. to a white oak, N30W 19 ch. to a white oak on side of a branch, down meanders to beginning; signed: **Ann (+) Roach, Absalom (X) Roach**; witness: **Reuben Smith, Thomas Bradshaw, Wm. Shaw**; proved February Term 1799 by **Smith**, delivd **James Crutchfield**.

P. 407, 19 September 1798, **Samuel Smith** of Orange to **Robert Haterack** of Rockingham, four hundred dollars, 253 1/2 acres, land **Smith** now lives on, part of 595 acres legated to him by his father **William Smith**, begin at a P. O., S 35 ch. to Divison Line between sd. land & **Widow Smith**, W 6 ch. to a hicory, N 3 ch. to a hicory, W 67 ch. along line to Back Line, N 5 ch. to a B. J. on **William Madkin's** line, E 12 1/2 to a P. O., N17E 43 ch. to **Cuningham Smith's** line, E 48 ch. along line to first station; signed: **Saml. Smith, Jane (X) Smith**; witness: **Samson Smith, Stephen Morriss**; proved February Term 1799 by **Samson Smith**, delivd. **Andrew McCully**.

P. 409, 4 October 1791, **James Baldridge** of Orange to **John Elliott** of same, one hundred pounds, [no acreage given], in Green County, Tennessee, within limits of **Baldridge's** entry of 5,833 acres, begin at 2 chesnut trees, E 290 p. to a stake, N 460 p. to a stake, W 290 p. to a stake, S 460 p. to first station; signed: **James Baldridge**, witness: **William Elliott, Malcomb Baldridge**; proved February Term 1799 by **William Elliott**, delivd. **William Elliott**.

P. 410, 22 August 1796, **Titus Atwater** of Chatham to **Moses Atwater** of Orange, one hundred pounds, 224 acres, on waters of Haw R., begin at a hicory **Jesse Nevill's** line, N to a black oak, W to a hicory, S to a hicory, E to a stake, S to a stake, E to first station; signed: **Titus Atwater**; witness: **Randolph Mabray, William (+) Willis**; acknowledged February Term 1799, delivd. **Titus Atwater**.

P. 412, 14 December 1798, **North Carolina** to **Isaac Dorris**, fifty shillings per hundred acres, 200 acres, on Scrub Br. of Quaker Cr., adjoins his other entry & **James Anderson**, begin at a black oak **Anderson's** cor., S85W 60 ch. to a black jack, S 10 ch. to a P. O., W 11 ch. to a stake in **King's** line, S 17 ch. to a stake on side of a branch a cor. of his other entry, E 74 ch. to a post oak, N 21 1/2 ch. to a post oak, N17W 10 1/2 ch. to first station, warrant dated 15 October 1779; signed: **W. R. Davie**; witness: **Will White**; [no probate record], delivd.

ORANGE COUNTY (NC) DEED BOOK 7

Colo. Jno. Ray.

P. 413, 30 March 1796, **Stephen Hart** of Orange to **William Elliott** of same, one hundred thirty seven pounds, 300 acres, on waters of Eno, bounded on N by **Paul & Armstrong**, on W by **Shepperd**, on S by **Collins**, on E by **Hart**, begin at a stone, W 50 ch. to a P. O., S 58 ch. to a hicory, E 61 ch. to a B. jack, N 10 ch. to a B. J., W 10 ch. to a B. J., N 48 ch. to beginning; signed: **Stephen Hart**; witness: **Willm. Hall, Thomas Faucett**; proved May Term 1796 by **William Hall**, delivered **Wm. Elliott**.

P. 414, 28 December 1798, **Thomas Carrington** of Orange to **Ephriam Carrington** of same, one hundred pounds, 125 acres, begin at 2 red oaks on N side of Flat R. on **John Taylor's** line, E to a branch, meanders of branch to **Ephriam Carrington's** on a white oak, N **Carrington's** line to **John Carrimgton Senr.'s** line on a red oak, West along **John Carrington Senr.'s** line to river on a white oak & black, down river to first station; signed: **Thomas (X) Carrington**; witness: **Jesse Rice, Jas. Walker**; proved February Term 1799 by **James Walker**.

P. 415, 10 January 1799, **John Casey** of Hillsborough to **Nelly Doherty & Fanny Doherty** daughters & coheirs of **George** late of Orange, five hundred pounds, confirm unto **Nelly Doherty & Fanny Doherty** as tenants in common & not as joint tenants, part of Lot # 25 in Hillsborough, begin at a point **Absalom Tatom's** cor. 80 feet N from the cor. of the Blue House at intersection of King & Churton Streets, W 55 feet, N 20 feet, W 110 feet to Lot # 24, N along lot to cer. of Lots # 24, 25, 34, & 35, E along Lot # 35 to Churton Street, S along Churton Street to beginning, also part of Lot # 35, begin at cor of Lot # 25 & 35 on Churton Street, W along Lot # 25 to cor. of Lots # 24, 25, 34, &35, N along Lot # 34 6 p. to **Thomas Person's** cor. on Lot, E along **Person's** line to Churton Street, S 6 p. to beginning, Also Lot # 34, bounded on N by Tryon Street, on E by Lot # 35, on S by Lot # 24, on W by Lot # 33; signed: **Jno. Casey**; witness: **Wm. Norwood**; proved February Term 1799 by **William Norwood**, sent **Misses Doherty** by **Cesar**.

P. 417, 20 February 1796, **Charles Powell** of Chatham to **Moses Atwater** of Orange, twenty five pounds, 40 acres, near Wilkinsons Cr. waters of Haw R., begin at a stake on County Line near **William Powell's** house, N with **Nevell's** line to a hicroy, nearly W to a willow on **Wolleys** Spring Br., down branch to a stake on **Malcom Smith's** line, nearly a S course with **Malcom Smith's** line to a hicory on County Line, E with County Line to beginning, original grant also transferred; signed: **Charles Powell**; witness: **Titus Atwater, William (X) Willis**; proved February Term 1799 by **Titus Atwater**, delivered **Moses Atwater**.

P. 419, 5 March 1798, **James Watson Senr., Margaret Watson, James Watson Junr.** of Orange to **William Riley** of same, fifty pounds, 40 acres, on waters of Seven Mile Cr., part of a tract from **Granville** to **James Watson Esq.** 17 June 1754, begin at a bunch of spice wood & willow on Watsons Cr., N along **Joseph Thompson's** line 27 ch. to his cor. a post oak on **Moor's** line, along same E 26 ch. to a bunch of maples on bank of creek, up meanders to first station; signed: **Jas. Watson Sr., Margaret (X) Watson, Jas. Watson Jnr.**; witness: **Joshua**

Thompson, Andrew Watson; proved February Term 1799 by Joshua Thompson, delivred Wm. Riley.

P. 420, 17 July 1797, John Carney of Orange to Jacob Rich of same, fifty pounds, 77 acres, on waters of Allamance, adjoins Jacob Rich & Luke Pryor, begin at a stake, N 30 ch. to a stake Henry McCulloh's line, W 8 ch. to a post oak Rich's cor., his line S 34 ch. to a hicory, E 19 ch. to a white oak, S 11 ch. to a black oak, E 6 ch. to a hicroy on line of Pryor, N 27 ch. to a stake, W 29 ch. to first station, North Carolina to Carney; signed: John (I) Carney; witness: Luke Pryor Senr., Luke Pryor Junr.; proved February Term 1799 by Luke Pryor Senr., delvd. John Loy.

P. 421, 30 December 1789, James Riggs of Orange to William Walker of same, one hundred forty pounds, 100 acres, on waters of Little R., begin at mouth of Black Jack Cr. the consentable line between James Riggs & John Riggs, up creek to a hicory, N to a post oak saplin, E to a black oak cor., N along Walker's line to a hicory on old line, the above mentioned line being made consentable between John Thomas & James Riggs & Thomas Riggs, being a tract of land willed to sd. Riggs by their father to be divided by them, W to a post oak, S to a hicory, W to a white oak, S to river, down river to first station; signed: James Riggs; witness: John Riggs, George Newton, Jno. Woods of Hugh; proved February Term 1799 by John Riggs, delivd. Robert Walker.

P. 423, 15 February 1799, William Courtney of Hillsborough to William Cain of Orange, five shillings, Negor man slave named Affrica, Courtney had mortgaged slave to Cain 28 November 1798 subject to equity of redemption, this deed quits all claim to equity of redemption and vests full title of slave in Cain; signed: William Courtney; witness: David Ray, James Yarbrough; proved November Term 1799 by Yarbrough, delivered Wm. Cain Junior.

P. 424, 5 March 1798, Ezra Cates, planter, of Orange to James Karr, planter, of same, one hundred fifty pounds, 232 acres, on waters of Newhope, bounded on lands of Jane Gray, begin at a post oak, S 75 ch. to a post oak, E 31 ch. to a black jack, N 75 ch. to a hicory, W 31 ch. to first station, part of the land of Robert Baker Deceased by deed bearing date 25 October 1782; signed: Ezra Cate, Mary Cate; witness: Jas. Mitchell, Rob. Cate; proved February Term 1797 by James Mitchell, delivd. James Karr.

P. 425, 27 February 1799, Edward Turner of Orange to John Carragan of same, seventy five pounds, 67 acres, on N side of Eno R., begin at a beach on bank of river at mouth of a small branch, up branch with a line of marked trees a NE course 24 1/2 ch. to a black oak, N65E 6 ch. 25 lk. to a spanish oak on William Courtney's line, with line due N 18 ch. 20 lk. to a black oak on Great Road, along road W 30 ch. to an elm on bank of Eno below & near the Ford, down river to beginning; signed: Edward Turner;; witness: John Pickard, Henry Fossett; proved February Term 1799 by Pickard, delivd. Jno. Carragan.

P. 426, 11 August 1798, Isaac Reynolds of Guilford to Robert Morrison of Orange, one hundred pounds, 207 acres, on S side of Haw R., adjoins Nathl.

ORANGE COUNTY (NC) DEED BOOK 7

Newlin & George Maddin, begin at a sassafras on side of Haw R., S28W 16 1/2 ch. to a spanish oak, S65W 11 ch. to a black oak, S 12 ch. to a spanish oak, W 54 ch. to a spanish oak, N 20 ch. to a white oak, E 20 ch. to a stake, N 13 ch. to a B. oak, E 15 ch. to a B. O., N 14 ch. to a hicory, E 6 ch. to a B. O., N 5 ch. to a B. O. on river, down meanders to first station; signed: **Isaac Reynolds**; witness: **Nathl. Carter, William Edwards**; proved February Term 1799 by **Carter**, delivd. **John Workman**.

P. 427, 29 December 1797, **Malcomb Smith** of Chatham to **Moses Atwater** of Orange, forty pounds, 100 acres, on waters of Terrices Cr., begin at a hicory on County Line, E 100 p., N 160 p. to a stake, W 100 p. to a hicory, S 160 p. to first station; signed: **Malcomb (+) Smith**; witness: **Chainal Pendergrass, Job Pendergrass**; proved February Term 1799 by **Job Pendergrass**, delivd. **Moses Atwater**.

P. 429, 3 December 1798, **George Johnston** of Orange to **Thomas Couch** of same, one hundred pounds, 141 1/2 acres, begin at a white oak, E 40 ch. to a B. jack, S 30 1/2 ch. to a stake, E 53 ch. to a white oak, S 5 ch. to a walnut, W 83 ch. to a stake, N 23 1/2 ch. to a post oak, W 10 ch. to a black jack, N 12 ch. to first station, 1/2 of tract from **North Carolina** to **Mark Patterson & John Cobb** 18 May 1789, on waters of Newhope, being the north half, sold by virtue of an execution by **James Freelnad** Esq. High Sheriff & purchased by **William Courtney, Courtney** to **George Johnston**; signed: **Geo. Johnston**; witness: **Saml. Couch, David (I) Hinchey**; proved February Term 1799 by **Samuel Couch**, delivd. **Thomas Couch**.

P. 431, 1 February 1799, **Benjamin Forrest Senr.** of Orange to **Benjamin Forrest Junr.** of same, five pounds, 117 acres, begin at a shugar [sugar] tree on the side of Eno R., S25E 15 3/4 ch. to a water oak, S15W 13 3/4 ch. to a dead red oak, S39W 45 1/4 ch. to a red oak, W 4 1/8 ch. to a stake, N 44 ch. to a pine in **Drusy Johnston's** line, E to Eno R., down river to first station; signed: **Benjamin (B) Forrest**; witness: **James Latta Junr., Josiah (X) Forrest**; proved February Term 1799 by **Josiah Forrest**, delivd. **Jno. Cain**.

P. 432, 27 September 1798, **Bryson Dobbins** of Orange to **Henry Thompson Junr.** of same, fifty four pounds five shillings, 1 old Negro slave named **Sarah** about 60 years of age, 1 malatto [mulatto] girl named **Nancy** about 7 years of age, 1 mulatto boy slave named **Dempsey** about 4 years of age, 1 cow, 1 bed & furniture, 1 large pott, 1 small pott, 1 dutch oven, 1 large tubb, 1 large pail, 8 chairs, 1 walnut table, 2 pine tables, 1 saddle & bridle, 6 knives & forks, 6 large plates, 5 small plates, 6 table spoons, 6 cups & saucers, 1 tea pott, 1 sugar dish, 1 decanter, 1 sugar cannister, 1 looking glass, 2 brass candle sticks, 2 pewter dishes, 1 diaper table cloth, 1 large pewter basin, 1 coffee mill, 1 coffee pott, 2 sad irons, 2 pott racks, 1 tea kittle, & tin quart measure, mortgage deed due 1 March next [1799], if property not sufficient to pay debt, **Dobbins** will pay balance; signed: **Bryson Dobbins**; witness: **Wm. Norwood**; proved February Term 1799 by **William Norwood**, delivd. **Randolph Segrove** pr. order.

P. 433, 11 November 1797, **Benjamin Rhodes** of Orange to **John Sheperd** of same, fifty seven pounds fifteen shillings, 92 1/2 acres, on waters of Ellebees Cr.

a branch of Eno, begin at a pine a cor. of **Sheperd's** land, S with **Lewis'** line 80 p. to a red & white oak, N75E 211 p. to a sweet gum on a branch, up branch to a sweet gum in **Sheperd's** line, his line S62 1/2W 136 p. to beginning; signed: **Benjamin Rhodes**; witness: **Francis Moreland, John (I) Edwards, William Edwards**; proved February Term 1799 by **John Edwards**, delivd. **Jno. Shepperd.**

P. 435, 17 April 1797, **Robert Scoby** & **Lucy Scoby** wife of **Robert** & mother of **Soloman Deboe** & **Stephen Deboe** orphans of **John Deboe** deceased to **Archibald Murphey** guardian of **Soloman** & **Stephen Deboe**, three hundred two pounds eight shillings, dower & right of dower to **John Deboe** Land on Eno, **William Lackey** to **John Deboe**, considerartion is amount due to orphans from settlement in 1797, mortgage deed, to be paid by 1 January 1798 or **Murphy** can sell right of dower; signed: **Robert Scoby, Lucy Scoby**; witness: **Abraham Thompson, William McMun**; proved February Term 1799 by **McMun**, delivd. **J. Scoby** pr. **Mr. Deboe's** order.

P. 436, 1 March 1799, **Henry Thompson Senr.** of Orange to son **Henry Thompson Junr.**, love & affection, a Negro boy slave named **Edmund**, **Edmund** is to remain in service of **Henry Thompson Senr.** during his lifetime; signed: **Henry Thompson Senr.**; witness: **William Mebane**; proved February Term 1799 by **Mebane**, delivd. **Henry Thompson Senr.**

P. 436, 17 April 1798, **Ann Cate** & **Stephen Cate** of Orange to **James Kirk** of same, thirteen pounds ten shillings, 6 1/2 acres, on S side of Cain Cr., begin at a red oak on bank of creek & on line of **Kirk**, W 6 ch. to a white oak, N 15 ch. to Turkey Hill Cr., down meanders to Cain Cr., down creek to first station in all 16 ch.; signed: **Ann (X) Cate, Stephen Cate**; witness: **Saml. Bradford, Thomas (X) Dixon**; proved February Term 1799 by **Samuel Bradford**.

P. 438, 22 March 1798, **Daniel Albright** of Orange to **Colba Jackson** of same, fourteen pounds, 64 1/2 acres, on waters of Grate Allamance & Gun Cr., begin at a post oak, S 31 ch. to a stake, W crossing Gun Cr. 15 ch. to a B. O., S 6 ch. to Allamance Cr., up creek to a mulberry & elm, N 39 ch. 50 lk. to a stake, E 19 ch. to beginning; signed: **Daniel Albright**; witness: **William Ray, Joseph Baker**; proved February Term 1799 by **Ray**, delivd. **Danl. Albrightt**.

P. 439, 22 March 1798, **Daniel Albright** of Orange to **Malachiah Hatmaker** of same, fourteen pounds, 64 1/2 acres, on Great Allamance Cr., begin at a red oak on bank of creek a cor. of **Malachiah Hatmaker**, his line N 36 ch. 50 lk. to a stake, S70E 5 ch. to a hicory, S25E 44 ch. to a sugar tree on bank of creek, up meanders to first station; signed: **Daniel Albright**; witness: **William Ray, Joseph Baker**; proved February Term 1799 by **Ray**, delivd. **Danl. Albright**.

P. 440, 31 September 1797, **William Carter** of Orange to **Robert Morison** of same, sixteen pounds, 34 acres, begin at a black oak saplin, N46W 32 p. to a branch, up branch to a P. O. bush in **John Shy's** line, E with line 125 p. to **John Shy's** cor., S 88 p. to beginning, part of a tract from **North Carolina** to **John Elliot** 9 November 1784, **Elliot** to **Carter**; signed: **William Carter**; witness: **Eli Harvey, Nathan Dicks**; proved February Term 1799 by affirmation of

Harvey, delivd. R. Morrison.

P. 441, 1 February 1799, **Benjamin Forrest Senr.** of Orange to **Josiah Forrest** of same, five pounds, 117 acres, begin at a pine in **Drury Johnston's** line **Benjamin Forrest Junr.'s** cor., S 44 ch. to a stake **Forrest's** cor., W 14 & then 8 ch. to a hicory, N30W 50 ch. to a dogwood on side of Eno R., E with **Drury Johnston's** line to first station; signed: **Benjamin (B) Forrest**; witness: **James Latta Junr., Benj. (B) Forrest Junr.**; proved February Term 1797 by **Benjamin Forrest Junr.**, delivd. **Jno. Cain.**

P. 442, 25 June 1798, **Thomas Lewellen L. Wall** of Orange to **Sally Wall** his wife [no residence given], for maintenance & support of herself & her children begotten by **Thomas Lewellen L. Wall**, Negro fellow named **Fendall**, Negro wench named **Lydia**, 1 gray horse, 1 bay mare & colt, an elegant 4 posted bedstead with screws & sacking bottom, 5 blankets, 1 feather bed, bolster, & 2 pillows, 1 trunk with all her wearing apparel, 1 small bedstead & bed to the satisfaction of **Sally Wall**, the two have "mutually agreed to separate & part their interests & concerns with each other forever, **Sally Wall** is given right of *femme sole* & relinquishes all claim of dower to property of **Thomas L. L. Wall** & grants **Thomas L. L. Wall** liberty to marry any other woman he pleases any law to the contrary notwithstanding, **Sally Wall** to petition the General Assembly for a divorce; signed: **Sally Wall, Thomas L. L. Wall**; witness: **Robert Thompson, Nancy S. Gilbert**; proved February Term 1799 by **Thompson**.

P. 444, 2 December 1797, **North Carolina** to **James McMun** [no residence given], fifty shillings per hundred acres, 97 1/2 acres, on waters of Back Cr., adjoins his own land, **William Smith, & Andrew Smith**, begin at a black oak **James McMun's** cor., E 16 ch. to a hicory **Andrew Smith's** cor., N 61 ch. to a black oak **William Smith's** cor., W 16 ch. to a stake on **Samuel Devenport's** line, S 61 ch. to first station, warrant dated 1 February 1796; signed: **Saml. Ashe**; witness: **J. Glasgow**; [no probate record], delivd. **Wm. McMun.**

P. 445, 13 June 1798, **North Carolina** to **William McQuiston** [no residence given], fifty shillings per hundred acres, 165 acres, on waters of Newhope, adjoins **William Couch** & **Burrows**, begin at a white oak **Couch's** cor., his line N 60 p. to a post oak **John Strayhorn's** cor., his line N54W 128 p. to a stake in **Strayhorn's** Field his cor., S18E 256 p. to a gum on a branch his cor. **Burrows'** line, his line E 180 p. to a post oak **Burrows'** cor., N 67 p. to a stake on **Couch's** line, W 100 p. to first station, warrant dated 28 February 1795; signed: **Saml. Ashe**; witness: **J. Glasgow**; [no probate record], delivd. **Jno. McKerrall.**

P. 446, 20 March 1799, **North Carolina** to **John McRorey** [no residence given], fifty shillings per hundred acres, 200 acres, on Boyds Cr., adjoins his own land, begin at a black jack a cor. to **McRorey**, his line S 26 ch. 50 lk. to a stake, along **Freeland's** line E 20 ch. to a stake on **Stockard's** line, along same N50E 18 ch. 50 lk. to a stake on **Alvin's** line, along same N45W 21 ch. to a stake, N50E 6 ch. 75 lk to a black jack or oak, N 46 ch. to a stake on the creek, W to beginning, entered 9 June 1795; signed: **W. R. Davie**; witness: [none]; [no probate record], delivd. **Jno. McRorey.**

P. 447, 10 July 1788, **North Carolina** to **Pomphrey Herndon** [no residence given], ten pounds per hundred acres, 82 acres, on Fills Cr. of Morgans Cr., bound on N by his own land, on S by **Jesse Nevell**, on W by **John Hightower**, begin at his own cor. red oak, W his line 76 ch. to a post oak, S 15 ch. to a black jack, E 31 ch. to a stake, N 7 ch. to a post oak, E 45 ch. to a stake, N 8 ch. to first station; signed: **Sam Johnston**; witness: **W. Williams**; [no probate record], delivd. **P. Herndon**.

P. 448, 8 December 1797, **North Carolina** to **Andrew McBroom** [no residence given], fifty shillings per hundred acres, 147 acres, on waters of Little R., adjoins **Thomas Persons, Zachariah Dickey,** & his own land, begin at a post oak, with a line of **McBroom's** Old Tract N 60 ch. to a stake, W at 21 ch. passing another of his cor. a black oak, along same S 60 ch. to a stake on **Dickey's** line, along same E to beginning, warrant dated 20 October 1796 & 7 February 1797; signed: **Saml. Ashe**; witness: **J. Glasgow**; [no probate record], delivd. **Andrew McBroom**.

P. 449, 8 December 1797, **North Carolina** to **Nathaniel Christmas** [no residence given], fifty shillings per hundred acres, 250 acres, adjoins lands of **Strudwick** lying in that part called The Gore between **Strudwick's** Lower & Middle Tracts, begin at a post oak a cor. of **Thomas Lasey**, his line E 12 ch. to a post oak on the Fayetteville Road, along another of **Lasey's** lines & the road S13E 7 ch. to a stake on **Strudwick's** line, along same N29E 61 ch. to a stake on Mocason Br., N50W 72 ch. to a stake on a line **Strudwick's** Middle Tract, along same 114 ch. to a stake **Lasley's** line, along same to beginning, warrant dated 17 [blank] 1797; signed: **Saml. Ashe**; witness: **J. Glasgow**; [no probate record], delivd. **Chs. Christmas**.

P. 450, 11 March 1799, **North Carolina** to **Charles Christmas** [no residence given], fifty shillings per hundred acres, 200 acres, between **Strudwick's** Lower & Middle Tracts, begin at a post oak on line of Lower Tract, with same N29E 98 ch. 50 lk. to a white oak, E 17 ch. 50 lk. to a white oak cor. of **James Thompson**, his line S26W 15 ch. 50 lk. to a maple on South Prong of Little Cain Cr., up same N34W 5 ch. 50 lk. to a B. oak near & above mouth of a small branch, up branch 15 ch. to a white oak, S5E 9 ch. to a post oak, S24W 45 ch. to a stake, to beginning, entered 19 March 1795; signed: **W. R. Davie**; witness: **Will. White**; [no probate record], delivd. **Chs. Christmas**.

P. 451, 11 March 1799, **North Carolina** to **Reubin Smith** [no residence given], fifty shillings per hundred acres, 110 acres, on waters of Little Cain Cr., adjoins **Nathaniel McLimore, Hugh Rea,** & his own land, begin at a sassafras, W 6 ch. 50 lk. to a post oak on a branch of Cain Cr., down meanders 19 ch. to a maple & cor. of **J. Thompson**, N4E 5 ch. 25 lk. to a black jack on a branch, W 9 ch. 75 lk. to a rock, N 32 ch. to a post oak, E 33 ch. to a stake, S 33 ch. to beginning, entered 11 July 1797; signed: **W. R. Davie**; witness: **Will. White**; [no probate record], delivd. **Reubin Smith**.

P. 452, 11 March 1799, **North Carolina** to **Acquilla Crompton** [no residence given], fifty shillings per hundred acres, 70 acres, on waters of Storm Cr. of North Hico, adjoins **Abraham Night, Vincent Roberts,** & County Line, begin at a pine **Roberts'** cor., his line N 40 ch. to a whitee oak on County Line, along same W 17 ch. 50 lk. to a white oak, S 40 ch. to a black jack on **Knight's** line, E 17 ch. 50 lk. to beginning; signed: **W. R. Davie**; witness: **W. White**; [no probate record], delivd. **Acquilla Crompton.**

P. 453, 14 December 1798, **North Carolina** to **Robert Stewart** [no residence given], thirty shillings per hundred acres, 200 acres, on waters of Eno, adjoins his own land & **Matthew Lindsay,** begin at a black jack **Stewart's** cor., S 56 1/2 ch. to a stake **Stewart's** cor., E 24 ch. to a black jack **Matthew Lindsay's** cor., S 20 ch. to **Lindsay's** cor., W 26 ch. to a black oak, N 107 ch. to a pine, E 40 ch. to a post oak bush, S 30 1/2 ch. to a stake, W 43 ch. to first station, warrant dated 20 June 1793; signed: **W. R. Davie**; witness: **Will. White**; [no probate record], delivd. **Robt. Stewart.**

P. 454, 14 December 1798, **North Carolina** to **Jacob Marshill** [no residence given], fifty shillings per hundred acres, 200 acres, on waters of Vernals Cr., begin at a hicory **Freeman's** cor., E 60 p. to 3 black oaks, N 240 p. to a black oak, W 114 p. to a post oak, S 8 p. to a post oak, W 71 p. to a white oak on **Lindley's** line, S 232 p. to a stake, E to first station, entered 22 February 1796; signed: **W. R. Davie**; witness: **W. White**; [no probate record], delivd. **D. Foust.**

P. 455, 14 December 1798, **North Carolina** to **Peter Foust** [no residence given], thirty shillings per hundred acres, 13 1/2 acres, on waters of Cain Cr., adjoins **Foust, Jacob Marshill,** & **George Foust,** begin at a stake in **Foust's** Field, W 5 ch. to a post oak **Peter Foust's** cor., N 27 ch. to a black oak, E 5 ch. to a black oak, S 27 ch. to first station, warrant dated 1 October 1793; signed: **W. R. Davie**; witness: **Will. White**; [no probate record], delivd. **D. Foust.**

P. 456, 6 April 1799, **Andrew Murdock** Esq. Sheriff of Orange to **John McKerell** of same, one hundred fifty five pounds, 276 acres, on Spirit Br. waters of Eno, begin at a white oak **John Estes'** cor. formerly **Hugh Woods',** E with **Estes'** line 42 ch. 50 lk. crossing Spirit Br. to a red oak **Lytle's** cor., S his line & by his cor. 40 ch. to **William Crabtree's** cor. white oak, continuing same course along his line in all 65 ch. to a black oak **Crabtree's** cor., W his line 20 ch. to his cor. stake, continuing same course along **David Strayhorn's** line in all 42 ch. 50 lk. to a black oak & hicory on **Conner's** line, his line N 11 ch. to a black oak **Conner's** cor., N 46 ch. to first station, levy on lands of **James Watson Junr.** for two hundred ten pounds two shillings one pence three farthings recovered by **Jeanny Watson** assignee, sold 22 February 1799; signed: **Andrew Murdock**; witness: **Wm. Norwood, James Baldridge;** acknowledged before **John Lewis Taylor,** JSCLE, 10 April 1799, delivd. **Jno. McKerell.**

P. 459, 11 March 1799, **North Carolina** to **John Armstrong** [no residence given], ten pounds per hundred acres, 200 acres, on waters of Little R., adjoins **David Gilson** & **John Allerson,** begin at a pine **David Gilson's** cor., W 55 ch. to a post oak **Gilson's** cor., N 56 ch. to a black oak **John Allerson's** cor., E 12 1/4 ch. to a white oak, S 33 1/2 ch. to a post oak, E 52 1/2 ch. to a pine, S 39 3/4 ch. to a post oak, W 10 ch. to a stake, N 17 ch. to first station, entered 10 August 1786; signed: **W. R. Davie**; witness: **Willm. White**; [no probate record], delivd. **Jno. Armstrong.**

P. 460, 5 April 1798, **North Carolina** to **John Armstrong** [no residence given], fifty shillings per hundred acres, 106 acres, on waters of Little R., adjoins his own land, begin at a white oak **Robert Jurdon's** cor., S 10 ch. to a pine **Jordon's** cor., E 30 ch. to a stake, S 14 ch. to a pine **John Armstrong's** cor., W 57 ch. to a pine **Armstrong's** cor., N 24 ch. to a stake, E 27 ch. to first station, entered 31 December 1796; signed: **Saml. Ashe**; witness: **J. Glasgow;** [no probate record], delivd. **Jno. Armstrong.**

P. 461, 8 December 1797, **North Carolina** to **James Baldridge** [no residence given], fifty shillings per hundred acres, 294 acres, on waters of Little R., adjoins **Thomas Person** formerly **Mulhollan, Wm. McKee, Thomas Rountree, Daniel McMahon, & Robert Berry,** begin at a hicory on **Rountree's** line, W crossing the Great Road 1 ch. to his cor. a black oak, N 4 ch. to a pine **Daniel McMahon's** cor., along his line W 45 ch. to a white oak on **McKee's** line, with line S 29 ch. to a black jack on **Person's** line, along same E 24 ch. to his cor. a hicory, S 51 1/2 ch. to a stake a cor. of **Person's** 200 acre tract, with a line of tract E crossing the road in all 37 1/2 ch. to a stake, W 16 ch. to a black oak **Berry's** cor., his line N 46 ch. to beginning, entry dated 18 May 1797; signed: **Saml. Ashe**; witness: **J. Glasgow**; [no probate record], delivd. **Jno. Armstrong.**

P. 462, 13 August 1798, **North Carolina** to **Robert Gray** [no residence given], fifty shillings peer hundred acres, 22 acres, on waters of Little R., adjoins **Henry Waggoner, Francis Baldridge, James Watson, Thomas Griffen, & Samuel Nelson,** begin at a pine **Watson's** cor., S 4 ch. 40 lk. to a post oak, E 50 ch. to a stake, N 4 ch. 40 lk. to a white oak **Watson's** cor., his line W 50 ch. to beginning, entered 8 November 1796; signed: **Saml. Ashe**; witness: **J. Glasgow;** [no probate record], delivd. **Robert Gray.**

P. 463, 11 March 1799, **North Carolina to Robert Dickens & William Waite** [no residence given], fifty shillings per hundred acres, 108 acres, on waters of Flat R., adjoins their own lines, begin at a hicory **Horton's** cor., S35W 38 ch. to a post oak another of **Horton's** cor., W 22 ch. to a pine, N 33 ch. to a stake, E to beginning; signed: **Willm. R. Davie**; witness: **Willm. Hill**; [no probate record], delivd. **W. Waite.**

P. 464, 25 January 1799, **Thomas Horton** of Orange to **James Horton** of same, 300 pounds, 133 acres, on both sides of Mountain Cr., begin at a dogwood formerly a red oak, W 27 1/2 ch. to a red oak saplin, N a dividing line 48 1/2 ch. to a black oak in **Commons'** line, E with line to his cor. 27 1/2 ch., S 48 1/2 ch. to first station; signed: **Thomas (H) Horton**; witness: **Saml. Turrentine, Edwd. Harris**; proved 18 April 1799 before **Spruce Macay**, JSCLE, by **Torringtine,** delivd. **Gavin Alves.**

P. 466, 2 February 1799, **James Horton** of Orange to **George Laws** of same, eight hundred dollars, 343 acres, begin at a dogwood formerly a red oak, W 27 1/2 ch. to a red oak saplin, N a dividing line 48 1/2 ch. to a black oak in **Commons'** line, E with line to his cor. 27 1/2 ch., S 48 1/2 ch. to first station, 133 acres, on both sides of Mountain Cr., **Thomas Horton** to **James Horton** 25 January 1799, another tract adjoining above on S side, begin at a stake in line of above **Thomas Latta's** cor., S along **Latta's** line about 42 ch. to a black oak **Stephen Willson's** cor., his line S16W 35 ch. to a hicory, W 18 ch. to a stake, N along **Moor's** line 78 ch. to a post oak, with line of above mentioned Old Tract E 29 ch. to first station, 210 acres, **Walter Alves** to **James Horton** 20 February 1796; signed: **James Horton**; witness: **Walter Alves, Henry Wood**; proved 18 April 1799 before **Spruce Macay**, JSCLE, by **Alves**, delivd. **Gavin Alves**.

P. 468, 19 April 1799, **Nancy Benton** Executrix of **Jesse Benton** deceased of Orange & **Joseph Taylor** of Granvville to **David Dickey** of Caswell, two hundred twenty dollars, 150 acres, **Absalom Tatom, William Watters,** & **Nancy Benton** appointed executors of estate of **Jesse Benton** by will, **Tatom** & **Watters** refused to serve, will authorized sale of land, **Jesse Benton** & **Joseph Taylor** purchased a tract from **James Freeland** Sheriff which adjoined **John Nichols, Joseph Ray,** & others & conveyed to **Benton** & **Taylor** as Joint Tenants not as Tenants in Common by deed dated 27 May 1785, this land being sold, [no metes & bounds description]; signed: **Ann Benton, Joseph Taylor**; witness: **John Wilkinson, Jesse Benton**; proved 19 April 1799 before **John Lewis Taylor** by **Jesse Benton** & acknowledged by **Joseph Taylor**, delivd. **Willm. Woods.**

P. 469, 19 April 1799, **Willm. McQuiston** of Hillsborough to **Catlet Campbell** of same, five shillings, 2 acres, mortgage deed, **McQuiston** owes **Robert** & **Walter Colquhoun** Merchants & Partners of Petersburg, Virginia, three hundred thirty pounds seventeen shillings six pence, Lots # 2 & 44 in Hillsborough, bounded by King Street on N, by Lot # 45 on E by Margaret Lane on S, by Public Lot # 1 on W, also 1 Negro woman slave named **Frank** about thirty five or forty years of age, property to be sold in debt not paid by 1 June next; signed: **William McQuiston**; witness: [none listed]; acknowledged before **Spruce Macay**, JSCLE, 19 April 1799, delivd. **Catlet Campbell.**

P. 472, 9 September 1797, **James Hogg** of Orange to **James Phillips** of Hillsborough, sixty one pounds five shillings, 12 1/4 acres, adjoins Town of Hillsborough, on N side of road leading E from Queen Street, begin at a stake the point of intersection of the Town Line with N side of road, E along N side of road 10 ch. 75 lk. to a stake on E side of an Old Crossroad, N 11 ch. 40 lk. to a stake on **Mr. Watter's** line, W along **Mr. Watter's** fence reduced to a straight line to a stake **Mr. Watter's** SW cor. being in the Town Line, S along line 11 ch. 40 lk. to beginning; signed: **James Hogg**; witness: **A. Tatom**; acknowledged 9 April 1799 before **Spruce Macay**, JSCLE, delivd. **Catlet Campbell.**

P. 473, 13 August 1798, **North Carolina** to **William Walker** [no residence given], fifty shillings per hundred acres, 275 acres, on waters of Stags Cr. & Quaker Cr., adjoins **John Criswell** & **George Faucett**, begin at a hicory **Faucet's** cor., his line E crossing the Fayetteville Road 53 ch. to a white oak **Bird's** cor., his line S 31 ch. to a post oak & white oak, W 23 ch. 50 lk. to a black jack, S 42 ch. to a black jack on **Bradford's** line, his line W 21 ch. crossing road to a stake on **Murrey's** line his line N 15 ch. to his cor. stake, W 20 ch. to a stake, N 8 ch. to a stake **Crisswell's** line, his line E 8 ch. 75 lk. to his cor. a post oak, N 50 ch. to beginning, Warrant No. 339 dated 1 October 1793 & No. 354 Entered 27 January 1797; signed: **Saml. Ashe**; witness: **J. Glasgow**;

ORANGE COUNTY (NC) DEED BOOK 7

[no probate record], delivd. **Wm. Walker**.

P. 474, 8 December 1797, **North Carolina** to **John Walker** [no residence given], fifty shillings per hundred acres, 75 acres, on Stags Cr., adjoins **James Murray**, begin at a hicory on **Hughes'** line, along line N39W 13 ch. 75 lk. to a burch on N bank of Stags Cr., up creek N34E 3 ch. 50 lk. to a poplar on **James Murrey's** line, along line W 45 ch. 50 lk. to a black jack, S 1 ch. 75 lk. to a willow oak a cor. to **Watkin's** Old Tract, with line of tract E 64 ch. 25 lk. to beginning, entered 27 January 1797; signed: **Saml. Ashe**; witness: **J. Glasgow**; [no probate record], delivd. **Wm. Walker**.

P. 475, 10 August 1797, **North Carolina** to **James Cheek** [no residence given], fifty shillings per hundred acres, 29 acres, on waters of Newhope, adjoins **George Long, James Mitchell, John Mitchell, Robert Cheek**, & his own land, begin at a B. O. **James Mitchell's** cor., his line N 21 ch. 75 lk. to a P. O. on **John Mitchell's** line, W 13 ch. 50 lk. to a B. O., S 21 ch. 70 lk. to a willow oak, E 13 ch. 50 lk. to beginning, entered 29 November 1796; signed: **Saml. Ashe**; witness: **J. Glasgow**; [no probate record], delivd. **James Cheek**.

P. 476, 11 March 1799, **North Carolina** to **James Carroll** [no residence given], fifty shillings per hundred acres, 30 acres, adjoins **William McCauley** & his own land, begin at a willow oak a cor. of **Wm. & Mathew McCauley**, E 13 ch. 60 lk. to a post oak, N 22 ch. to a post oak, W 13 ch. 60 lk. to a stake on **William McCauley's** line, S 22 ch. to beginning, entered 29 November 1796; signed: **W. R. Davie**; witness: **Will. White**; [no probate record], delivered **James Cheek**.

P. 477, 11 March 1799, **North Carolina** to **Barnard Cate** [no residence given], fifty shillings per hundred acres, 350 acres, on Cain Cr., adjoins **Thomas Cate & John Cate**, begin at a white oak on a branch on **John Cate's** line, along line E 345 ch. 50 lk. to a white oak, N30E 8 ch. to a post oak, E 5 ch. 50 lk. to a black oak on the branch of Cain Cr., up meanders 28 ch. to a white oak at mouth of a branch, up branch 20 ch. to a spanish oak, N 11 ch. to a post oak, W 60 ch. to a black oak, S 36 ch. 50 lk. to a post oak at head of a branch, down branch to beginning; signed: **W. R. Davie**; witness: **Will. White**; [no probate record], delivd. **Barnard Cate**.

P. 478, 5 April 1798, **North Carolina** to **Absalom Willhoit** [no residence given], fifty shillings per hundred acres, 306 acres, on waters of Cedar Cr., begin at a hicory on side of Cedar Cr., E 12 ch. 50 lk. to a post oak, S 19 ch. to a stake, W 2 ch. to a stake, S43W 22 ch. to a post oak, W 37 ch. to a white oak, N28W 6 ch. 50 lk. to a white oak, N20W 14 ch. to a red oak **Holt's** cor., N24E 16 ch. to a post oak, N77E 4 ch. to a post oak, N27E 30 ch. to a spanish oak, N 15 ch. to a post oak, S62E 26 ch. to a hicory on side of Cedar Cr., down meanders to first station, warrant dated 18 November 1778; signed: **Saml. Ashe**; witness: **J. Glasgow**; [no probate record], delivd. **W. Raney**.

P. 480, 11 March 1799, **North Carolina** to **William Nunn** [no residence given], fifty shillings per hundred acres, 68 acres, on waters of Eno R., begin at a white oak **John Daniel's** cor., his line E 35 p. to a hicory his cor. on **Cabe's** line, his line N 58 p. to a white oak in **Nunn's** line, his line W 134 p. to a white oak **David**

Rainey's cor., his line S 90 p. to a black jack, E 99 p. to a stake **John Daniel's** cor. on **Couch's** line, N with **Daniel's** line to beginning, entered 7 December 1797; signed: **W. R. Davie**; witnes: **Will. White**; [no probate record], delivd. **W. Nunn**.

P. 481, 11 March 1799, **North Carolina** to **Mathias Willson** [no residence given], fifty shillings per hundred acres, 100 acres, on waters of Back Cr. & Buckhorn Br. & on E side of his own plantation, adjoins **James Gill** & **Moses Fortune**, begin at 2 persimmons, N 6 ch. to a black jack Gill's cor., N80W 13 ch. to a spanish oak on Hasting's line, S10W 46 ch. to a post oak, S80E 22 ch. to a gum, N10E 44 ch. to a white oak, to beginning, entered 25 February 1795; signed: **W. R. Davie**; witness: **Will. White**; [no probate record].

P. 482, 11 March 1799, **North Carolina** to **Abner Marsh** [no residence given], fifty shillings per hundred acres, 100 acres, on waters of Linches Cr., adjoins **Acquilla Crompton, A. Lee, Mabane, & James Lee**, begin at a post oak on Caswell County Line, with **Crompton's** line S 37 ch. to a pine his cor., E 10 ch. to a pine, S 20 ch. 50 lk. to a post oak,E 11 ch. 50 lk. to a post oak on **Lee's** line, along same N 57 1/2 ch. to a pine on County Line, along same W to beginning, warrant No. 443 entered 8 September 1797; signed: **W. R. Davie**; witness: **Wm. White**; [no probate record], delivd. **Abner Marsh**.

P. 483, 20 April 1797, **George Holt Senior** of Orange to **Keziah Low** [no residence given], one hundred pounds, Negro woman **Phillis**; signed: **George (H) Holt**; witness: **Thomas Low, George Garrett, Harmon (X) Low**; proved May Term 1797 by **Harmon Low**.

P. 483, 22 August 1797, **John Hogan** of Montgomery County, Tennessee to **William Hogan** of Orange, three hundred dollars, Negro woman named **Tamer** about 20 years of age; signed: **John Hogan**; witness: **Willm Stroud, David Hogan**; proved before **Spruce Macay**, JSCLE, by **William Stroud** [no date given], delivd. **Wm. Nunn**.

P. 484, 21 August 1797, **John Hogan** of Montgomery County, Tennessee, to **William Hogan** of Orange, two hundred pounds, 143 acres, on waters of Bolans Cr., adjoins lands formerly belonging to **John Hogan** on S land belonging to heirs of **Stephen Lloyd** on W & N known as Rocky Spring Tract, [no metes & bounds description]; signed: **John Hogan**; witness: **William Stroud, Thomas Hogan**; proved before **Spruce Macay**, JSCLE, [no date givven], delivd. **Wm. Nunn**.

P. 485, 13 August 1797, **Thomas Hogan** of Montgomery County, Tennessee, to **William Hogan** of Orange, sixty pounds, Negro man slave named **Ned**, now in possession of **Thomas Brewer**; signed: **Thomas Hogan**; witness: **John Hogan, Willm. Stroud**; proved before **David Stone**, JSCLE, [no date given], delivd. **Wm. Nunn**.

P. 486, 13 September 1798, **Thomas Lloyd** of Sumner County, Tennessee to **William Hogan** of Orange, power of attorney, to receive from **Thomas Armstrong** or any other person in possession of estate of **James Armstrong** his wife's share of estate; signed: **Thomas Lloyd;** witness: none listed; acknowledged before **Thomas Donnall & James Douglas,** Justices of Sumner County, Tennessee, 13 September 1798; certification of **David Shelby,** CSC, Sumner County, Tennessee, that **Douglass & Donnell** are justices dated 14 September 1798, delivd. **Wm. Nunn.**

P. 487, 11 March 1799, **North Carolina** to **William Lingo** [no residence given], fifty shillings per hundred acres, 26 3/4 acres, adjoins **P. Madison, James Baxter,** & Granville County Line, begin at a pine a cor. to **Lingo's** other tract, N 3 ch. 33 lk. to a stake on **Madison's** line, E 29 ch. 50 lk. to his cor. black oak on Granville County Line, with line S 45 ch. 83 lk. to a stake, W 4 ch. to **Baxter's** cor. post oak, N 44 ch. 50 lk. to a gum, W 25 ch. 50 lk. to beginning, entered 24 June 1796; signed: **W. R. Davie;** witness: **Will. White;** [no probate record], delivd. **Jacob Umpstead.**

P. 488, 9 November 1784, **North Carolina** to **John & Edward King** [no residence given] , fifty shillings per hundred acres, 400 acres, on Deep Cr. a branch of Stoney Cr., adjoins a claim of **Samuel Means,** begin at a post oak, N 66 ch. to a stake, E 67 ch. to a post oak, S 56 ch. to a white oak, W 43 ch. to a white oak, S 10 ch. to a black oak, W 24 ch. to first station; signed: **Alexander Martin;** witness: **J. Glasgow;** [no probate record], delivd. **Jno. King.**

P. 489, 9 November 1784, **North Carolina** to **John & Edward King** [no residence given], fifty shillings per hundred acres, 150 acres, on waters of Deep Cr., begin at a white oak, N 30 ch. to a post oak, W 50 ch. to a black oak, S 30 ch. to a white oak, E 50 ch. to first station; signed: **Alex: Martin;** witness: **J. Glasgow;** [no probate record], delivd. **Jno. King.**

P. 490, 14 December 1798, **North Carolina** to **John Patton** [no residence given], thirty shillings per hundred acres, 100 acres, on the Dray Br. of Vernals Cr., begin at a post oak, E crossing the Dray Br. 22 1/2 ch. to a stake, N 25 ch. to a black oak, E 5 ch. to a black oak, N 19 1/2 ch. to a black oak, W crossing branch 22 1/2 ch. to a stake, S 19 1/2 ch. to a post oak, W 5 ch. to a stake, S 25 ch. to first station, warrant issued 1 October 1793; signed: **W. R. Davie;** witness: **Will. White;** [no probate record], delivd. **Jno. Patton Junr.**

P. 491, 6 November 1784, **North Carolina** to **Thomas Patton** [no residence given], fifty shillings per hundred acres, 320 acres, on Vernals Cr. of Haw R., adjoins **John Patton** & **Robert Hunter,** begin at a hicory on side of Vernals Cr., N45E 40 ch. to a P. O., S45E 65 ch. to a P. O., S62W 7 ch. to a P. O., S 20 ch. to a R. O., W 54 ch. to a B., N 40 ch. to a P. O., W 7 ch. to a P. on side of Vernals Cr., up meanders to first station; signed: **Alexr. Martin;** witness: **J. Glasgow;** [no probate record], delivd. **Jno. Patton Junr.**

P. 492, Ended May 30th 1799, **J. Estes** P. Register.

ORANGE COUNTY (NC) DEED BOOKS 6 & 7

PERSONAL NAME INDEX

Citation is to the book and page number found in the original books. The names of a few of the witnesses were written in German script. The Public Register, who apparently could not read German script, attempted to copy the original script. These names have been reproduced in the text and copies of the names are included at the end of this index.

Abercrombie, 6:343
Abercromby, Charles, 6:87
Adams, James, 6:83
   John, 7:27, 7:363
   Margaret, 7:27
   Susanah, 6:469
   William, 6:469, 7:285
Adkinson, Thomas, 6:161
Ailsworth, George, 6:152
Alan, see Allen
Albright, Daniel, 6:48, 6:457, 6:464, 7:76, 7:83, 7:438, 7:439
   George, 6:14, 6:464
   John, 6:12, 6:112, 6:115, 7:90
   L., 6:295, 6:329
   Ludwick (Lodwick), 6:69, 6:79, 6:457, 6:464
Allen, 6:156, 6:412
   Abraham, 6:226
   George, 6:13
   Jacob, 6:18, 6:345, 6:346, 6:348, 7:74, 7:227
   James, 6:319
   John, 6:20, 6:140, 6:190, 6:198, 7:313
   Samuel, 6:173, 6:226
   Sherrod, 6:429
Allerson, see Allison
Alley, Samuel, 6:173
Allison, 7:392
   David, 7:257
   John, 7:5, 7:246, 7:284, 7:287, 7:459
   Joseph, 6:309, 6:344, 7:287
Alston, John, 6:116
Alsworth, George, 6:85, 6:152
Alves, Emilia, 6:35
   Gaven (Gavin), 6:94, 7:380, 7:379, 7:464
   Walter, 6:35, 6:94, 6:118, 6:440, 7:246, 7:303, 7:369, 7:380, 7:466
Alvin, 7:446
Anderson, Alexander, 7:357, 7:358 Daniel, 6:367
   Jane (Mrs.), 6:85, 6:184, 7:96
   James (Jas.), 6:85, 6:184, 6:228, 7:96, 7:412

Anderson,
   Mary, 6:99
   Thomas, 7:357, 7:358
   William, 6:93, 6:184
Andrew, James, 6:442
Andrews, James, 7:397
   William, 6:446
Ansley, 6:353
   David, 7:370
   Gilbert, 7:367, 7:360, 7:370
   William, 7:35, 7:75, 7:360, 7:367, 7:370
Armstrong, 6:57, 7:98, 7:413
   James, 7:267, 7:486
   John (Jno.), 7:459, 7:460, 7:461
   Thomas, 7:265, 7:486
Ashe, Samuel (Saml.), 6:3, 6:17, 6:18, 6:19, 6:20, 6:21, 6:22, 6:23, 6:24, 6:25, 6:26, 6:27, 6:28, 6:30, 6:31, 6:32, 6:33, 6:34, 6:56, 6:71, 6:77, 6:81, 6:186, 6:215, 6:216, 6:218, 6:225, 6:289, 6:298, 6:344, 6:345, 6:346, 6:347, 6:348, 6:349, 6:350, 6:351, 6:352, 6:353, 6:354, 6:355, 6:356, 6:357, 6:360, 6:362, 6:363, 6:364, 6:365, 6:420, 6:421, 6:447, 6:440, 7:18, 7:19, 7:22, 7:24, 7:25, 7:87, 7:265, 7:281, 7:282, 7:283, 7:316, 7:317, 7:318, 7:320, 7:322, 7:323, 7:343, 7:358, 7:383, 7:384, 7:385, 7:386, 7:387, 7:388, 7:389, 7:391, 7:394, 7:398, 7:444, 7:445, 7:448, 7:449, 7:460, 7:461, 7:462, 7:473, 7:474, 7:475, 7:478
Ashley, Charles, 6:314
Atkinson, Thos., 6:141
Atwater, Moses, 7:410, 7:417, 7:427
   Titus, 7:410, 7:417
Atwood, Thomas, 7:356
Backer, Lenalhase, 6:325
Bagley, Willm., 7:247
Bailey, James, 6:389, 7:27, 7:30
   John, 7:271
   Mrs., 6:389
   William, 7:271

Baker, Joseph, 7:330, 7:338, 7:366, 7:438, 7:439
    Robert, 7:424
Baldridge, Elizabeth, 7:402
    Francis, 6:407, 7:462
    James, 6:57, 6:109, 6:442, 7:392, 7:393, 7:397, 7:402, 7:409, 7:456, 7:461,
    John, 7:3
    Malcomb (Malcom), 6:109, 6:442, 7:392, 7:393, 7:394, 7:397, 7:409
Baldwin, 7:93
Baley, see Bailey
Balldin, Samuel, 6:365
Balrie, Marcom, 7:205
Barbee (Barbey), 6:66, 6:446
    Christopher (Christo), 6:226, 6:378, 6:411, 6:438, 6:461
    Gray, 6:391, 6:432
    Henry Christopher, 6:378
    John, 6:343
    Mr., 6:411
Barber, Allen, 6:448
    Joseph (Jo.), 6:91, 6:97, 7:301
Barker, George, 7:52
    Israel, 6:328, 7:52
Barlon, Sampson, 7:292
Barnett, John, 6:187
Barnhill, John, 6:354, 6:355, 7:330
    Robert, 6:354, 6:355
    William, 7:292
Barns, William, 6:3
Barnwell, John, 6:449
    Robert, 6:90
Barton, John, 6:169
Bason, Jacob, 7:351
    John, 7:3
Baxter, James, 7:274, 7:276, 7:332, 7:487
    John, 7:332
    Reuben, 6:393
    Rosannah, 7:274, 7:276
    Rose, 7:332
Beasley, Henry, 6:393
Beason, 6:223
Bedford, Thomas, 6:1
Bell, Robert (R.), 6:37, 6:48, 6:52, 6:222, 6:397, 6:401
Benehan (Bennehan), 6:178
    Richard, 6:41, 6:94, 7:274, 7:276, 7:332
    Wm., 7:274, 7:276
Bennett, Henry, 6:271
    John, 6:187
Bentham, James, 6:271
Benton, 7;9
    A., 6:410, 6:465, 7:6
    Ann, 7:468

Benton,
    Asa, 6:409
    Augustus, 6:372
    Jacob, 6:404
    Jesse, 7:238, 7:241, 7:468
    L., 7:17
    Nancy, 7:468
    Robert, 6:118
    S., Col., 6:227, 7:6
    Samuel (Saml.), 6:93, 6:160, 6:217, 6:227, 6:321, 6:374, 6:401, 6:436, 6:438, 7:43
Berry, Robert, 7:461
Bevell (Bevill), Elisha, 6:199
Beverly, Robert, 6:81
Bickell, Benj., 6:294
Bird, 7:473
    Empson, 6:24, 6:34, 6:101
    James, 7:245
Blackwood, James, 6:333
Blair, James, 7:14
Blake, Isham, 7:328
Blount, Jacob, 6:250
Blyth, Joseph, 6:266
Bobbitt, Sihon (Sion), 6:314
Bogan, William, 6:379
Boggs, Andrew, 7:376
    Ezekiel, 7;376
    Joseph, 7:376
    Susannah, 6:294
Booth, Daniel, 6:219, 6:376, 7:345
    Joseph, 6:230
Borland, 7:216
    Alexander (Alexr.), 7:23, 7:229, 7:231, 7:233, 7:234
    Andrew, 6:343
    James, 7:23
Boughton, Ann, 6:463
    John, 6:463
    Susannah J., 6:463
    Thomas, 6:463
Bowen, Green, 7:305
Bowles, Benjamin, 6:452
    John, 6:21
Bowls, Thos., 7:316
Boyd, A., 6:234
    George, 6:23
Boyle, James, 7:301
    Lasinal, 6:328
    Thomas, 7:283
    William, 6:97, 6:373, 6:456
Boyles, John, 6:347
Bozwell, James, 6:207
Bracken (Brackin), Isaac, 6:310, 6:328
    Thomas, 7:389

ORANGE COUNTY (NC) DEED BOOKS 6 & 7

Bracken (Brackin),
   William, 7:60, 7:389
Bradford, 7:473
   Samuel, 7:356, 7:436
   Thomas (Thos.), 6:1, 6:341, 7:302, 7:316
Bradley, Enoch. 7:5
Bradshaw, Thomas, 6:107, 7:32, 7:406
Brandford, Thos., 7:405
Bray, John, 6:7
Breeze, John, 6:369
Brewer, 7:34
   Ezekiel, 7:343
   Sackfield, 6:363, 7:343
   Thomas, 7:485
   William, 6:221, 7:34
Brittain, Joseph, 7:367
Brown, 7:298
   Charles, 6:266, 6:280
   George, 6:396, 7:270
   Jas., 7:64
   John, 6:145, 6:407, 7:298
   Joseph (Jos.), 6:266, 6:271, 6:275,
      6:280, 6:284
   William, 7:247
Browning, John, 6:351
   Samuel, 6:15
Bruce, Abner B., 6:60, 7:260
Bruse, John, 6:427, 7:11
Bryant, James, 6:454
Buckingham, 6:294
Bullock (Bullack), Gaiht., 6:245
   John (Jno.), 6:386, 7:203, 7:286
   Leonard Henly, 6:60, 6:118, 6:245, 7:62
   Micajah, 6:118, 6:178
   Richard, 6:118
Bunch, 6:223
   George, 6:233
   Henry, 7:75, 7:222
   John, 6:233
   Thomas, 6:382, 7:214, 7:222
Burges, Will:, 6:228
Burke, Andrew, 6:184, 6:235, 6:243, 7:96,
      7:379
Burney, Robt., 6:81
Burns, Andrew, 6:381
   James, 6:381
   William, Senr., 6:381
Burros, James, 6:381
Burroughs, James, 6:381
Burrow, 6:381
   Garrald, 6:68
   Jarrett, 6:384
   Jarral, 6:386, 7:300
   John, 7:34
   William, 7:300

Burrows, 7:445
Burton, David H., 6:183
   Jett, 6:182
   Robert, 6:118, 6:253
Byrn, Thomas, 7:59, 7:68
Byrns, Mary, 7:59
Cabe, 7:480
   John, 6:399, 7:219, 7:224, 7:225, 7:228
   William, 7:23, 7:225, 7:233
Cable, Anthony, 7:37, 7:41, 7:201
   Jacob, 6:444
   see also Coble
Cadle, Zachariah, 6:175
   see also Kyadle
Cain & Ray, 6:416
Cain, James, 7:373
   John (Jno.), 6:110, 6:357, 6:440, 7:35,
      7:431, 7:441
   John Kelly, 6:349
   Timothy, 6:110
   William (Willm., Wm.), 6:110, 6:367,
      6:391, 6:416, 7:5, 7:35, 7:318, 7:321,
      7:373, 7:395, 7:423
   William, & Company, 6:35, 6:399, 7:91
Caldwell, John, 6:143, 6:219, 6:321, 6:323,
      6:333, 7:212, 7:213, 7:215
   Revd. Joseph, 7:38 Campbell, 7:221
Campbell, Archibald, 6:148, 6:158
   Catlett (Ca.), 6:367, 6:414, 6:441, 7:263,
      7:324, 7:325, 7:327, 7:363, 7:469,
      7:472
   Charles, 6:230
   Henry, 6:344
   John, 6:223, 7:24, 7:251, 7:359
   Martha, 7:359
   Robert, 6:238, 6:392, 6:433, 6:463,
      6:466, 7:213
   Samuel, 7:333
Campble, William, 6:165
Cantrel, 6:186
Cantrell, James, 6:214, 7:298
Caps, Cason, 6:242
Caragan, see Carragan
Carey, Samuel, 6:189
Carlton, Leonard, 6:387, 6:444, 6:463, 6:466
Carmichael, Thomas, 6:91, 6:97
Carney, John, 7:420
Carragan, 6:35
   John, 6:228, 7:9, 7:425
Carrall, Betty, 6:228
Carrigan, see Carragan
Carrington, 6:89, 6:137
   Ephriam, 7:414
   George, 7:318, 7:367, 7:369
   James, 6:376, 7:215

ORANGE COUNTY (NC) DEED BOOKS 6 & 7

Carrington,
  James, Junr., 6:8, 6:9, 6:235, 6:243
  James H., 7:247
  John, 6:8, 6:9, 6:154, 6:200, 6:235,
    6:243, 6:300, 7:35, 7:75, 7:213,
    7:215, 7:247, 7:414
  Thomas, 7:414
  William, 6:192
Carrol, Stephen, 6:110, 7:373
Carroll, James, 7:476
Carson, James, 6:60, 6:235, 6:243, 7:64,
    7:77
  Moses, 7:335
Carter, John (Jno.), 6:10, 6:13, 6:118
  Landon, 6:118
  Nathaniel (Nathl.), 6:168, 7:426
  William, 6:10, 6:440
Cary, George, 7:250
  Samuel, 7:250
Casey, 6:414
  George, 7:250
  John (Jo.), 6:367, 6:441, 7:415
Castlebury, Polly, 7:345
Caswell, Richd. (Rd., R.), 6:335, 6:390,
    7:210, 7:319
Cate (Cates), Ann, 7:436
  Barnard, 7:477
  Elizabeth, 7:71
  Ezra, 7:424
  Jesse, 6:161, 6:303, 6:365, 7:205
  John, 7:305, 7:336, 7:337, 7:477
  Lazarus, 6:421, 7:19
  Mary, 7:424
  Moses, 6:341
  R., Junr., 7:374
  Richard, 7:35, 7:75
  Robert (Rob.), 7:71, 7:205, 7:317, 7:374,
    7:424
  Stephen, 7:436
  Thomas, 6:365, 7:305, 7:336, 7:337,
    7:343, 7:374, 7:477
Chance, Rachel, 6:431
Chandler, Daniel, 7:225
  John, 6:173
Chapman, Benjamin, 6:67
Charles, George, 6:444
  Michael, 6:54, 7:84, 7:297
Cheek, 7:287
  James, 7:475, 7:476
  Robert, 7:475
Chizenhall, Samuel, 6:133
  Clement, 6:133
  William, 6:133
Christmas, Charles (Chs.), 6:107, 6:222,
    6:322, 6:389, 6:462, 6:467, 7:32,

Christmas, Charles, 7:449, 7:458
  J., 7:39
  John, 6:227
  James, 7:9
  Mary, 6:462, 6:467
  Noial Graves, 6:227
  Nathaniel, 6:227, 6:322, 6:372, 6:462,
    6:467, 7:449
  Richard, 7:339, 7:377
  Thomas, 6:227
  William, 6:227
Churton, W., 6:2
  William, 7:311
Cilley, Chs., 6:158
Cimb, Henry, 7:286
Clack, Joseph, 7:27, 7:30
Claney, George, 6:169
Clap, Barnet (Barnett), 6:12, 7:223
Clark (Clarke), Jas., 7:257
  Jesse, 7:347, 7:348
  John, 6:384, 7:79
  Joseph, 7:79
  Mary, 7:402
  Nathl., 7:247
  Patrick, 6:41
  Sarah, 7:98
  Thomas, 7:347, 7:348
  William, 6:349, 7:98, 7:347, 7:348
Clements (Clemments), John, 6:133
  Richard, 6:133
Clendennen, 7:339, 7:341
  James, 6:431, 7:311
  Joseph, 7:311, 7:320, 7:333
  William, 6:141, 7:311
Clenney (Clenny), George, 6:160
  James, 6:160
  Jonathon, 6:110
  Samuel, 6:63, 6:65, 6:110, 7:373
  William, 6:110, 7:373
Clinton, 6:353, 7:370
  Matthew, 6:420
Cloud, 6:186
  Daniel, 7:395
Clower, Jonathon, 7:252
Coale, see Cole
Coales, Meremons, 7:35
Cobb, John, 7:429
  Joseph, 6:156
Coble, Adam, 7:207, 7:208
  Anthony, 7:56
  David, 6:217, 7:203, 7:286
  John, 6:217, 7:37, 7:207, 7:259
  Margaret, 7:207, 7:208
  Nicholas, 6:443
  see also Cable

Cochran, Richard, 7:295
   Coglin, James, 6:397, 6:401, 6:410, 6:465, 7:89
Cohen, Soloman, 6:275
Cole, 6:296
   John (Jno.), 6:296, 7:317
   Soloman, 6:363
   Thomas, 6:305, 6:313, 6:365, 7:48
Collins, 7:274, 7:413
   Andrew, 7:395
Eli, 7:308
   Enoch, 7:265, 7:267
Colquhoun, Robert, 7:469
   Walter, 7:469
Colter, Mathew, 6:411
Colther, Mathew, 7:25
Combs, 6:186
Commissioners, 6:182, 6:192
Commons, 7:464, 7:466
   James, 7:369
Compton, Thos., 6:451
Conger, Sten., 7:291
   Stephen, 6:150, 7:17, 7:291, 7:293, 7:296
Connally, 6:333
   Thomas, 6:221
Conner, 7:456
Connor, John, 7:218
Cook, Ephriam, 6:112
   H., Junr., 7:49, 7:51
   Henry, 7:49, 7:51
   John, 7:49, 7:51, 7:388
   Wm., 7:229
Cope (Coop), Horatio, 6:449
   Richard (Richd.), 6:23, 6:90, 6:134, 6:449
Copeland (Copland, Coupland, 6:289, 6:382, 6:419
   David, 6:419, 6:429
   Jonathon, 6:316
   William, 6:404
Cornelius, J., 6:266
Cornell, Benjamin, 6:223
   Sarah, 6:223
Cother, 7:350
   Matthew, 7:212
Cotner, Daniel, 7:57
Cotton, Mr., 7:357, 7:358,
Couch, 7:360, 7:480
   John, 6:410, 6:465, 7:38
   Samuel (Saml.), 6:459, 7:429
   Thomas, 7:429
   William, 7:445
Coulter, 6:21
   Henson, 6:393
   Mathew, 6:378

Courtney, 6:192
   Jo., 6:156, 7:9
   William, 6:156, 6:337, 6:391, 7:9, 7:69, 7:246, 7:262, 7:321, 7:325, 7:327, 7:423, 7:425, 7:429
   William, (Bricklayer), 7:262 Courtney,
Cox, Deborah, 6:424
   Moses, 6:132, 6:136
   Rachel, 6:424
Cozart, James, 7:303
Crabtree, James, 7:230
   Thomas, 7:9, 7:218
   William, 7:15, 7:231, 7:238, 7:456
Cradick, John, 6:412
Craig, James, 6:3
   John, 6:2, 6:3
   William, 6:2
Crawford, James, 6:365
   Moses, 6:223
Creather, Samule, 6:359
Criswell, John, 7:473
Crompton, Acquilla, 7:452, 7:482
Crutchfield, James, 6:107, 7:406
   William, 7:88
Culberson, 7:19
Cummings, William, 7:260
Curry, John, 7:376
Dale, 7:313
Dalgett, Wilson, 6:275
Dalzell, Wilson, 6:275, 6:280, 6:284, 7:64
Daniel, 7:19
   Christopher (Chris.), 7:221
   George, 6:391, 6:432
   Henry O., 6:462, 6:467
   John, 6:230, 6:409, 6:420, 6:433, 6:461, 7:89, 7:218, 7:221, 7:317, 7:350, 7:353, 7:358, 7:480
   Penney, 6:432, 7:221
   Robert T., 6:230, 6:432, 6:433, 7:221
   Samuel, 6:433, 7:89
Davie, William (W.) Richardson (R.), 6:8, 6:9, 6:321, 6:436, 6:438, 7:335, 7:336, 7:375, 7:392, 7:393, 7:412, 7:446, 7:450, 7:451, 7:452, 7:453, 7:454, 7:455, 7:459, 7:463, 7:476, 7:477, 7:480, 7:481, 7:482, 7:487, 7:490
Davis, Abraham, 6:200
   James, 7:211
   John, 6:199, 6:203, 6:210, 6:266, 7:323
   Robert, 6:454
Deboe, John, 7:435
   Soloman, 7:435
   Stephen, 7:435
Dellesseline, Francis G., 6:210

Denning, John, 7:301
    Margaret, 7:301
    Widow, 6:97
Dennis, Edward, 6:402
    Isaac, 6:402, 6:404
    John, 6:402, 6:404
    Mary, 6:402
    Rebecca, 6:404
Derham, Mark, 7:289
    see also Durham
Deshays, William, 6:87
Devenport, Samuel, 7:444
Dickens, Robert, 6:137, 7:463
    William, 6:89, 6:137
Dickey (Dickie), David, 7:468
    James, 6:28, 6:168, 6:196, 6:361, 7:248, 7:300
    William, 6:28, 6:81, 6:181, 7:248, 7:300
    Zachariah, 7:448
Dicks, John, 6:50
    Nathan, 7:440
Dickson, 6:223
    Robert, 7:100
    William, 6:69, 6:112
    see also Dixon
Dickt, James, 7:389
Dixon, 6:355, 7:80
    Benjamin, 7:97
    C., 6:414
    J., 6:461
    James (Jas.), 6:372, 7:354, 7:366
    John, 7:401
    Joseph (Jos.), 6:372, 6:385, 6:410, 6:465, 7:216
    Robert (Robt.), 7:48, 7:76, 7:80, 7:83, 7:100
    Thomas, 6:200, 6:370, 7:436 Tilman, 7:216
    William, 6:112, 6:115, 7:48, 7:100
Dobbins, Bryson, 6:8, 6:9, 6:367, 6:374, 7:432
Dodd, William, 6:396
Doherty, Fanny, 7:415
    George, 6:414, 7:238, 7:241, 7:319
    Mary, 7:238, 7:241
    Misses, 7:415
    Nelly, 7:415
    Polly B., 7:238, 7:241
Donaldson, Col., 6:245
    Robert (Robt.), 6:275, 6:280, 6:284
    Stokley, 6:118
Doning, Saml., 6:303
Donnall, Thomasa, 7:486
Dorris, Isaac, 6:25, 7:412
    Joseph, 6:150, 7:17

Dorris,
    Joseph, Junr., 6:150
    William, 6:354
Dossett, William, 6:353
Douglas (Douglass), James, 7:486
    John, 6:63, 6:101
    Margaret, 6:63
Downing, James, 6:13
Dozer, Leonard, 6:210, 6:266, 6:269, 6:271, 6:275, 6:280, 6:284
Dranberry, David, 6:218
Dry, William, 6:60, 6:210, 6:245, 6:249, 6:250, 6:253, 6:256, 6:263, 6:266, 6:269, 6:271, 6:275, 6:280, 6:284, 7:62, 7:64
    William, Col., 6:261
Duffy, William (Wm.), 6:367, 6:374, 6:390, 6:397, 6:399, 6:401
Duk, Taylor, 6:314
Duke, 6:39
    John, 6:45
Duncan, 6:412
Dunnagan, Charles, 6:76,
    James, 6:76
    John, 6:350
    Sharwood, 6:76
    William, 6:76, 6:358, 7:318
Dunnavan, John, 6:81, 6:448
Dupee, Cornelius, 6:269
Durham, 6:322
    John, 6:26
    Mark, 7:289
    Thomas (Thos.), 6:462, 6:467
    see also Derham
Dyer, 7:265
Eagan, Robert, 7:77
Ebouch, Henry, 7:64
Eccles, John, 6:325
    William, 6:325, 7:330, 7:386
Ector, 6:352
    Samuel (Saml.), 7:254, 7:298
Edge, Nehemiah, 6:39
Edwards, Allen, 6:317, 6:319
    Henry, 6:365
    John, 7:205, 7:433
    Nathaniel, 6:168
    William, 6:425, 7:426, 7:433
Effland, John, 6:5
Ellimon, 7:281
Elliot, Jane, 6:10
Elliott, James, 7:5
    John, 6:10, 7:409, 7:440
    William, 6:10, 7:409, 7:413
Ellis, John, 7:257
Elmore, John, 7:364

ORANGE COUNTY (NC) DEED BOOKS 6 & 7

Emery, Moses, 6:168
English, David, 7:394
Estes, Burras, 7:26
   Burrows, 7:26
   John (J.), 6:35, 6:192, 6:335, 6:469,
     7:15, 7:211, 7:456, 7:492
   Thomas, 6:228
Eubank, 7:47
 George, 6:130, 6:146, 6:149
   Thos., 6:149
Evans, John, 7:263
Faddis, John, 6:332, 6:376, 7:215, 7:225,
   7:231
Fairman, John, 6:374, 6:401
Fann, John, 6:393, 6:396
   Mark, 6:396
   Rebekah, 6:396
Fanning, Edmund, 6:182, 6:192, 6:335,
   6:398, 7:210
Farmer, Conrod, 6:444, 7:37
   Lannad, 6:444
Faucett, 6:81
   George, 7:473
   James, 6:181, 6:192, 6:382, 6:419, 7:362
   Lucy, 7:362
   Ralph, 6:106
   Thomas, 7:413
   William, 6:301, 6:456
   see also Fossett
Fegiman, John, 6:374
Ferrill, Barnabus O., 6:414
Finley, Hugh, 6:96
   Thomas, 7:309
Fitch, William, 6:109
Flint, Thomas, 6:193
Flintham (Flintom), John, 7:216, 7:229,
   7:233
Flowers, Jacob, 6:378, 6:411
   Mary, 6:378, 6:411
Forrest, 7:367
   Benjamin, 7:431, 7:441
   John, 6:453, 7:33
   Josiah, 7:431, 7:441
   Matthew, 6:132
   Shadrack, 6:116, 6:183
Forsyth, Willm., 6:406
Fortune, Moses, 7:481
Fossett, George, 6:24
   Henry, 6:315, 7:15, 7:425
   Ralph, 6:78
   William (Wm.), 6:373, 6:448, 6:456
   see also Faucett
Foster, Richard, 6:113
Foust, Cathana, 6:12
   D., 7:454, 7:455

Foust,
   Daniel, 7:278, 7:285
   George, 6:167, 6:194, 7:258, 7:261,
     7:290, 7:445
   John, 6:113, 7:33
   Peter, 7:290, 7:455
   Phillip, 6:12
   Stephen, 7:35
Frazier, Arthur, 6:200
   Ephriam, 6:89, 6:137, 6:154, 6:200
   Willm., 6:154
Freeland, 6:216, 7:446
   James, 6:57, 6:337, 7:87, 7:90, 7:273,
     7:351, 7:429, 7:468
   Jno., 7:87
   Joseph, 6:337
Freeman, 7:454
   Daniel, 7:313
   William, 7:357, 7:358
Freeor, Rd. W., 6:93
Friddle, George, 6:21, 6:52, 6:205
Fruit, 6:412
Fulton, 7:317
   James, 6:358, 7:317
Gaddis, 6:184
   Hannah, 7:96
   Isaac, 6:93, 7:96
   James, 7:323,
Gaines, Edward, 6:149
Galbreath (Gailbreath0, 6:341
   Catherine, 7:90
   John, 6:223, 6:225
   William, 7:90
Gamblin, James, 7:17, 7:291
Garner, Lewis, 6:209
Garrett, Everard, 6:69, 6:112, 6:115
   George, 7:483
   James, 6:5
   William, 6:112
Gassins, Stephen, 6:327
Gattis, Alexander, 6:291, 6:293, 7:344,
     7:345
   Ann, 7:345
   James, 7:344, 7:345
   John, 7:344
   Margaret, 6:291, 6:293
   Samuel, 6:291, 6:293
   William (Wm.), 6:291, 6:293, 7:345
George II, 7:343, 7:347
Gess, William, 6:297
Gibbons, James, 6:145
Gibins, 6:137
Gibson, 6:89
   Andrew, 6:54, 6:91, 6:97, 7:83, 7:351,
     7:377 William, 6:228

Giford, Henry, 6:249
Gilbert, Nancy S., 7:442
Gill, James, 7:481
Gilson, David, 7:459
Gipson, Thomas, 6:154
Glasgow, James (J.), 6:3, 6:16, 6:17, 6:18,
    6:19, 6:20, 6:21, 6:22, 6:23, 6:26,
    6:27, 6:28, 6:29, 6:31, 6:33, 6:34,
    6:30, 6:32, 6:56, 6:71, 6:77, 6:186,
    6:214, 6:215, 6:216, 6:217, 6:218,
    6:219, 6:220, 6:225, 6:289, 6:290,
    6:335, 6:343, 6:344, 6:347, 6:350,
    6:351, 6:352, 6:354, 6:355, 6:356,
    6:359, 6:360, 6:361, 6:362, 6:363,
    6:364, 6:365, 6:366, 6:390, 6:421,
    6:426, 6:440, 6:447, 7:22, 7:23, 7:25,
    7:87, 7:210, 7:237, 7:243, 7:244,
    7:245, 7:281, 7:282, 7:283, 7:317,
    7:319, 7:322, 7:328, 7:323, 7:343,
    7:383, 7:384, 7:385, 7:386, 7:389,
    7:390, 7:391, 7:394, 7:444, 7:445,
    7:448, 7:449, 7:460, 7:461, 7:462,
    7:473, 7:474, 7:475, 7:478, 7:488,
    7:489, 7:491
Goodloe, Jno., 7:332
Gordon (Gorden), 7:42
    James, 7:302
    John, 7:302
    William, 6:161, 7:302
Gortner, David, 7:49, 7:51
    Peter, 7:49, 7:51
Gott, 6:341
Governor of North Carolina, 6:37, 6:39,
    6:45, 6:48, 6:50, 6:52, 6:54, 7:43
Gracie, Archibald, 6:367
Gradner, John, 6:234
Graham, John, 7:389
Granville, 6:2, 6:67, 6:101, 6:103, 6:140,
    6:168, 6:228, 6:293, 6:305, 6:404,
    6:417, 7:279, 7:234, 7:306, 7:419
Graves, 7:203
    Boston, 6:5, 7:286
    Jacob, 6:5, 7:53
    John, 6:5, 7:53
    Robert, 7:247
Gray, George, 7:251
    Jane, 7:424
    John, 6:2
    Robert, 7:462
    Thomas, 6:7, 6:392, 6:433
Green, 7:221
    Daniel (Danl.), 7:225
    Edmund, 6:14, 6:294, 6:295, 6:396,
        6:329, 7:68
    James, 6:37, 6:48, 6:52, 6:86, 6:235,

Green,
    James, 6:237, 6:240, 6:243, 7:43
    John, 6:7, 6:154, 7:274, 7:276
    Obed, 6:14, 6:295, 6:306, 6:307, 6:329,
        7:68, 7:76, 7:79, 7:314
    William Wills, 6:433
Griffeth, Jennet, 6:101
    John, 6:101
Griffin (Griffen), 6:332
    Andrew, 6:81
    Thomas, 6:303, 7:462
Griffis, 6:352
Grimes, Barnaby, 6:63
Grisham, 7:367
    Littleberry, 6:4
Guess, George, 7:274
Guinn, 7:283
Guisse, 6:178
Gwin (Gwinn), 7:283
    Alexander, 7:269
    Edward, 7:55
    James, 7:269
    Mordicai, 7:269
Hackney, John, 6:319
Hagan, James, 6:145
Hagwood, Benjamin, 6:221
    George, 6:311
Hairiot, William, 6:210
Haise, 6:425
Haley, David, 6:385
Hallburtin, William, 6:377
Hall, 6:156, 7:368
    David, 6:7, 6:387, 6:392, 6:394, 6:459,
        6:460, 7:2
    Isaac, 6:325
    Levi, 7:245
    Nancy, 6:459
    Nanny, 6:7
    Robert, 6:165, 7:252
    Sheriff, 7:89
    Thomas, 6:7, 6:343, 6:394, 6:459, 6:460,
        7:2
    William, 6:43, 6:145, 6:165, 7:3, 7:413
Hallaway, see Holloway
Hamilton, Joseph, 7:211
Hamlin, Peter, 7:11
    Stephen, 7:11
    William, 7:11
Haney, John, 6:150, 6:209
Hanley, Daniel, 7:90
    Elmore, 7:27, 7:30
Harden, John, 7:55
Harder, Jacob, 6:56
Hargess, William, 6:451
Hargis, Susanah, 6:451

Hargraves, Richard, 6:196
Harlot, George, 6:266, 7:64
Harmen, Peter, 7:371
Harper, Reuben, 6:24
Harris, Archer, 6:330
    Edward, 6:435, 7:8, 7:464
    James, 6:94
    Nathaniel, 6:83
    Richmond, 6:94
    Robert, 6:39, 6:50
    S., 6:316
    Sterling, 6:101, 7:58, 7:74 Hart, 7:360
Hart, Ann, 6:392
    Catherine, 6:315
    David, 6:60, 6:118, 6:245, 7:62
    Ellenor, 6:78
    James, 6:78, 6:96, 6:106, 6:196, 6:454, 7:205
    John, 6:337
    Joseph, 6:118, 6:392, 7:60, 7:255
    Morgan, 6:402, 6:404, 7:43, 7:238, 7:241, 7:398
    Nathaniel, 6:60, 6:118, 6:245, 7:62
    Peter, 6:78, 6:96, 6:106
    Samuel, 6:96
    Stephen, 6:96, 6:315, 7:373, 7:413
    Thomas, 6:60, 6:78, 6:101, 6:118, 6:245, 6:256, 6:263, 7:62
Harvey, 6:456, 7:389
    Caleb, 6:186
    Eli, 6:317, 7:399, 7:440
    Isaac, 6:317
    William, 7:399
    Zephaniah, 6:402
Hastings, John, 7:271
    Joseph, 6:347, 7:27, 7:30, 7:395
Hatch, Alexander, 6:366
Hatchett, Edmund, 6:339
    Edward, 6:260
    William, 6:260, 6:336, 6:339, 6:340
Haterack (Hatrick), Robert, 7:405, 7:407
Hatmaker, Francis, 7:273
    Malachiah (Malachi), 7:80, 7:439
    Mary, 7:80
Hawkins, Isham, 6:296
Hays (Hayes), 6:199, 6:203
    Samuel, 6:86, 6:143, 6:203, 6:409
    William, 6:391, 6:432, 6:436
Haywood, J., 7:64
    John, 6:8, 6:9, 6:253, 6:321, 6:436, 6:438, 7:69
    Willm. H., 6:323, 6:333, 7:1
Heflin, James, 7:219
Heiling, Willm., 6:130
Helms, William, 6:13

Henderson Company, 6:275, 6:280, 6:284
Henderson, 6:333
    Archibald, 6:118
    H., 7:38
    John, 6:118
    Leonard, 6:118
    Richard, 6:60, 6:118, 6:245, 7:62
    Richard, & Company, 6:118, 6:245, 6:249, 6:250, 6:253, 6:256, 6:263, 6:266
Henley, Elmore, 6:410
Henly, David, 7:3
Heriot, Col. Robert, 6:210
    George, 6:210, 6:269, 6:275, 6:284, 6:288
    John, 6:210, 6:284
    Mary, 6:210, 6:284
    Robert, 6:210, 6:284
    William, 6:284, 7:64
Herndon, Edmond, 6:187
    James, 6:387, 6:392, 6:463, 6:466
    Pomfret, 6:311, 7:7, 7:447
    William, 7:85
    Zachariah, 6:7, 6:187
Hesse, H., 7:262
    Henry, 7:26
    John Henry, 6:347
Hickman, Capt., 7:265
Hicks, Zebedee, 6:134
Hightower, Austin, 6:333
    John, 7:447
Hill, Samuel, 6:10, 7:91
    Thomas H., 6:256
    William, 6:24, 6:25, 6:28, 6:81, 6:85, 6:152, 6:345, 6:346, 6:348, 6:349, 6:353, 6:357, 6:358, 6:428, 7:18, 7:19, 7:24, 7:316, 7:318, 7:393, 7:463
Hilton, 7:295
Hinchey, David, 7:360, 7:429
Hobbs, Nicholas, 7:59
Hobson, Georeg, 7:401
    Richard, 6:377
    Thomas, 6:377
Hodge, 6:341
    George, 7:351
    Jo., 7:3, 7:353
    Joseph, 6:374, 7:3, 7:17, 7:291, 7:293, 7:339, 7:341, 7:354, 7:364, 7:366, 7:377
    Margaret, 7:351
    Robert, 7:354
    William, 7:354, 7:364, 7:366
Hodges, Philemon, 6:143, 6:203, 6:409, 6:425
Hogan, David, 7:483

Hogan, John, 6:332, 6:402, 6:446, 7:483,
  7:484, 7:485
  Thomas, 7:484, 7:485
  William, 7:483, 7:484, 7:485, 7:486
Hogg, James, 6:60, 6:85, 6:118, 6:152,
  6:245, 6:249, 6:256, 6:261, 6:263,
  6:275, 6:280, 6:284, 7:62, 7:284,
  7:308, 7:472
  John, 6:60, 6:160
Holden, John, 6:419
  Thomas, 6:419
Holdeness, Anne, 6:63
  John, 6:63
  Thomas, Junr., 6:63
Holder, Isaac, 6:63, 6:65
Holeman, Richard, 7:252
Holgan, Thomas, 7:354
Hollaway, see Holloway
Holliberton (Holliburton), David, 6:116,
  6:187
  William, 6:377
Holliway, see Holloway
Holloway, Bermillial, 6:357
  Bremelion, 7:75
  Samuel, 7:95
  Thomas, 6:348, 7:35, 7:58, 7:74, 7:75
  Widow, 7:308
Holmes, John, 6:167, 6:194
  Joseph, 6:14, 6:74, 7:68
  Moses, 7:320, 7:333
  Samuel A., 6:461
Holms, James, 6:14
Holstead, John, 7:57
Holt, 7:478
  Absalom, 6:305, 6:313
  Christopher, 6:71, 6:305
  George, 6:71, 6:305, 7:483
  J., 6:457
  Jacob, 7:100
  Jeremiah, 6:69, 6:464, 7:80, 7:314
  John, 6:69, 6:112, 6:115, 7:35, 7:59,
    7:219
  Joshua, 6:5, 7:53, 7:202
  Michael, 6:69, 6:71, 6:305, 6:395, 7:40,
    7:51, 7:53, 7:90, 7:95, 7:202, 7:300,
    7:314
  Nicholas, 6:295, 6:306, 6:307,
  Nicholas, 7:79
  Reuben, 6:305, 7:293, 7:296
  Shadrack, 6:54, 7:297
Homes, see Holmes
Hooper, William, 6:449, 7:379, 7:380
Hopkins, 6:300
  Chuza, 6:300
  Francis, 6:385
Hopkins,
  Jane, 6:385
  Samuel, 6:226, 6:320, 6:327, 6:362,
    6:385, 6:425, 7:345
  William, 6:19
Horn, James, 7:220, 7:224, 7:238
  Thomas, 6:348, 7:58, 7:74, 7:220, 7:224
  William, 7:220, 7:224
Hornaday, Christopher, 7:207, 7:208, 7:401
  John, 7:57, 7:207, 7:208
  Lewis, 6:231, 7:313
Horne, James, 7:227
Horner, George, 6:235, 6:237, 6:243
  James, 6:314
Horton, 7:463
  Charles, 6:41
  Henry, 6:330
  James, 7:369, 7:464, 7:466
  Thomas, 6:172, 7:464, 7:466
  Willm., 6:50
Houlden, 6:290
House, George, 6:340
  Peter, 6:466
Houseman, Joseph, 6:48
Howard, C. D., 6:275, 6:280, 6:284
Howell, Benjamin, 6:359
Huffhines, Christopher, 7:56
Huffman, Andrew, 7:364
  John, 6:12, 7:48, 7:391
  Peter, 7:223
Huggams, Jacob, 6:28, 6:220
Hughes, 7:474
  John, 6:15, 6:209
Humphries, John, 6:183
Hunt, Henry, 6:357, 6:358
  John, 6:357
  Memucan, 6:118, 6:182, 6:414
Hunter, Christian, 6:314
  James, 6:314
  Jesse, 7:398
  Mary, 6:310
  Rachel, 6:310
  Robert, 7:491
Hurdle, Hardy, 6:30, 6:43, 6:56, 6:81, 6:150,
    6:176, 6:181, 6:223, 6:225, 6:350, 6:351,
    6:352, 6:361, 7:17, 7:248, 7:291, 7:293,
    7:296, 7:309, 7:383, 7:384, 7:385, 7:386,
    7:387, 7:388
  Martin, 6:150, 6:176, 7:293, 7:296, 7:388
Hust, John, 6:392, 6:459, 6:460
  Joseph, 6:394, 7:2
Hutchell, Wm., 6:209
Hutcheson, James, 7:48, 7:351
Hutchins, Moses, 7:85
  Thomas, 7:85

Ivey, John, 6:302
Jackson, Benjamin, 7:203
　Colba, 6:205, 7:403, 7:438
　James, 7:91
　Thomas, 6:402
　William, 7:5, 7:91
Jacob, Henry, 7:384
James, Abner, 7:41, 7:201
　Emanuel, 6:234
　Samuel, 6:444, 7:84
Jamison, William, 7:375
Jenking, John, 6:189
Jenkins, 7:250
　Ephriam, 7:214
　John, 6:193, 6:296, 7:214, 7:289
　Samuel, 7:214
　William, 7:357, 7:358
Johnson, William, 6:118, 6:245
Johnston, 7:360
　Drury, 7:431, 7:441
　George, 6:156, 6:204, 6:226, 6:320,
　　6:323, 6:327, 6:333, 6:337, 7:322,
　　7:323, 7:429
　Henry, 7:93
　James, 7:42
　Samuel, 6:83, 6:220, 6:343, 7:237, 7:447
　Thos., 6:103
　William, 6:60, 6:118, 7:62, 7:69
Jolley, Boling, 6:302
　John, 6:302
Jones, 7:247
　Alston, 7:1
　Edmund, 6:221, 7:1
　Edward, 7:1
　Fowler, 6:99
　Johnston, 7:399
　Jonathon, 6:164, 6:441
　Mathew, 6:249
　Thomas, 6:164, 7:399
Jordan (Jordon, Jourdan, Jurdon), Isham,
　　7:292
　Robert, 6:16, 6:57, 7:402, 7:460
　Thomas, 7:397, 7:402
Jouett, John, 7:55
Justiss)Justus), John, 6:296, 7:42
Kaling, William, 6:146
Karr, James, 7:424
Kaydle, Benjamin, 6:101
　Zachariah, 6:101
　see also Cadle
Keeling, William, 6:146, 6:149
Keith, John, 6:269
Keling, William, 6:130
Kelley, 6:349
　Charles, 6:17, 6:27, 7:3, 7:71, 7:374

Kelley,
　John, 6:63, 6:65, 6:67, 6:110, 6:207,
　　6:289, 6:290, 6:404, 7:373
　Thomas, 6:63
Kennedy, John, Senior, 6:141
　Thomas, 6:141
　William, 6:389
Kennon, Charles, 6:435, 7:8
Kiding, William, 6:146
Kilpatrick, Alexander, 7:3
Kimb (Kime), Henry, 6:386, 7:286
Kimbroe (Kimro), Frederick, 7:202, 7:295
King, 7:412
　Baxter, 6:144, 6:293, 6:332, 7:363
　Charles, 6:100, 6:144
　Edward, 6:196, 7:383, 7:384, 7:385,
　　7:488, 7:489
　John, 6:56, 6:100, 6:105, 6:332, 7:330,
　　7:384, 7:385, 7:386, 7:488, 7:489
　Julius, 6:330
　Nathaniel, 6:291, 6:293
　Sarah, 6:100, 6:105
　Thomas, 6:29, 6:39
　William, 6:144
Kinnon, J., 6:377
Kirk, James, 6:363, 7:436
　Lewis, 7:337
Kirkland, William, 6:184, 6:367, 6:399
　William, & Company, 6:35, 6:367, 6:399
Kirkpatrick, Alexander, 6:132, 6:136, 7:351,
　　7:354
Knight, 7:452
　John, 7:369
Lackey, James W., 6:374, 6:401
　William, 7:435
Lafferty, Thomas, 6:209
Lapsley, David, 6:103
　Thomas, 6:101, 6:103, 6:175
Larimer, Thomas, 6:310
Lasey, Thomas, 7:449
Lasley, 7:449
　Barnard, 7:97
　Bernard, 7:88
　Thomas, 6:31, 6:240
Latta, 7:317
　James, 6:163, 6:170, 6:349, 7:20, 7:373,
　　7:402, 7:431, 7:441
　John (Jno.), 6:59, 6:179, 6:197, 6:297,
　　6:300, 6:358, 7:362
　Thomas, 6:297, 7:466
Latty, see Latta
Laughlin, Hugh, 6:317
Laws, George, 6:178, 7:466
　William, 6:178
Lawson, James, 6:145

Lay, Geo., Senr., 6:194
Laycock, Thomas, 6:207
   William, 6:421
Lea, Absalom, 6:422, 6:452
   James, 6:422
Lee, A., 7:482
   James, 7:482
   John, 6:7
Leigh, John, 6:387, 6:394, 7:2
   Sullivan, 6:387
Lett, James, Junr., 6:97
Lewis, David, 7:253
   Robert, 6:118
   William, 6:382, 6:419
Ley, Francis, 6:271
Linch, see Lynch
Lindley (Lindly), 7:454
   J., 6:167
   Jonathon, 6:319
   Owen, 6:96, 6:106, 6:315, 7:98
   Thomas, 6:317, 6:319, 7:98, 7:339
Lindsay, 6:26
   Matthew, 6:309, 7:453
Lindsey, William, 6:309
Linge, William, 7:332
Lingo, William, 7:487
Lloyd (Loyd), 6:366, 7:305
   Frederick, 6:22, 7:356
   James, 6:302
   Stephen, 6:332, 7:484
   Thomas, 6:175, 6:366, 6:446, 7:486
   William, 6:359
Lockhart (Lochart, Locheart), William
     (Wm.) 7:9, 7:324, 7:327, 7:392
Logue, John, 6:309
Long, Davis, 6:402
   George, 7:26, 7:475
   John, 6:217, 7:300, 7:313
Love, James, 6:456
   William, 6:214, 6:301, 6:373, 6:456
Lovel, Colstin, 7:301
   William, 6:448
Low, Harmon, 7:483
   Keziah, 7:483
   Thomas, 7:483
Loy, John, 7:371, 7:403, 7:420
Loyd, 6:366, 7:305
   Frederick, 6:22
   James, 6:302
   Stephen, 6:332
   Thomas, 6:446
   William, 6:359
Lutterloh, Henry Lewis, 6:239
Luttrell, John, 6:60, 6:118, 6:245, 6:249, 7:62

Lynch (Linch), David, 6:453, 7:33
   Edward, 6:103
   John, 6:196, 7:383, 7:384
   Moses, 6:90, 6:453
   Thomas, 6:90, 6:447, 6:453
Lytle, 7:456
   Archibald, 7:238, 7:241
   Capt., 7:15
   William, 6:169, 6:414, 7:15, 7:77, 7:210,
     7:216, 7:238, 7:2417:262, 7:265,
     7:267, 7:328
Mabane, see Mebane
Mabray, Randolph, 7:410
MacPerson, John, 6:190
Macay, Spruce, 7:464, 7:466, 7:469, 7:472,
   7:483, 7:484
Macpherson, Enoch, 6:190
Maddin, George, 7:426
Maddon, Stephen, 7:24
Maden, Samuel, 6:309
Madison, P., 7:487
Madkin, William, 7:407
Mahon, 6:113
   Alexander, 7:341
   Archibald, 7:339
Mains, Robert, 6:196
Malcom, 7:360
Malcomb, John, 6:113
Mallett, 6:447
   Peter, 7:211
Man, Malachi, 7:597:79
Mangum, Arthur, 6:237, 6:314
   Betsy, 6:370
   John, 6:300
   William, 6:193
Marchill, Jacob, 7:455
Marcom, 6:343
   Richd., 6:394, 7:2
   Thomas, 6:459
   William, 6:343
Marley, 7:387
   Adam, 6:43, 7:17, 7:293, 7:296
   Martha, 6:67
   Robert, 6:43, 6:67, 6:176, 6:484, 7:293,
     7:296
Marsh, Abner, 7:482
Marshall, 7:401
Marshill, Jacob, 7:454
Marten, Zachariah, 6:168
Martin, 6:347
Martin, Alexander, 6:16, 6:214, 6:427, 7:243,
   7:244, 7:245, 7:488, 7:489, 7:491
Mason, Henry, 7:287
   Thomas, 6:426
Mathews, James, 6:319

May, 7:370
   Barnet, 7:223
   John, 6:12, 7:367
   Southerland, 7:370
   Sutherland, 7:370
Maze, Zachariah, 7:369
McAdam, Hugh, 6:202
McAdams, 6:301
   James, 7:3, 7:90
McAllister, H., 6:409
McAnless, William, 6:442
McBride, James, 6:31
McBroom, Andrew, 7:257, 7:448
McCallister, James, 6:379
McCandless, David, 6:57
   Jane, 7:394
   John, 6:57
   William, 7:397
McCauley, 6:3
   Andrew, 6:24
   John, 6:100, 6:105, 6:226, 6:327, 6:328, 6:376, 6:416, 7:212, 7:213, 7:215
   John, (Irish), 6:21, 6:86, 6:143, 6:144, 6:156, 6:204, 6:219, McCauley, 6:221, 6:238, 6:243, 6:291, 6:621, 6:323, 6:327, 6:333
   Mathew, 6:221, 6:323, 6:333, 6:376, 6:396, 6:446, 7:34, 7:215, 7:476
   William, 6:219, 6:299, 7:26, 7:69, 7:351, 7:476
McClary, James, 7:269
McClure, 6:340
   Henry, 6:336
McCollum, Henry, 6:316
McCool, 7:91
McCoy, Henry, 7:257
McCracken, Jeremiah, 6:161, 7:311
   Thomas, 7:211
McCraw, George, 6:81
McCrory, John, 6:215, 6:216
McCulley, Joseph, 7:255
   Thomas, 6:352
McCulloch, 7:393
McCullock, 6:37, 6:39, 6:356, 6:357 James, 7:392
   Robert, 6:165
McCulloh, 6:48, 6:50, 6:52, 6:57, 6:237, 7:247
   Andrew, 6:350, 6:351
   Henry, 6:5, 6:73, 6:112, 7:206, 7:311, 7:420
   Henry Eustace, 6:41, 6:68, 6:69, 6:115, 6:167, 6:427, 7:35, 7:55, 7:258, 7:313, 7:319, 7:391
   John, 6:442, 7:397

McCulloh
   Joseph, 6:351, 6:350
   Patrick, 7:15
   Robert, 6:59
McCully, Andrew, 7:407
   see also McCauley
McDaniel, 6:132, 7:225
   Eli, 6:132, 6:136, 6:240, 7:14
   Mitch, 6:17
McFarlan, Willm., 6:314
McFarlin, John, 6:330
   Thomas, 6:330
McGuire, Patrick, 7:98
McKamey, Francis, 6:374
McKee, William, 7:281, 7:461
McKerrall, 7:456
   John, 6:43, 6:79, 6:110, 6:414, 7:260, 7:263, 7:445
McLaughlin, Hugh, 6:319
McLimore, Nathaniel, 7:451
McMahon, Daniel, 7:461
McManamy (McMiminy), John, 6:23, 7:225
McMannes, John, 7:362
McMasters, Lewis, 6:443
McMullan, Alex, 6:330
McMullin, Samuel, 6:364
McMun, James, 7:444
   William, 7:435, 7:444
McMurrey, John, 6:130, 6:146, 6:149
McNair, Ralph, 6:228, 6:402
McPherson, Jno., 6:140, 6:190
McQuiston, William, 7:246, 7:284, 7:445, 7:469
McRorey, John, 7:446
McSwaine, David, 7:306
McVinch, 7:19
   Catherine, 7:222
   John, 7:222
   Widow, 7:18
Meacham, 7:205
   John, 6:87, 6:466
Means, Samuel, 7:364, 7:488
Mebane, 7:392, 7:482
   Alexander (Alexr.), 6:2, 6:101, 6:156, 6:184, 6:321, 6:436, 6:438, 6:447, 7:213
   Dd., 7:88, 7:97, 7:271
   David, 7:47
   James, 6:16, 6:57, 6:233, 6:299, 6:447, 7:271, 7:308
   William, 6:313, 7:48, 7:351, 7:436
Medison, Peyton, 6:178
Melican, see Millikin
Melton, Ancil, 7:223
Merrett, John, 6:4

Merritt, William, 6:230, 7:1, 7:353
Millican, see Millikin
Millikin, 7:306
    Charles, 6:27, 6:148, 6:158, 6:365
        James, 6:27, 6:148, 6:158, 7:289 ,
    John, 6:26, 6:27, 6:148, 6:158, 7:205
    Robert, 6:148
    Thos., 6:158
Millington, John, 6:28
Ming, Joseph, 6:150, 6:176
Mitchell, Andrew, 7:90
    David, 7:287
    James, 6:100, 6:105, 7:398, 7:424, 7:475
    James, Capt., 6:269
    John, 6:100, 6:105, 6:271, 7:475
    Mr., 6:275
    Robert, 6:301
    Rt., 7:255
Mitchem, John, 6:87
Mize, Kedrick, 6:189
    Sack, 6:189
Montgomery, William, 6:39, 6:45, 6:50, 6:349
Moody, Joel, 7:270
Moor, 7:419, 7:466
Moore, 7:27
    Alexander Duncan, 7:6
    Alfred, 6:8, 6:9, 6:321, 6:417, 6:436, 6:438, 6:454
    Geo., 7:363
    Henry, 6:172
    James, 6:172, 6:227, 7:52, 7:306, 7:316
    John, 7:12, 7:289, 7:316
    John, Oldfield, 7:279, 7:306 John, Capt., 7:279, 7:306
    Joseph, 6:103, 6:152, 6:441, 7:96, 7:324
    Martha, 7:337
    Phillip, 7:376
    Robert, 7:52
    Roger, 7:211
    Sterling, 6:141, 7:42
    Thomas, 7:316
    William, 6:148, 6:158, 6:303, 7:71, 7:374
Moreland, Francis, 7:433
Morgan, 6:409
    Hardy, 6:21, 6:86, 6:226, 6:320
    J., 7:350
    John, 6:378, 6:411, 7:270, 7:353
    Mark, 6:378, 6:393
Morow, John, 7:278
Morris, Henry, 6:359
Morrison, Nathaniel, 6:319
    Robert, 6:10, 6:168, 7:426, 7:440
Morriss, Stephen, 7:405, 7:407
Morrow, Andrew, 6:231, 7:278, 7:285

Morrow,
    John, 6:469, 7:285
Moseley, Saml., 6:144
Moses, Abijah, 6:393
Mosley, John, 6:144
Mulhollan, 7:271, 7:461
    Hugh, 6:337, 6:389, 6:417
    Thomas, 6:364, 6:384, 6:469, 7:281, 7:283, 7:285, 7:287, 7:300
Mumford, James, 6:103
Murdock, Andrew, 6:35, 6:37, 6:39, 6:41, 6:43, 6:45, 6:48, 6:50, 6:52, 6:54, 6:79, 6:235, 6:237, 6:240, 6:243, 6:299, 6:399, 6:412, 7:43, 7:77, 7:91, 7:456
    James, 7:283
    Margaret, 6:412
Murphey, Archibald, 7:435
    Gabriel, 6:369, 6:422, 7:11
    William, 6:369, 6:427, 7:11
Murray, 6:354, 7:330, 7:473
    Henry, 7:254
    James, 6:301, 6:313, 7:48, 7:243, 7:244, 7:245, 7:254, 7:298, 7:474
    John, 7:399
    Walter, 6:449, 7:357
Muzzell, William, 6:369, 6:422, 6:427, 6:451, 6:452
Nash, Genl., 6:454
Neal, James, 6:469
Neese, Jacob, 6:21, 6:37
Neill, Thomas O., 7:77
Nelson, 7:72
    Abraham, 7:234, 7:382
    Arch., 7:82
    James, 7:82, 7:205
    John, 7:308
    Samuel, 7:462
    Thomas, 7:234
Nesley, John, 7:375
Nevell, 7:417
Nevill, Benjamin, 6:311, 7:7
    J. Junr., 6:406, 7:7
    Jesse, 6:311, 6:323, 6:406, 7:7, 7:410, 7:447
Newcomb, Betty, 7:231
Newlin Newland), James, 6:13
    John, 6:13, 6:29
Nathl., 7:426
Newman, Benjamin, 7:235
Newmon, 7:231
Newton, George, 7:421
Nichols, 6:93
    John, 6:163, 6:170, 6:414, 6:454, 7:468
    Jonathon, 6:179, 6:197, 7:91

Night, Abraham, 7:452
　Absalom, 7:259
Nix, Joseph, 6:87
Noey (Noe), George, 68
　John, 6:68, 6:370, 6:386
　Joseph, 6:68
Nolner, Henry, 6:89, 6:137
North Carolina, 6:3, 6:4, 6:16, 6:17, 6:18,
　6:19, 6:20, 6:21, 6:22, 6:23, 6:24,
　6:25, 6:26, 6:27, 6:28, 6:29, 6:30,
　6:31, 6:32, 6:33, 6:34, 6:56, 6:59,
　6:71, 6:77, 6:79, 6:81, 6:83, 6:90,
　6:109, 6:116, 6:132, 6:136, 6:156,
　6:182, 6:183, 6:184, 6:186, 6:196,
　6:209, 6:214, 6:215, 6:216, 6:217,
　6:218, 6:219, 6:220, 6:223, 6:225,
　6:289, 6:290, 6:294, 6:309, 6:325,
　6:333, 6:335, 6:337, 6:343, 6:344,
　6:345, 6:346, 6:347, 6:348, 6:349,
　6:350, 6:351, 6:353, 6:354, 6:355,
　6:357, 6:358, 6:359, 6:360, 6:361,
　6:362, 6:363, 6:365, 6:366, 6:389,
　6:398, 6:412, 6:420, 6:421, 6:426,
　6:427, 6:440, 6:443, 6:444, 6:447,
　6:352, 6:356, 6:364, 6:469, 7:11,
　7:15, 7:18, 7:19, 7:22, 7:23, 7:24,
　7:25, 7:30, 7:37, 7:48, 7:55, 7:85,
　7:87, 7:203, 7:207, 7:210, 7:233,
　7:237, 7:243, 7:244, 7:248, 7:259,
　7:273, 7:274, 7:276, 7:278, 7:281,
　7:282, 7:283, 7:289, 7:292, 7:298,
　7:306, 7:309, 7:313, 7:316, 7:317,
　7:318, 7:319, 7:320, 7:322, 7:323,
　7:324, 7:332, 7:333, 7:335, 7:336,
　7:339, 7:341, 7:343, 7:345, 7:359,
　7:360, 7:362, 7:364, 7:375, 7:376,
　7:383, 7:384, 7:385, 7:386, 7:387,
　7:388, 7:389, 7:390, 7:391, 7:392,
　7:393, 7:394, 7:399, 7:402, 7:403,
　7:412, 7:420, 7:429, 7:440, 7:444,
　7:445, 7:446, 7:447, 7:448, 7:449,
　7:450, 7:451, 7:452, 7:453, 7:454,
　7:455, 7:459, 7:461, 7:460, 7:462,
　7:463, 7:473, 7:474, 7:475, 7:476,
　7:477, 7:478, 7:480, 7:481, 7:482,
　7:487, 7:488, 7:489, 7:490, 7:491
Norwood, William, 6:182, 6:239, 7:3, 7:265,
　7:267, 7:328, 7:395, 7:415, 7:432,
　7:456
Nugent, Jacob, 6:231, 7:261, 7:290, 7:399
Numah, William, 7:311
Nunn, William, 7:91, 7:234, 7:480, 7:483,
　7:484, 7:485, 7:486
O'Daniel, Henry, 6:365, 6:462, 6:467
　Saml., 6:240

O'Ferrell, Barnabas, 6:414, 7:363
　Dr., 7:263
O'Kelly, John, 6:377
　William, 6:230, 6:377
O'Neal, William, 6:112
O'Neil, William, 7:55
O'Neill, Thomas, 7:77
Oneil, Jas., 7:367
Orsbon, Edwin, 6:461
Owen, Thomas, 6:182
Owens, Only, 6:189
Ozbern (Ozburn), Margaret, 6:176
　William, 6:150, 6:176
Pace, Joseph Baker, 7:330, 7:386
Palmer, James, 7:263, 7:324
　William, 6:182
Parish, Callam, 7:34, 7:270
Parker, Abraham, 6:154, 6:200
　David, 7:303
Parkes, Alexr., 7:92
　Mary, 7:93
　Samuel, 7:92, 7:93
Parks, Nancy, 7:93
Parrish, Elijah, 6:99
Partin, Martin, 6:424
　William, 6:221, 7:25, 7:212
Pasmore, David, 6:26, 6:29
Patten, 7:211
Patterson, Andrew, 7:322
　Chesley Page, 7:12
　David, 6:217, 6:386
　J. S., 6:384, 6:386, 7:300
　J. V., 6:68
　James, 6:54, 6:226, 6:320, 6:327, 6:362,
　　6:370, 7:59, 7:273, 7:377
　Jesse, 6:443
　John, 6:384
　Mann, 6:204, 7:12, 7:390
　Mark, 6:156, 6:337, 7:429 Nancy, 7:12
　Page, 7:85, 7:390
Patton (Patten), John, 7:14, 7:490, 7:491
　Jno., Junr., 7:490, 7:491
　Robert, 7:354, 7:366
　Thomas, 7:491 Paul, 7:413
Paul, John, 6:196
Peace, William, 7:212
Peake, B., 6:377
Pearce, Moses, 6:15
Peavey, Joseph, 7:55
Peck, Frederick, 6:382, 6:429
Peeler, Christian, 7:234
Pendergrass, Chainal, 7:427 Job, 7:427
　Luke, 7:292
　William, 6:378, 6:393, 6:396, 6:411,
　　7:350, 7:353

Perkins, Thos. H., 7:55
   Thomas Hardin, 7:377
   Thomas Hardy, 6:427
Person, 7:281, 7:283
   Thomas, 6:344, 7:281, 7:282, 7:283,
      7:287, 7:415, 7:448, 7:461
Petigrew, William, 7:332
Pevey, Joseph, 7:55
Phelps, Amos, 6:412
Phillips, 7:282
   A., 6:310
   Amos, 6:412
   Ann, 7:92, 7:93
   James, 7:324, 7:325, 7:380, 7:472
   Jesse, 6:444, 7:37
   Rachel, 7:92
   Rainey, 7:92, 7:93
   T. H., 7:213
   William, 7:80
Phipps, 6:183
Phips, John, 6:435, 7:8
Pickard, John, 6:31, 7:425
Pickett, Benjamin, 6:306, 6:307
   Joshua, 6:306, 6:307, 6:329
   Edward, 6:175
   William, 7:85, 7:350, 7:353
Piggott, Benjamin, 6:140
   Jeremiah, 6:294
   Joshua, 6:306
Pike, 7:401
Pile, Conrad (Conrod), 6:52, 7:76, 7:83,
   7:403
Pinnier, Thomas, 6:50
Piper, Abraham, 6:221, 7:34
   Alexander, 6:21, 6:221
   Rebekah, 7:34
   Samuel, 6:221
   Sarah, 6:221
Pitman, John, 7:269
Pleasant, William, 7:292
Poor, Peter, 7:202
Powell, Charles, 7:417
   Elias, 6:73
   James, 6:221
   John, 6:69, 6:71, 6:73, 6:112, 6:115,
      6:205, 6:112
   Mary, 6:73
   William, 7:417
Powk, Temple, 6:337
Pratt, George, 7:39
   James, 7:39, 7:395
Prosser, James, 6:19
Pryor, Luke, 6:242, 7:420
Puckett, Jane, 6:226, 6:385
   John, 6:320, 6:385, 6:425

Pugh, Ezra, 6:269
   John, 6:161, 7:42, 7:71
Purviance, Henry, 6:118
Quesenberry, Nicholas, 6:378
Quince, Richard, 6:60
Rae, see Ray
Ragsdale, Benj., 6:373, 6:456
Rainey (Raney), Benjamin, 6:71, 6:457,
   6:464, 7:41, 7:56, 7:80, 7:100, 7:201,
   7:297, 7:354
   David, 7:480
   Nancy, 6:71
   William, 6:73, 6:457, 6:464, 7:3, 7:41,
      7:55, 7:56, 7:90, 7:100, 7:201, 7:478
Rawls, Isaac, 6:220
Ray, David, 6:1, 6:41, 6:79, 6:367, 6:379,
   6:399, 6:416, 7:423
   Hugh, 6:32, 6:360, 6:431, 7:451
   James H., 6:167, 6:194, 6:242, 7:20
   James, 6:454, 7:347, 7:348 Ray, John,
      7:14, 7:211, 7:347, 7:348, 7:359,
      7:412
   Joseph, 7:468
   Martha, 6:167
   Robert, 6:194, 7:20
   William, 6:14, 6:19, 6:21, 6:41, 6:83,
      6:167, 6:205, 7:20, 7:22, 7:84, 7:253,
      7:258, 7:438, 7:439
Rea, see Ray
Reaves, Archibald, 6:416
Reding, John, 7:220, 7:224, 7:227, 7:228,
   7:233
   Stephen, 7:227
   Thomas, 7:220, 7:224, 7:227, 7:230
Redman, John, Junr., 7:228
Reed, John, 7:259
Rebecca, 7:259
Reeves, 6:347
   George, 6:228
   Henry, 6:118
   John, 6:34, 7:235, 7:265, 7:267
   see also Reaves
Regans, W., 7:270
Reid, William, 6:2
Rencher, Ann, 7:234
   John Grant, 6:332, 7:38, 7:82, 7:234
Ress, George, 7:362
Reynolds, Isaac, 6:426, 7:426
Rhea, John, 6:39, 6:45
   see also Ray
Rhodes, Benjamin, 7:433
   John, 6:4
   Leaven, 7:32
   Levan, 7:32
   Thomas, 7:18, 7:19

ORANGE COUNTY (NC) DEED BOOKS 6 & 7

Rhodes, William, 6:4, 6:87, 6:156, 6:204, 7:85
Rice, Adam, 6:253
　Jesse, 6:83, 7:414
Rich, Jacob, 6:242, 7:68, 7:76, 7:311, 7:320, 7:371, 7:403, 7:420
　Joseph, 6:68
　Peter, 7:371, 7:403
　Philepina, 6:242
　Thomas, 7:371
Richards, Jacob, 6:207
Rickets, Anthy., 6:19
Ricketts, Reason, 6:50
Rider, William, 6:106, 7:327
Riggs, James, 6:197, 7:421
　John, 6:59, 6:179, 6:197, 7:375, 7:421
　Thomas, 6:197, 7:421
Riley (Rielly), John, 6:16, 6:57, 7:72, 7:75, 7:219, 7:228
　Robert, 7:205
　William, 6:16, 6:57, 7:222, 7:284, 7:419
Rivers, James, 6:370
Roach, Absalom, 7:406
　Ann, 7:406
　James, 7:406
　William, 7:337
Roan, James, 6:296
　Lewis, 6:296
Roark, William, 6:407
Robbs, Alexander, 6:28, 6:30, 6:181, 7:248, 7:291, 7:309
Roberts, James, 6:316, 7:351
　Vincent, 7:259, 7:452
　William, 6:77, 6:178
　Willis, 7:247
Robertson, Nathaniel, 7:279
　Thomas, 7:306
Robinson, 7:362
　James, 6:379
　Michael, 6:59, 6:165, 6:179, 6:379
　Nathaniel, 6:26, 7:289, 7:306
　Thomas, 7:279, 7:289, 7:306
Rogers, William, 6:341
　William, Capt., 7:319
Romley, Joseph, 6:336
Roney, Benjamin, 6:202
　James, 6:202
Ross, Alex., 6:81
　Andrew, 6:79
　Jacob, 6:37
　James, 6:91, 6:97
　Sarah, 6:336
Rountree, Thomasa, 7:461
Rowan, James, 6:296
Rudolph, John, 6:217, 7:203

Rugley, 7:392
Russell, Alexander, 6:113, 7:33
　John, 6:89, 6:137
Rutherford, John, 7:343, 7:347
Sample, Alexr., 7:332
　James, 7:332
Saunders, James, 6:1
Scarlett, James, 6:228
　Thomas, 7:229
Scoby, J., 7:435
　Lucy, 7:435
　Robert, 7:435
Scoggin, John, 6:187
Scott, J., 6:372
　James, 6:214
　Thomas, 6:367
Sears, Joseph, 6:116, 6:173
Segrove, Randolph, 7:432
Seley, Martin, 7:84
Senate, 7:367
Shaddy, John, 7:202
Shankland, 7:380
Shanks, 7:387
Shannon, Hugh, 7:335, 7:354
Sharp (Sharpe), 6:356
　Aaron, 6:74, 7:258, 7:273
　Adam, 6:134
　Elizabeth, Sr., 6:239
　John, 6:21
　Joseph, 7:260
Shaw, Hugh, 7:33
　Samuel, Senr., 6:341
　William, 6:107, 7:406
Shelby, David, 7:486
Shelton, Edmund, 7:344, 7:345
Shepperd, 7:205, 7:413
　Eliza, 6:164
　H., 7:47, 7:74, 7:88, 7:96, 7:97
　Henry, 7:42, 7:263
　Jno., 7:433
　Samuel, 7:82
　William, 6:74, 6:83, 6:205, 6:307, 6:463, 6:466, 7:83, 7:210, 7:314, 7:379
　William, Col., 6:222
Sheridan, George, 6:29, 6:426, 7:5
Sheriff, 6:79, 6:93, 6:156, 7:215, 7:262
Shoemaker, 7:367
Shoffner (Shofner), Frederick, 6:395, 7:95
　Michael, 6:395, 7:51, 7:95
Shugart, Issac, 6:13
Shy, 7:282
　Jesse, 6:10
　John, 6:10, 6:168, 7:440
Sillivan, Joseph, 6:260
Simmons, Caleb, 6:448

Simmons (Simons), David, 6:302
  Shadrach, 6:210, 6:266, 6:269, 6:271,
    6:275, 6:280, 6:284
Sims, Hubert, 7:369
Sinnet, 7:367
Slave - Abraham, 7:238
  Affrica, 7:423
  Africa, 7:321
  Black Tom, 6:416
  Cesar, 6:217, 7:415
  Davie, 6:222
  Dempsey, 7:432
  Diles, 6:416
  Doll, 6:222
  Edmund, 7:436
  Else, 7:71
  Esther, 6:367
  Fann, 6:222
  Fendall, 7:442
  Fillis, 6:239
  Frank, 7:469
  Hannah, 7:302
  Harry, 6:230, 7:238
  Hester, 6:222
  Jack, 6:367
  John, 7:238
  Key, 7:302
  Let, 7:302
  Luce, 6:416
  Lydia, 7:442
  Mingo, 7:89
  Molley, 6:416
  Nancy, 7:432
  Naney, 7:238
  Ned, 7:485
  Nelse, 6:227
  Peter, 6:227
  Phillis, 6:416, 7:483
  Polley, 7:238
  Princess, 7:238
  Rose, 7:253
  Sarah, 6:367, 7:432
  Simon, 6:416
  Sophia, 6:222
  Stephey, 6:416
  Suxy, 6:222
  Tamer, 7:483
  Will, 7:32
Sloss, John, 6:30, 6:81, 6:181
  Joseph, 6:91
Smallwood, William, 6:237
Smith, 6:217, 6:220
  Adam, 6:71, 6:217
  Andrew, 6:220, 7:444
  Benjamin, 6:60, 6:261, 6:263

Smith, Benjamin, General, 7:62
  Cuningham, 7:407
  Elias, 7:59, 7:79
  George, 7:279, 7:305, 7:306
  Henry, 7:51
  James, 6:76, 6:233
  Jane, 7:407
  John, 6:28
  Malcom (Malcomb), 7:417, 7:427
  Mary, 7:405
  Reuben, 6:32, 6:33, 6:161, 6:431, 7:77,
    7:321, 7:406, 7:451
  Robert, 6:93, 6:152, 7:96
  Sampson, 7:405
  Samson, 7:407
  Samuel, 6:233, 6:299, 7:405, 7:407
  Sarah, 6:462, 6:467, 7:62
  Stephen, 6:165
  Tobias, 7:223
  Widow, 7:407
  William, 7:405, 7:407, 7:444
Smothers, Ann, 6:260
  John, 6:260, 6:339, 6:340
  Nancy, 6:340
  Susannah, 6:339
  William, 6:260, 6:340
Snotterly, Henry, 6:52
Sothberry, 7:3
Spaight, Richd. Dobbs, 6:29, 6:217, 6:219,
    6:359, 6:361, 6:366, 6:426, 7:23
Sparrow, John, 6:378, 6:396, 6:411
Spoon, John, 7:376
Springer, 6:218, 6:443
Squires, John, 7:354, 7:364, 7:366
Stalcup, William, 6:30, 7:17, 7:291
Standford, 6:223
  Charles, 6:225
Staneman, James, 7:313
Steel, Jno., 7:69
  Joseph, 6:107
  Thomas, 6:13
Stephens (Stevens), Daniel, 6:311, 7:7
  Samuel, 7:7
Stewart, Robert, 7:453
Stile, Henry, 6:93
Stockard, 7:377, 7:446
  James, 7:338
Stone, David, Judge, 7:265, 7:267, 7:274,
    7:276, 7:287, 7:295, 7:485
Stout, Jacob, 6:20, 6:140, 6:190
  Judith, 6:190
  Margaret, 6:140
  Peter, 6:140, 7:278, 7:285
Strader, Henry, 7:41, 7:201
  Jno., 7:56

Strain, Thomas, 6:341
Strayhorn, 7:445, 7:456
   David, 7:218, 7:382
   Gilbert, 6:293, 7:218, 7:382
   James, 7:234, 7:382
   John, 6:381, 7:205
   Wm., 7:205
Strother, John, 6:96
Stroud, Anderson, 6:446
   William, 6:302, 7:483, 7:484, 7:485
Strudwick, 6:17, 6:27, 6:158, 6:225, 6:363,
   7:211, 7:449, 7:450
   Martha, 7:308
   Samuel, 7:308
   William Francis, 6:161, 6:164, 6:322,
     6:441, 6:462, 7:42, 7:47, 7:88, 7:97,
     7:308
Stubbs, Isaac, 6:424
   Joseph, 6:424
   Thomas, 6:424
   Zilpah, 6:424
Summer, Robert, 6:250
Sutton, Thomas, 6:440
Suver, Henry, 6:313, 7:48
Swaffere, James, 6:168
Swann, John, 6:160
Swanney, 6:449
Tate, 7:389
   James, 7:251, 7:308
   John, 7:60, 7:255, 7:316
   Richard, 7:60
   Robert, 7:316
Tatom (Tatum), Absalom, 6:35, 6:60,
   6:78, 6:96, 6:110, 6:192, 6:414,
   7:238, 7:241, 7:263, 7:325, 7:327,
   7:363, 7:415, 7:468, 7:472
   Morning, 6:189, 7:250
   Stephen, 6:99, 6:193, 7:250
   William, 6:99
Taylor, Charles, 6:15
   Frederick, 7:395
   John, 6:85, 6:152, 6:217, 6:227, 6:416,
     6:454, 7:15, 7:43, 7:414
   John Lewis, 7:456, 7:468
   Joseph, 6:85, 6:152, 6:178, 7:468
   Robert, 6:152
Tedford, Hugh, 6:234
   Robert, 6:234
Thomas, Senr., 6:234
Telfair, John, 6:228
Tepson, Lenuel Cox, 6:328
Terrell, Henry, 6:169
Thedford, Josiah, 7:309
Thomas, Griffeth, 7:3
   John, 7:3, 7:421

Thomas, Thomas, 7:251
Thompson, 6:186, 6:453, 7:33
   Abraham, 7:435
   Benjamin, 6:106
   Henry, 7:9, 7:27, 7:30, 7:432, 7:436
   James, 6:315, 6:431, 7:303, 7:333, 7:450
   John, 6:107, 6:109, 6:360, 6:431, 7:14,
     7:32, 7:47, 7:88, 7:97
   Joseph, 6:103, 6:175, 7:47, 7:419
   Joshua, 7:419
   Josia, 7:47
   Laurence, 6:168
   Richd., 7:278, 7:285
   Robert, 6:314, 6:424, 7:442
   Samuel, 6:152, 6:389, 6:448, 7:231
   Simon, 7:97
   Theophilus, 6:93
   Thomas, 7:97
   Wm. F., 6:381, 7:382
Thornbury, David, 6:384, 6:443
Thornton, Benjamin, 6:78
Tilley, Lazarus, 6:19
Tinnin, 6:167
   James, 6:194, 7:258
   John, 6:101
   Robert, 6:101
Torrentine, see Turrentine
Toundson, Joseph, 6:420
Toweln, Jesse, 7:399
Townsand, Joseph, 6:420, 7:235
Trice, Charles, 6:433, 7:221
   Edward, 7:85
   James, 6:432
   Thomas, 6:463, 6:466, 7:12, 7:89
   William, 7:12
Trotter, Robert, 6:406
   William, 6:406
Trousdale, Jas., 7:338
   John, 7:20, 7:359
   Robt., 6:136
   William, 6:132, 6:136, 6:356
Troxler, Barnet, 7:391
   Barnaby, 7:253
   Barnet, 7:237
   Barney, 7:253
   Jacob, 7:253
**Trustees of the University of North
   Carolina**, 6:8, 6:9, 6:74, 6:83, 6:205,
   6:235, 6:243, 6:307, 6:436, 6:438,
   6:461, 7:80, 7:83, 7:213, 7:215, 7:314
Tucker, 6:116
   B. W., 6:210
   Daniel, 6:210, 6:261, 6:284, 7:64
   Ethed., 6:116
   Harris, 6:459, 6:460

Turner, 6:116, 6:183, 6:385
   Edward, 7:9, 7:425
   Elias, 6:435, 7:8
   Robert, 7:364, 7:387, 7:388
Turrentine, Alexander, 6:145
   Daniel, 7:339, 7:341, 7:354, 7:364, 7:366
   James, 6:407
   Samuel, 6:145, 7:39, 7:252, 7:328, 7:464
Ulias, 6:386
   Phillip, 6:370, 7:376
Umpstead, Jacob, 7:487
   John, 6:93, 6:118, 7:96
Varnel, Jesse, 6:168
Vaughan, James, 7:82, 7:205
   Spencer, 7:216
Vincent, Thomas, 6:43
Waggoner, Henry, 6:145, 7:462
   Jacob, 6:145
   John, 6:165
Waite, William, 7:463
Waldraven, John, 6:202
Walker, 7:298
   Andrew, 6:101
   Conally, 7:254
   Henry, 6:189
   James, 6:330, 7:414
   John, 6:101, 6:179, 6:197, 6:202, 6:393, 6:396, 7:24, 7:474
   Peter, 6:101, 6:175
   Philip, 7:255
   Robert, 6:59, 6:179, 6:197, 7:421
   William, 6:103, 6:175, 6:179, 6:197, 6:234, 6:310, 7:421, 7:473, 7:474
Wall, John, 6:63
   Margaret, 6:63
   Sally, 7:442
   Thomas Lewellin Lechmere (Lechmear), 7:27, 7:30, 7:442
Wallace (Wallis), 7:367
   John Allen, 7:360
   William, 6:94, 7:291, 7:293, 7:370
Waller, Joseph, 6:193
Ward, Stephen, 7:207, 7:208
   Sutton, 6:28
   William, 7:207
Warnion, James, 6:234
Warnock, James, 6:310
Warren (Warrin), 7:367, 7:378
   Boswell, 6:369, 6:427
   John, 6:43
Warson, Daniel, 6:25
Wason, Daniel, 6:25
Wasson, Robert, 6:57
Watkins, 7:474
Watson, Andrew, 6:417, 7:246, 7:303, 7:419

Watson, Bennet, 6:391, 7:344
   Daniel, 6:204
   James, 6:172, 6:407, 6:417, 7:15, 7:462
   James, Esq., 7:419
   James, Junr., 7:246, 7:284, 7:303, 7:419, 7:456
   James, Senr., 6:172, 7:419
   Jeanny, 7:456
   John, 6:172
   Mack, 6:7
   Margaret, 7:419
   Robert, 6:113
   Samuel, 6:113
Watters, 7:472
   Henry, 7:380
   Mrs. Mary, 6:217
   W., 6:9
   William, 6:8, 6:9, 6:35, 6:227, 6:321, 6:390, 6:436, 6:438, 7:6, 7:9, 7:379, 7:468
Watts, Josiah, 7:69
   Thomas, 6:237, 6:322, 7:69
Webb, Thomas, 6:94
Weel, Elisha, 6:422
Weems, John, 6:219
Wells, Elisha, 6:452
   Miles, 6:422, 6:427, 6:452
   Nathan, 7:401
Wheeler, John, 7:57
Whelley, Benjamin, 6:146
   John, 6:130
Whinney, Abraham, 7:333
   Martha, 7:333
Whitacre, Abraham, 7:227
White, 6:412, 7:220
   Henry, 6:361
   Joseph, 7:224
   Pennery, 7:248
   Stephen, 7:338, 7:354, 7:366
   William, 7:336, 7:375, 7:387, 7:388, 7:392, 7:412, 7:450, 7:451, 7:452, 7:453, 7:454, 7:455, 7:459, 7:476, 7:477, 7:480, 7:481, 7:482, 7:487, 7:490
   see also Whyte
Whitehead, John, 6:35
   Mr., 7:241
   William, 6:35, 6:289, 6:315, 6:382
Whithead, Thomas, 7:14
Whitney, Lebious, 6:454
Whitsell, Adam, 6:79
   James, 6:23, 7:359
   John, 6:134
   Samuel, 7:251
Whitted, 6:186, 6:289

ORANGE COUNTY (NC) DEED BOOKS 6 & 7

Whitted, Jas., 6:78, 6:96, 6:106, 6:192, 6:335
   John, 6:78, 7:236
   Thomas, 6:205, 7:286
   William, 6:78, 6:96, 6:106, 6:192, 6:419, 6:429, 7:9
Whyte, Will., 7:335
Wilborn, 6:193
Wilbourn (Wilburn), John (Jno.), 7:250
Wilhoit (Wilhite), Absalom, 7:478
   Elias, 7:391
   Jacob, 6:54, 7:223
Wilkins, 7:338
Wilkinson, Daniel, 7:72
   James, 7:347, 7:348
   John, 7:72, 7:468
   William, 7:72
Williams, 6:417
   Elizabeth, 6:316
   Frederick, Capt., 7:336
   James, 6:19, 6:37, 6:39, 6:41, 6:45, 6:48, 6:50, 6:52, 6:54, 6:222, 6:237, 6:240, 7:43, 7:76, 7:83
   John, 6:60, 6:71, 6:118, 6:245, 6:249, 6:250, 6:253, 6:261, 6:263, 7:62, 7:376
   Ralph, 6:152, 7:347, 7:348
   Thomas, 7:298
   Umphrey, 6:294
   William, 6:83, 6:382, 6:427, 6:447
Willis, Augustine, 7:295
   John, 7:295
   Miles, 6:427
   Plummer, 7:295
   William, 7:410, 7:417
Wilson (Willison), Archelus, 6:407
   Edward, 7:302
   James, 7:269, 7:297
   John, 6:161, 6:311, 6:406, 7:7
   Mathias, 7:271, 7:481
   Mathis, 7:271
   Samuel, 6:81
   Stephen, 6:297, 7:466
   William, 7:302
Winslow, Jos., 6:280, 6:284
Winston, Jos., 6:275
Wire, James, 6:443
Witherspoon, David, 6:93
Wittie, Joshua, 7:260
Wolf, Ann, 7:203
   William, 7:203
   see also Woolfe
Wood, Charles, 7:269, 7:297
   Fanny, 6:63, 6:65
   Freeman, 7:251

Wood, Henry, 7:466
   John, 6:63, 6:65, 6:289, 6:290, 7:373
   Joseph, 7:375
   Levin, 7:68
   Lewis, 7:59
   Thomas, 6:133
   William, 6:382, 7:203
Woodrow, James, 7:397
Woods, David, 6:163, 6:170
   Hugh, 7:362, 7:421, 7:456
   John (Jno.), 6:163, 6:170, 7:421
   Richard, 6:424
   Thomas, 6:163, 6:170
   William, 6:170, 7:468
Woody, James, 6:319
   Joseph, 6:364
Woolfe, Peter, 6:240
   William, 7:290
   see also Wolf
Workman, John, 7:426
Woroon, Willm., 6:466
Wright, John, 6:140
Yarbrough, James, 6:1, 6:41, 7:263, 7:321, 7:423
Yeargan, Benjamin, 6:86, 6:143, 6:199, 6:203, 6:219, 6:320, 6:327, 6:362
   Charlotte Hinton, 6:199
   Garret, 6:86
   Jarratt, 6:143
Young Miller & Company, 6:414
Young, John, 7:322

GERMAN SIGNATURES

Signature	Reference
Jonas P. Albright	**6:295**
Lu Dangeble	**7:37**
unfoje Pavlo	**7:55**
fen Cobyt oford	**7:273**
Jannyo albright	**7:329**
Jacob Gerngt	**7:395**
brwd x Heeilar	**7:395**

PLACE NAME INDEX

Citations are to the original book and page number.

Allamance Creek, 7:258, 7:420
Autor Creek, 7:338
Back Creek, 6:23, 6:101, 6:103,
 6:134, 6:215, 6:220, 6:225, 6:233,
 6:299, 6:341, 6:453, 7:3, 7:24,
 7:33, 7:292, 7:354, 7:359, 7:366,
 7:444, 7:481
Back Line, 7:407
Banks Cabbin, 7:1
Barbee's Tract, 6:446
Bartie County, 7:359
Batts Creek, 6:2
Baxters Creek, 7:332
Bear Creek, 7:336
Belvidere, 7:62
Benton's Mill, 7:9
Bertie County, 7:359
Big Creek, 6:186, 6:260
Big Road, 7:393
Bird Branch, 6:311
Black Creek, 7:282
Black Jack Creek, 6:197, 7:421
Blown Fork Branch, 7:257
Blue House, 6:414, 7:263, 7:415
Bolands Creek, 6:327, 6:320, 7:25
Bolans Creek, 6:362, 7:484
Bolings Creek, 6:21, 6:446
Borlands Creek, 7:212
Boyds Creek, 6:56, 6:216, 7:87,
 7:364, 7:446
Bradley Lick Creek, 6:1
Brunswick County, 6:60, 6:210,
 6:245, 6:249, 6:250, 6:253, 6:256,
 6:261, 6:263, 6:266, 6:269, 6:271,
 6:275, 6:280, 6:284, 7:62, 7:64,
Buck Quarter Creek, 6:67, 6:402,
 6:404
Buck Water Creek, 6:110, 6:289,
 6:290, 6:382
Buckhorn Branch, 7:481
Buffalow Creek, 6:141
Cabbin Branch, 7:35
Cain (Cane) Creek, 6:13, 6:20, 6:27,
 6:140, 6:190, 6:231, 6:317, 6:319,
 7:208, 7:282, 7:336, 7:436, 7:451,
 7:455, 7:477

Cain (Cane) Creek Settlement,
 6:231, 7:401
Caintucky, 6:245
Camp Creek of Nap of Reeds, 6:99,
 6:189, 6:193, 7:247, 7:250
Carrigan's Old Place, 6:35
Carson's Old Line, 7:335
Caswell County Line, 6:15, 6:83,
 6:134, 6:369, 6:422, 6:428, 6:451,
 6:452, 7:11, 7:216, 7:225, 7:247,
 7:259, 7:292, 7:468, 7:482
Caswells Creek, 6:406
Cate's Old Tract, 7:336
Cates Creek, 7:39
Cedar Fork, 7:323
Cedar Creek, 7:391, 7:478
Chapel Road, 6:226
Chappel, 6:427
Charles Dunnagan's Spring Br.,
 6:76
Charleston (Charles Town), 6:263,
 6:271, 7:64
Charleston District, 6:271
Chatham County Line, 6:13, 6:20,
 6:198, 6:218, 6:190, 6:221, 6:226,
 6:239, 6:249, 6:302, 6:320, 6:327,
 6:378, 6:411, 6:443, 7:7, 7:98,
 7:270, 7:410, 7:417, 7:427
Cherokee Indians, 6:18, 6:249,
 6:263
Cherokee Nation, 6:60, 6:245
Cherokee Nation of Indians, 7:62
Chesnut Creek, 6:385
Church, 7:263
Churton Street, 6:414, 7:263, 7:415
Cleared Ground, 6:228
Cleared Land, 6:339
Clinch River, 6:60, 6:118, 7:62
Collins Creek, 6:26, 6:365, 6:366,
 7:305, 7:337
Columbia County, 6:424
Cool Spring, 6:35
Cother's Field, 7:350
County Line, 6:173, 6:234, 6:435,
 7:8, 7:392, 7:393, 7:417, 7:427,
 7:452

Courthouse, 7:246
Crooked Run, 6:358
Crooked Run Creek, 7:35
Crosscreek Road, 7:270
Crows Road, 7:305
Cumberland County, 6:143, 6:203,
  6:275, 6:280, 6:284, 6:409, 6:425
Cumberland River, 6:60, 6:118,
  6:245, 7:62, 7:265
Cunalls Creek, 6:240
Dan River, 7:402
Davidson County, 6:454, 7:68,
  7:265
Deep Creek, 6:43, 6:89, 6:137,
  6:150, 6:154, 6:176, 6:196, 6:200,
  6:325, 6:361, 7:17, 7:248, 7:291,
  7:293, 7:296, 7:309, 7:383, 7:384,
  7:385, 7:386, 7:488, 7:489
Division Line, 7:405, 7:407
Division No. 1, 6:106
Dog Creek, 7:84
Draft, 7:370
Drailght, 6:303
Dray Branch, 7:490
Dry Creek, 6:444, 7:222, 7:390
Duck River, 7:238
Dutchmans Branch, 6:435
Dyals Creek, 6:3146:330
Dyer's Camp, 7:265
East Fork, 6:1
Elder Spring, 7:382
Ellibees Creek, 6:116, 6:173, 6:183,
  6:435, 7:8, 7:225, 7:433
Eno River, 6:18, 6:78, 6:85, 6:94,
  6:96, 6:106, 6:152, 6:184, 6:309,
  6:335, 6:344, 6:345, 6:346, 6:348,
  6:353, 6:356, 6:420, 6:421, 6:424,
  7:9, 7:15, 7:18, 7:19, 7:23, 7:35,
  7:96, 7:98, 7:216, 7:218, 7:222,
  7:227, 7:230, 7:231, 7:233, 7:234,
  7:235, 7:317, 7:335, 7:367, 7:382,
  7:413, 7:425, 7:431, 7:433, 7:435,
  7:441, 7:453, 7:456, 7:480
Entry No. 361, 6:233
Eubank's Tract, 7:47
Fayetteville Road, 6:194, 6:303,
  7:449, 7:473
Fills Creek, 7:447
First Creek, 7:85
Fishing Creek, 6:234

Flat River, 6:45, 6:50, 6:77, 6:83,
  6:89, 6:94, 6:137, 6:154, 6:200,
  6:237, 6:330, 6:442, 7:303, 7:392,
  7:397, 7:414, 7:466
Ford, 7:425
Foresters (Forresters) Creek, 6:93,
  6:454, 7:91, 7:96
Fourth Creek, 7:285
Fousts Creek, 6:469, 7:278
Franklin Street, 6:321, 6:372, 6:376,
  6:391, 6:432, 6:436, 7:213, 7:215
Franklin County, 6:227
Georgetown (George Town), 6:210,
  6:266, 6:275, 6:280, 6:284, 7:64
Georgetown (George Town)
  District, 6:218, 6:261, 6:266,
  6:269, 6:271, 6:275, 6:280, 6:284,
  7:64
Georgia, 6:402, 6:404, 6:424, 7:219,
  7:376
Grant #319, 6:389
Granville County, 6:89, 6:118,
  6:137, 6:154, 6:178, 6:182, 6:200,
  6:245, 6:250, 6:253, 7:27, 7:30,
  7:250, 7:468
Granville County Line, 7:247, 7:487
Grays Creek, 7:27, 7:30
Great Allamance Creek, 6:12, 6:37,
  6:48, 6:52, 6:54, 6:194, 6:242,
  7:20, 7:223, 7:319, 7:371, 7:376,
  7:377, 7:391, 7:403, 7:438, 7:439
Great Canaway, 6:245
Great Flat Rock, 7:255
Great Road, 6:81, 7:72, 7:387, 7:425
Great Road Leading to
  Hillsborough, 6:134, 7:90
Great Road from Hillsborough to
  Dan River, 7:402
Great Road from Hillsborough to
  Halifax, 6:357, 6:419
Green County, 7:409
Green River, 6:60, 7:62
Guilford County, 6:43, 6:91, 6:97,
  6:176, 6:234, 6:310, 6:370, 6:384,
  6:443, 7:293, 7:300, 7:377, 7:426
Guilford County Line, 6:54, 6:384
Gun Creek, 6:427, 6:464, 7:76, 7:80,
  7:83, 7:314, 7:438
Gunn Creek, 6:79
Hagwood's Cabbin, 6:311

Halifax County, 6:296, 6:357, 6:419
Hancock County, 6:402, 6:404
Harmon's Road, 6:295, 6:306
Haw Branch, 6:302, 7:350, 7:353
Haw Creek, 6:113, 6:130, 6:136,
　6:141, 6:161, 6:233, 6:299, 6:441,
　7:338, 7:341
Haw River, 6:5, 6:10, 6:13, 6:14,
　6:29, 6:33, 6:34, 6:68, 6:71, 6:73,
　6:74, 6:101, 6:130, 6:136, 6:168,
　6:233, 6:234, 6:240, 6:260, 6:299,
　6:305, 6:310, 6:313, 6:336, 6:360,
　6:364, 6:426, 6:431, 6:444, 7:3,
　7:5, 7:14, 7:37, 7:48, 7:55, 7:76,
　7:83, 7:84, 7:87, 7:90, 7:92, 7:93,
　7:98, 7:208, 7:244, 7:269, 7:279,
　7:282, 7:306, 7:319, 7:356, 7:364,
　7:377, 7:399, 7:410, 7:417, 7:426,
　7:491
Hawfields, 7:302
Hawfields Branch, 6:130, 6:136
Hayes Creek, 7:238
Hazell Street, 6:169
Henry McCulloh's Boundary, 7:208
Hickmans Creek, 7:265
Hico, 6:149, 6:451, 7:11, 7:259,
　7:335
Hico Road to Hillsborough, 7:96
Highland Pond, 7:23
Hillsborough, 6:35, 6:57, 6:78,
　6:96, 6:110, 6:134, 6:154, 6:156,
　6:160, 6:169, 6:182, 6:192, 6:200,
　6:316, 6:335, 6:337, 6:357, 6:374,
　6:367, 6:390, 6:397, 6:399, 6:401,
　6:414, 6:416, 6:419, 6:465, 7:6,
　7:9, 7:15, 7:43, 7:96, 7:210,
　7:246, 7:260, 7:262, 7:263, 7:264,
　7:324, 7:325, 7:327, 7:328, 7:363,
　7:379, 7:380, 7:402, 7:415, 7:423,
　7:469, 7:472
Hillsborough Road, 6:456, 7:47,
　7:88, 7:97, 7:283
Holsten River, 6:245
Horse Creek, 6:172
Hugh Shannon's Old
　Improvement, 7:335
Indian Purchase, 7:62
Isle of Wight County, 7:292
J. Pratt's Old Tract, 7:39
Jacob Rich's Mill, 7:403

James Watson's Old Tract, 6:417
John Ivey's Spring Branch, 6:302
John Moore's Old Field, 7:289
Joseph Moore's New Survey, 6:152
Jourdans Creek, 6:30, 6:181, 6:214,
　7:389
Jumping Run, 7:370
Kenedays Branch, 7:42
Kennedys Branch, 7:42
Kentucky River, 6:60, 7:62
King & Queen County, 6:463
King Street, 6:316, 6:374, 6:390,
　6:399, 6:401, 6:414, 7:6, 7:260,
　7:263, 6:397, 7:415, 7:469
Laughlins Cr., 7:52
Lick Branch, 6:99, 7:250
Lick Creek, 6:86
Linches Creek, 6:422, 6:428, 6:452,
　7:482
Little Allamance Creek, 6:69, 6:112,
　6:115, 6:305, 6:427, 7:55, 7:100
Little Back Creek, 6:164, 7:271
Little Cain Creek, 6:31, 6:32, 6:148,
　6:158, 6:322, 6:363, 6:462, 6:467,
　7:343, 7:450, 7:451
Little Creek, 6:154, 6:200, 6:226,
　7:488
Little River, 6:16, 6:19, 6:39, 6:41,
　6:57, 6:59, 6:76, 6:93, 6:81,
　6:109, 6:145, 6:163, 6:165, 6:170,
　6:179, 6:197, 6:379, 6:407, 6:440,
　6:442, 6:454, 7:35, 7:281, 7:283,
　7:287, 7:318, 7:347, 7:348, 7:362,
　7:375, 7:392, 7:393, 7:394, 7:397,
　7:402, 7:421, 7:459, 7:460, 7:461,
　7:462 Long Branch, 6:377
Long Island, 6:245
Lot 1, 6:118
Lot 1A, 6:118
Lot 1B, 6:118
Lot 1C, 6:118
Lot 1D, 6:118
Lot 1E, 6:118
Lot 1F, 6:118
Lot 1G, 6:118
Lot 1H, 6:118
Lot 1I, 6:118
Lot 1L, 6:118
Lot 1O, 6:118
Lot 2, 6:118

Lot 2A, 6:118
Lot 2C, 6:118
Lot 2D, 6:118
Lot 2E, 6:118
Lot 2F, 6:118
Lot 2G, 6:118
Lot 2H, 6:118
Lot 2K, 6:118
Lot 2N, 6:118
Lot 2P, 6:118
Lot 2Y, 6:118
Lot #2, 6:438, 6:461, 7:246, 7:284
Lot #4, 6:391, 6:432, 6:436
Lot #6, 7:215
Lot #8, 6:9, 6:243, 6:376
Lot #9, 6:8, 6:235, 7:213, 7:215
Lot #11, 7:215
Lot #15, 6:372, 6:390, 7:6
Lot #16, 6:230
Lot #18, 6:399
Lot #19, 7:38
Lot #21, 6:374, 6:397, 6:401, 7:379
Lot #22, 6:182, 6:374, 6:397, 6:401, 7:379
Lot #23, 7:328, 7:379
Lot #24, 6:321, 6:414, 7:328, 7:415
Lot #25, 6:414, 7:263, 7:415
Lot #31, 6:374, 6:397, 6:401, 6:465, 7:379
Lot #32, 7:379
Lot #33, 7:2107:328, 7:379
Lot #34, 7:415
Lot #35, 7:415
Lot #44, 7:246, 7:284
Lot #45, 7:469
Lot #73, 6:169
Lot #74, 6:169
Lot #82, 7:324, 7:327
Lot #83, 7:324, 7:325
Lot #84, 7:324, 7:235
Lot #92, 6:160, 6:169
Lot #93, 6:160, 6:169
Lot #94, 6:160
Lot #99, 7:327
Lot #100, 7:327
Lot #101, 7:325, 7:327
Lot #102, 7:324, 7:325, 7:327
Lot #103, 7:324, 7:325
Lot #111, 6:160
Lot #112, 6:160

Lot #121, 6:160
Lot #128, 7:260
Lot #129, 6:316
Lot #130, 6:316
Lot #135, 7:43
Lot #136, 7:43
Lot #137, 7:43
Lot #138, 7:43
Lot #139, 7:43
Louisa River, 6:245
Low Grounds, 7:390
Lowgrounds of Morgan, 6:226
Macklenburg County, 6:1
Main Fork, 6:199, 6:203, 6:409, 7:359
Main Street, 6:230
Mangum's Entry, 6:370
Marcom Bairies Branch, 7:205
Margaret Lane, 6:316, 6:399, 7:43, 7:268, 7:469
Market House, 6:337, 6:367
Marrowbone Creek, 7:282
Marshalls Branch, 6:17, 6:383, 7:374
Mary Anderson's Branch, 6:99
McBroom's Old Tract, 7:448
McCool's Tract, 7:91
McCullock's Land, 6:37
Meadow, 7:370
Meadow Creek, 7:47, 7:88
Meadow Fork, 6:311, 7:7
Meadow Spring, 7:370
Mecklenburg County, 6:1
Meeting House Road, 7:374
Middle Fork of Hico, 6:149
Mile Branch, 7:332
Mill Creek, 6:178, 6:223, 6:323, 6:341, 6:412, 6:447, 7:367
Mill Dam, 6:317, 6:319
Mill Pond, 7:43
Mill Race, 6:313
Mill Seat, 6:89, 6:137, 7:1, 7:403
Mill Tract, 7:377
Mill, 6:156, 6:313
Mississippi, 7:238
Mocason Branch, 7:449
Montgomery County, 6:5, 7:483, 7:484, 7:485
Moore County, 7:377
Morgans Creek, 6:22, 6:105, 6:144,

ORANGE COUNTY (NC) DEED BOOKS 6 & 7

Morgans Creek, 6:221, 6:226, 6:332, 6:359, 6:378, 6:393, 6:406, 7:1, 7:34, 7:278, 7:363, 7:398, 7:447
Morgans Wagon Path, 6:226
Mountain, 7:79
Mountain Creek, 6:297, 7:369, 7:464, 7:466
Mulberry Branch, 7:42
Nap of Reeds, 6:189, 7:247, 7:250, 7:332
Narrow Street, 6:391, 6:432
Nevill's Mill, 6:323
New Bern, 6:93
New Hanover County, 6:160, 7:211, 7:380
New Road, 7:42
Newhope, 6:2, 6:3, 6:4, 6:21, 6:87, 6:105, 6:156, 6:187, 6:199, 6:219, 6:228, 6:203, 6:204, 6:337, 6:343, 6:347, 6:377, 6:381, 6:382, 6:409, 6:410, 6:433, 6:446, 6:466, 7:12, 7:26, 7:85, 7:221, 7:322, 7:323, 7:345, 7:360, 7:390, 7:398, 7:424, 7:429, 7:445, 7:475
North Carolina, 6:65, 6:68, 6:169, 6:210, 6:269, 6:271, 6:280, 6:284, 7:238
North East Creek, 6:343
North East Creek of Newhope, 6:187
North East Fork, 6:377
North Fork, 6:16, 6:379, 7:402
North Fork of Little River, 6:165
North Hico, 6:369, 6:422, 6:428, 6:452, 7:452
Obeds Creek, 6:393, 7:353, 7:350
Occaneechee (Occoneechy) Mountain, 6:35, 6:192, 6:335
Oglethorpe County, 7:219
Ohio River, 6:68, 6:118, 6:210, 6:245, 6:269, 6:271, 7:62
Old Corner, 6:209, 7:248, 7:373
Old Crossroads, 7:472
Old Deeded Land, 7:278
Old Field, 6:194, 6:293, 6:311, 6:333, 6:409, 7:211, 7:284, 7:300, 7:351
Old Halifax Road, 7:380
Old Holts Spring Branch, 6:71

Old Indian Town, 6:118
Old Last Line, 6:228
Old Line, 6:197, 6:228, 6:301, 6:345, 6:393, 7:58, 7:306, 7:363, 7:373
Old Mill Path, 6:89, 6:137
Old Road, 6:320, 7:380
Old Sand Pit, 7:213
Old Shoemaker's Corner, 7:367
Old Survey, 6:152
Old Tract, 6:209, 7:466
Orange County, 6:2, 6:4, 6:5, 6:7, 6:8, 6:9, 6:10, 6:12, 6:13, 6:14, 6:15, 6:35, 6:37, 6:39, 6:41, 6:43, 6:45, 6:48, 6:50, 6:52, 6:54, 6:57, 6:59, 6:60, 6:63, 6:67, 6:68, 6:69, 6:71, 6:73, 6:74, 6:76, 6:78, 6:79, 6:81, 6:83, 6:85, 6:86, 6:87, 6:90, 6:91, 6:93, 6:94, 6:96, 6:97, 6:99, 6:100, 6:103, 6:105, 6:106, 6:107, 6:109, 6:112, 6:113, 6:115, 6:116, 6:130, 6:133, 6:134, 6:136, 6:140, 6:141, 6:143, 6:144, 6:146, 6:148, 6:150, 6:152, 6:154, 6:156, 6:158, 6:161, 6:163, 6:164, 6:165, 6:167, 6:168, 6:170, 6:172, 6:173, 6:175, 6:176, 6:178, 6:179, 6:181, 6:182, 6:183, 6:184, 6:187, 6:189, 6:190, 6:192, 6:193, 6:194, 6:196, 6:197, 6:199, 6:202, 6:203, 6:204, 6:205, 6:207, 6:208, 6:209, 6:217, 6:221, 6:222, 6:223, 6:226, 6:228, 6:230, 6:231, 6:233, 6:234, 6:237, 6:240, 6:242, 6:243, 6:256, 6:260, 6:263, 6:291, 6:293, 6:294, 6:295, 6:296, 6:297, 6:299, 6:300, 6:301, 6:302, 6:303, 6:305, 6:306, 6:307, 6:309, 6:311, 6:313, 6:314, 6:315, 6:316, 6:317, 6:319, 6:320, 6:321, 6:322, 6:323, 6:325, 6:327, 6:328, 6:329, 6:330, 6:332, 6:333, 6:336, 6:337, 6:339, 6:340, 6:341, 6:370, 6:372, 6:373, 6:374, 6:276, 6:377, 6:378, 6:379, 6:381, 6:382, 6:385, 6:386, 6:387, 6:389, 6:391, 6:392, 6:393, 6:394, 6:395, 6:396, 6:399, 6:402, 6:404, 6:406, 6:407, 6:409, 6:410, 6:411, 6:412, 6:416, 6:417, 6:419, 6:424, 6:425, 6:429, 6:431, 6:433, 6:435, 6:438, 6:441, 6:442, 6:444, 6:446, 6:448, 6:449, 6:453, 6:454,

ORANGE COUNTY (NC) DEED BOOKS 6 & 7

Orange County, 6:456, 6:457,
  6:459, 6:460, 6:461, 6:462, 6:463,
  6:464, 6:465, 6:466, 6:467, 6:469,
  7:1, 7:2, 7:3, 7:5, 7:6, 7:8, 7:9,
  7:12, 7:14, 7:15, 7:17, 7:26, 7:27,
  7:30, 7:32, 7:33, 7:34, 7:35, 7:38,
  7:41, 7:43, 7:47, 7:48, 7:51, 7:52,
  7:53, 7:55, 7:56, 7:57, 7:58, 7:60,
  7:68, 7:69, 7:71, 7:72, 7:74, 7:75,
  7:76, 7:77, 7:80, 7:82, 7:83, 7:84,
  7:85, 7:88, 7:89, 7:90, 7:91, 7:93,
  7:95, 7:96, 7:97, 7:98, 7:100,
  7:201, 7:202, 7:203, 7:205, 7:207,
  7:208, 7:211, 7:212, 7:213, 7:215,
  7:216, 7:218, 7:219, 7:220, 7:221,
  7:222, 7:223, 7:224, 7:225, 7:227,
  7:228, 7:229, 7:230, 7:231, 7:233,
  7:234, 7:235, 7:238, 7:241, 7:246,
  7:247, 7:248, 7:250, 7:251, 7:252,
  7:253, 7:254, 7:255, 7:257, 7:258,
  7:259, 7:260, 7:261, 7:263, 7:265,
  7:267, 7:271, 7:273, 7>274,
  7:276, 7:278, 7:279, 7:285, 7:286,
  7:287, 7:289, 7:290, 7:291, 7:293,
  7:295, 7:296, 7:297, 7:298, 7:300,
  7:301, 7:302, 7:303, 7:305, 7:306,
  7:308, 7:309, 7:311, 7:313, 7:314,
  7:321, 7:324, 7:328, 7:330, 7:332,
  7:333, 7:337, 7:338, 7:341, 7:344,
  7:345, 7:347, 7:348, 7:350, 7:351,
  7:353, 7:354, 7:356, 7:357, 7:358,
  7:359, 7:360, 7:362, 7:363, 7:364,
  7:366, 7:367, 7:369, 7:370, 7:371,
  7:373, 7:374, 7:376, 7:379, 7:380,
  7:382, 7:395, 7:397, 7:398, 7:399,
  7:401, 7:402, 7:403, 7:405, 7:406,
  7:407, 7:409, 7:410, 7:413, 7:414,
  7:415, 7:417, 7:419, 7:420, 7:421,
  7:423, 7:424, 7:425, 7:426, 7:427,
  7:429, 7:431, 7:432, 7:433, 7:436,
  7:438, 7:439, 7:440, 7:441, 7:442,
  7:456, 7:464, 7:466, 7:468, 7:472,
  7:483, 7:484, 7:485, 7:486
Orange County Line, 6:137, 6:190,
  6:218, 6:422, 6:443, 6:452
Original Survey, 6:234
Original Tract, 6:228
Otter Creek, 7:338, 7:351
Owens Creek, 6:301, 6:352, 7:243,
  7:244, 7:245, 7:254

Parson County, 6:130
Parson County Line, 6:149
Patterson Tract, 6:226
Paynes Tavern, 6:57
Peach Orchard, 7:255
Pee Creek, 6:296, 6:348
Person County, 6:130, 6:137, 6:146,
  6:149, 6:452, 7:247
Person County Line, 6:149
Petersburg, 6:89, 6:137, 7:469
Pickett's Old Line, 7:250
Pine Hill, 6:130, 6:136
Pittsylvania County, 6:385
**Pomfret Herndon;s Old Wagon
  Road,** 6:311, 7:7
Powells Mountain, 6:245
Powells River, 6:118, 7:62
Powells Valley, 6:60, 6:118
Pratt's Old Corner, 7:395
Presswoods Creek of Newhope,
  6:1996:203, 6:293, 7:344
Prices Creek, 6:311, 7:7
Prosser's Old Tract, 6:19
Public Brick Spring Lot, 7:246
Public Lot, 7:246
Public Lot #1, 7:469
Public Property, 7:327
Quaker Cr., 6:90, 6:202, 6:354,
  6:355, 6:449, 7:292, 7:330, 7:357,
  7:358, 7:412, 7:473
Queen Street, 6:169, 7:324
Race Paths, 7:289
Raibons (Raiborns) Creek, 6:302,
  6:359
Raleigh, 7:62
Randolph County, 6:443
Randolph County Line, 6:218
Road, 6:3617:19, 7:228, 7:309,
  7:377
**Road Leading East from Queen
  Street,** 7:472
**Road from Granville to
  Hillsborough,** 6:154, 6:200
**Road from Hillsborough to Paynes
  Tavern,** 6:57
Road from Hillsborough, 7:9
**Road from John Carrington to
  William Ansley's Mill,** 7:35, 7:75
Robinson County, 6:150
Rock Creek, 6:306, 6:329, 7:57

Rock Land, 7:292
Rockingham County Line, 6:310
Rockingham County, 6:234, 6:310, 7:407
Rocky Branch, 6:113, 6:463, 6:466, 7:235
Rocky Creek, 6:294
Rocky Spring Tract, 7:484
Rowan County, 6:113
Saint Thomas District, 6:291
Saw Mill, 6:320, 7:293
Schoolhouse Branch, 6:143
Scrub Branch, 7:412
Scrub Creek, 6:25, 6:202
Second Creek, 6:4, 7:85
Seven Mile Creek, 6:417, 7:27, 7:30, 7:419
Shirleys Branch, 6:83
South Carolina, 6:210, 6:233, 6:261, 6:263, 6:266, 6:269, 6:271, 6:275, 6:280, 6:284, 7:64
South Fork, 6:59
South Hico, 6:146
South Prong, 7:450
Spartanburgh, 6:233
Spirit Branch, 7:456
Spoons Creek, 7:300
Stags (Staggs) Creek, 6:2, 6:24, 6:28, 7:473, 7:474
Steel's Old Tract, 6:107
Still House, 6:327, 6:362
Stinking Quarter Creek, 6:5, 6:205, 6:395, 6:443, 7:49, 7:51, 7:53, 7:95, 7:202, 7:273, 7:376
Stones Creek, 6:83, 7:229, 7:234, 7:259, 7:382
Stones River, 6:1
Stoney Creek, 6:150, 6:176, 6:196, 6:350, 6:351, 7:17, 7:52, 7:60, 7:255, 7:291, 7:301, 7:388, 7:488
Storm Creek, 7:452
Strayhorn's Field, 7:445
Strudwick's Lower Tract, 7:449, 7:450
Strudwick's Middle Tract, 7:449, 7:450
Suggs Creek, 6:34
Sullivan County, 6:12
Sumner County, 6:1, 7:486
Surry County, 6:469, 7:11

Tennessee, 6:1, 6:12, 6:150, 6:454, 7:60, 7:265, 7:409, 7:483, 7:484, 7:485, 7:486
Terrices Creek, 7:427
The Gore, 7:449
Theophilus Thompson's Tract, 6:93
Third Fork Creek, 6:463
Third Fork, 6:466
Thompson's Old Tract, 7:97
Thompsons Branch, 6:107
Toms Creek, 6:448
Top Ridge, 6:245
Town Commons, 6:192, 7:324, 7:325
Town Creek, 6:385
Town Land, 7:69
Town Line, 7:472
Tract #11, 7:311
Tract #22, 6:163
Tract #28, 6:163
Tract #47, 6:68
Tract No. 28, 6:170
Tract No. 29, 6:170
Tract No. 30, 6:170
Trading Road, 6:395
Transylvania, 6:210, 6:245, 6:269
Traveses Creek, 7:41, 7:56, 7:201
Tryon Street, 6:160, 6:169, 6:465, 7:210, 7:325, 7:327, 7:379, 7:415
Tucker's Corner, 6:116
Turkey Hill Creek, 7:436
Turner's Road, 6:385
Ullas Creek, 6:68, 6:370, 6:386
University & Hillsborough Road, 7:88
University Lands, 6:327, 6:362, 7:1
University, Village adjacent to the buildings of the, 6:8, 6:9, 6:235, 6:321, 6:362, 6:372, 6:376, 6:391, 6:432, 6:436, 6:438, 6:461, 7:38, 7:213, 7:215
Vernals Creek, 6:14, 6:295, 7:59, 7:79, 7:311, 7:333, 7:454, 7:490, 7:491
Virginia, 6:1, 6:5, 6:89, 6:137, 6:385, 6:463, 7:292, 7:469
Virginia Line, 6:245
Wake County, 6:116, 6:187, 6:328, 6:377, 6:391, 6:392, 6:436, 7:8,

Wake County, 7:38
Wake County Line, 6:116, 6:183
Wake Street, 6:160, 6:169, 6:374,
    6:397, 6:399, 6:401, 6:465, 7:43
Walnut Ford, 7:72
Washington County, 7:376
Watery Branch, 6:463, 6:466
Watkin's Old Tract, 7:474
Watsons Creek, 7:255, 7:316, 7:419
Wattery Branch, 6:392
Wells Creek, 7:313
West Fork, 6:101, 6:309
Whittel Branch, 7:301
Wikes Spring Branch, 6:311
Wilkinsons Creek, 7:417
William Courtney's Still House Lot,
    7:246
William Courtney's Tavern, 7:246
William Faucett's Old Line, 6:456
Willm. Merritt's Mill Seat, 7:1
William Powell's House, 7:417
Wolleys Spring Branch, 7:417
Woolf Branch, 6:116, 6:173, 6:183
Woolfe Pit, 6:311

www.ingramcontent.com/pod-product-compliance
Lightning Source LLC
Chambersburg PA
CBHW020654300426
44112CB00007B/373